COMMON NONSENSE

Glenn Beck and the Triumph of Ignorance

Alexander Zaitchik

WILEY

John Wiley & Sons, Inc.

For Mom and Pops

Published by John Wiley & Sons, Inc., Hoboken, New Jersey
Published simultaneously in Canada

For general information about our other products and services, please contact our Customer Care Department within the United States at (800) 762-2974, outside the United States at (317) 572-3993 or fax (317) 572-4002.

Wiley also publishes its books in a variety of electronic formats. Some content that appears in print may not be available in electronic books. For more information about Wiley products, visit our web site at www.wiley.com.

Library of Congress Cataloging-in-Publication Data:

Zaitchik, Alexander, date.
   Common nonsense: Glenn Beck and the triumph of ignorance / Alexander Zaitchik.
     p. cm.
   Includes index.
   ISBN 978-0-470-55739-6 (cloth); ISBN 978-0-470-63040-2 (ebk); ISBN 978-0-470-63064-8 (ebk); ISBN 978-0-470-63065-5 (ebk)
   1. Beck, Glenn—Influence. 2. Beck, Glenn—Political and social views.
   3. Conservatism—United States. 4. Ignorance (Theory of knowledge)—Political aspects—United States. 5. Political culture—United States. 6. Popular culture—United States. 7. Radio personalities—United States—Biography. 8. Television personalities—United States—Biography. 9. Authors, American—Biography. 10. Mormons—United States—Biography. I. Title.
   CT275.B5463Z35 2010
   320.52092—dc22
   [B]

2010003425

Printed in the United States of America
10 9 8 7 6 5 4 3 2 1

Sentimentality, the ostentatious parading of excessive and spurious emotion, is the mark of dishonesty, the inability to feel; the wet eyes of the sentimentalist betray his aversion to experience, his fear of life, his arid heart; and it is always, therefore, the signal of secret and violent inhumanity, the mask of cruelty.

—James Baldwin, *Notes of a Native Son*

CONTENTS

Introduction

The Man with the Plan

History will record that on the third Saturday of November 2009, Glenn Beck unveiled his hundred-year plan to save the republic at a golf-cart retirement community just north of Orlando.

The day began at a highwayside Borders Bookstore in Tampa, a short drive up the road from the Clear Channel studio complex that incubated Beck's talk-radio career in the final year of the Clinton administration. A shorter drive in the opposite direction blinked the purple neon lights of the city's most famous strip club, Mons Venus, against which Beck waged a culture war as a younger man.

Monuments to Beck's past were everywhere in the sleepy midsized Florida city, but the host's schedule brooked no appointments with nostalgia. The ground-rules flyer handed out in the Borders parking lot explained that Beck was too rushed even for chitchat with his longest-listening fans. Another bullet point instructed the assembled not to expect personalized autographs. Those in line would receive a mere scrawl of their hero's initials. Photographs were allowed, but no poses—and be quick about it.

Glenn Beck's devotees understood. Although it was clear that not everyone would reach the signing desk, a neat line of one thousand snaked patiently through the massive lot and then onto the sidewalk along the six lanes of Dale Mabry Boulevard, quiet with Saturday morning traffic. Armed with books, the waiting were happy just to be

1

there. Stretching out before and behind them was proof of something that Beck had told them again and again: *You are not alone.*

After two hours of signing books and issuing curt hellos, Beck boarded his *Arguing with Idiots* tour bus—sporting a two-sided mural of the author as Colonel Klink—and headed north to the day's main event. Throughout the hourlong journey up I-275, the bus passed colorful caravans of cars and trucks owned by members of Beck's conservative civic initiative, the 9.12 Project. The 9.12 vehicles were easy to identify: U.S. flags flapped in the wind, cardboard signs denounced socialism from the backs of trunks, and messages announced in soap and shoe polish, WELCOME HOME GLENN!

More than just a homecoming, Beck's Florida visit had been billed as a personal culmination and a national turning point. At the sprawling retirement community known as the Villages, Beck was scheduled to unveil the future of Glenn Beck Nation. Beck had been methodically teaspooning out the hype for weeks. His legions had been led to expect something very big and possibly epic, a historic proclamation to redirect the course of human events. It would have to be. Only something approaching the level of the Rapture could have capped what had been a breakout year for the forty-five-year-old host.

Since launching a revamped *Glenn Beck* on Fox News on the eve of Barack Obama's inauguration, Beck had become an unlikely power broker at the intersection of national media and politics. For his bombast, biliousness, and brio, the former Top 40 radio deejay was the talk of the nation, reviled or revered by millions of Americans on each side of a yawning cultural chasm—the Glenn Beck divide. It had been a remarkable journey, completed in just ten months, from cable news curio in professional limbo to *Time* magazine cover subject and named public enemy on Whitehouse. gov. Among conservatives, the polls showed Beck's influence ranking second only to that of Rush Limbaugh, whose mantle he now stood poised to inherit.

But all this was just for starters. With his speech in the Villages, the host promised to unveil the next stage in the evolution of Glenn Beck: the media brand, the political movement, and the psychosocial demographic. To those willing to join him and make what he called "hard sacrifices," Beck would offer a role in the crusade to rebuild, to *refound*, the republic. In the language of dispossession that defines the new conservative grassroots, he would show them how to "take their country back." Thirty thousand people made the Beck pilgrimage from across Florida and nearby states to receive the word.

The site of the revelation was a gazebo in the Villages' shopping district. If the scene bore a strong resemblance to nearby Disney World's Main Street attraction, it's because "retiring to Disney" is how residents refer to their golden years in the Villages, a manicured suburb that markets itself as "America's friendliest hometown." It is best known for its twenty-four golf courses, 99 percent white population, and two registered Republicans for every Democrat.

Developed by GOP megadonor Gary Morse, the Villages is a Potemkin village poetically suited to Beck's Potemkin populism. Dripping with the ersatz trappings of simpler-time nostalgia, its streets are designed not for cars but for the town's preferred mode of transportation: golf carts, known locally as "club cars." The main shopping drag hosts pricey quilteries and crafts stores, a club car dealer, a Johnny Rockets diner, and a Hallmark store. The local galleries do brisk and redundant trades in the oil-painted homilies of Thomas Kinkade.

Beck is no stranger here. The Villages has long been a favored stop-over for conservatives on book tours. The host last visited the previous November, when he descended by helicopter into the Barnes & Noble parking lot to sign copies of his bestselling fiction debut, *The Christmas Sweater*. Now, one year later, the town handed its entire commercial center over to Beck, welcoming him with everything short of trumpets. "Beck to announce plan to 'Save the Republic,'" declared the front page of the *Villages Daily Sun*.

It was a fine day to start a second American revolution in a retirement community. The temperature, like most of the crowd, hovered in the low seventies. A sound system set the mood with upbeat patriotic jukebox anthems, including a double helping of an old Beck favorite: Lee Greenwood's "God Bless the USA." It was to Greenwood's song that Beck arrived at the scene twenty minutes late. To the sound of cheers, the star emerged from an underpass separating Lucky Charm Antiques and Starbucks.

Although he flew to Florida on a private jet, Beck wore the coach-class outfit he favors for speaking events: jeans, Converse, and an untucked baby blue button-down. Flanked by a heavy security detail—there had been the usual threats—his soft six-foot-four frame moved slowly through the adoring throng. There was no sign of the bulletproof vest he is rumored to wear on the streets of New York City.

"Glenn Beck for President!" they screamed. "We love you, Glenn!"

Beck beamed under the love, his face flush and caught in a toothy, winsome grin rarely seen on Fox News. *This is why bands tour even when they no longer have to*, the former Top 40 deejay might have been thinking. Except for the gray at his temples, he could have been an over-grown thirteen-year-old, lumbering through a gymnasium on his way to accept an eighth-grade achievement award. The ovation only grew louder after Beck took the stage, where over the noise he slowly allowed his grin to fade. He opened with a joke: "Is this the ACORN rally?"

Clearly it was not. The crowd was uniformly white, middle class or higher, and dressed like suburbia. Peppering their number were members of the new breed of conservative costume-box activists who, in their American-flag shirts, tricorner hats, and media-hungry disgust for the establishment, might be said to bear an empty resemblance to the play-ful 1960s radicals known as the Yippies. Also present were sprinklings of active-duty military personnel and bandanna-wearing bikers, who stood out among an otherwise solid mass of aging preppy housewives.

Beck surveyed the crowd with a father's pride. Only when the raucous response to his ACORN reference faded did he begin his performance. It was a very familiar show, designed to please, covering his full repertoire of themes and obsessions. Beck's fans know these well from the host's broadcasts, books, and stage shows. His detractors know them equally well from the work of Comedy Central satirists, who must employ ever more refined strategies to exploit the nanoscopic space that separates Beck from Teflon self-caricature. But know them America does.

There was the obligatory skip across Beck's redemptive biographical rainbow, crunched down to the length and depth of a three-act, soft-focus *700 Club* reenactment. There were bits from his Frankenstein burlesque of libertarianism, equal parts Ron Paul, Dick Cheney, and Mormon elder. There were "boo!" lines about minor and nonsystemic corruption scandals involving minorities and liberals. There was a heavy single-note riff on the federal deficit. There was a hypocritical paean to personal thrift, an apocalyptic admonition to stock canned goods in fruit cellars, and a plug for Beck's personal three-G survivalist triad of God, gold, and guns.

Finally, inevitable as gravity, there was the florid signature that appears somewhere at least once, often twice, in every Beck performance.

This is the moment when the voice catches, the eyes mist, and it seems, for one or two excruciating moments, that the reluctant patriot might not be able to hold back the tears, so *verklempt* has he become at his rote invocation of love of country, or the brave troops, or George Washington, or, more likely, his four children—one of whom, it must be said, is afflicted with palsy, and all of whom, it must also be said, suffer daily for the father's gold-plated success.

Only when this obligatory medley was complete did Beck turn to the much awaited announcement. No, he would not be running for office. Not this time. What he had in mind was bigger than any one politician, more important than any single off-year election. What Beck had was a plan. *The* plan. This plan would take a century to see through to completion—maybe more. What began in March 2009 with the founding of the 9.12 Project, he explained, would enter a new stage in March 2010. The animating idea behind the plan, Beck explained, is to educate, organize, and think long-term—"like the progressives, like the Chinese." Throughout the coming century, conveniently encompassing the rest of Glenn Beck's natural life, the host would direct this plan. He wished it weren't necessary to burden himself and his family in this way, but he saw no choice. It was necessary if true patriots, like those gathered in the Villages, were to counter and crush the long-standing bipartisan goal to transform the United States into what Beck called a "socialist utopia."

The host knows of this bipartisan plan, he explained, because he had been reading history books.

"I've done a lot of reading on history in the last few years," Beck told the crowd. "I was amazed to find that what we're experiencing now is really a ticking time bomb that *they* designed about a hundred years ago, beginning in the Progressive movement."

Ah, yes. The Progressives. Beck's fans knew all about them. The host had discovered their turn-of-the-last-century perfidies early in 2008, after reading Jonah Goldberg's *Liberal Fascism*. Beck was so excited by the Progressives' starring role in Goldberg's revisionist history that he mentioned it almost daily for months. As a result, Goldberg found himself with an unlikely best seller on his hands. Ever since, Beck's ideas about the founders and Woodrow Wilson have formed the plastic piggybank bookends of his historical understanding.

Beck's narrative of the fall is a simple tale. It begins with the Christian supply-side vision of John Adams and ends with the Marx-inspired

Progressive plot of Teddy Roosevelt, Woodrow Wilson, and a young Walter Lippmann. Today, Beck believes, small *p* progressives continue the devil's work begun by their capital *P* predecessors, all of whom, Beck believes, were little more than proto-Nazis in reformers' clothing. Beck does not deny that his grasp of the progressive plot remains incomplete. As late as June 2009, he innocently asked a stunned Goldberg, "What is the difference between Marxism and progressivism?"[1] But Beck knows enough to know that the Progressives injected evil into America. It was they who released the European "virus" of social justice into the previously pure land. They took on the inequities and deformities of the Gilded Age—and what could be more American than gold? In their successful crusades to abolish child labor, reduce financial panics, break up monopolies, and give women the vote, they opened the door to feminism, the EPA, the income tax, and the popular election of senators ("Abolish the Seventeenth Amendment!" is a frequent battle cry on the 9.12 Project circuit). Worst of all, they created the Federal Reserve.

These abominations, in turn, have spawned the scarecrows that famously haunt the cornfield of Beck's imagination: Reverend Jeremiah Wright (Barack Obama's former minister), Van Jones (Barack Obama's former green jobs czar), and the hulking hard-to-kill root of Beck's "tree of radicalism," ACORN. Beck has taken it upon himself to do battle with these satanic agents and in the process rescue the republic. "I'm going to be a progressive hunter like the old Nazi hunters," Beck has promised. "I don't care where they are. If they destroyed us from the inside, they'll slither away. Progressivism will kill you."[2]

In response to the time bomb planted by the Progressives, Beck had come to the Villages to announce a time bomb of his own. He was, he said, in the process of organizing a series of seven educational conventions.* They would be held across the country, and the first was scheduled for March 2010 in nearby Orlando. The conventions, he explained over rising cheers, would present the views of handpicked

---

*In February 2010, Beck announced that this first phase of the plan had been scaled back to events in Orlando and Phoenix. Titled American Revival, the modest two-city tour offered the chance to see Beck and three guests speak on the themes of faith, hope, and charity. For $134.75, American Revivalists received a day of sermons and a workbook, which Beck described as "an American survival guide for American evangelist[s]." For everyone else, American Revival T-shirts are available at glennbeck.com for $19.95.

experts working on a range of issues, from national security to the economy (but not the environment).

"What I've done," he said, "is I've found two really smart people in each category, two really—oh, they just have all kinds of experience. And then I have coupled them with one rebel, one radical. I hear that it's popular to be a radical now."

The work of these experts would culminate in a book by Beck, ominously titled *The Plan*. The release party would be something extraordinary. It would force the entire nation to take notice. On August 28, 2010, Beck explained, he would address his legions from the foot of the Lincoln Memorial. "It isn't easy to get a permit for the National Mall," said Beck. But he did it—and for August 28, no less. Beck pointed out that Martin Luther King Jr. had delivered his "I Have a Dream" speech on August 28, in 1963, and had become immortal. Beck spoke of his intention to build on the meaning of this date with a dreamlike vision of his own. From then on, August 28 would mark "the unveiling of *The Plan* and the birthday of a new national movement to restore our great country."

With that, Beck left the stage to sign copies of his latest best seller, *Arguing with Idiots*.

"God bless you," he told the Villages. "And God bless the United States of America."

Throughout the summer of 2009, Beck had made cryptic references to his plan as a slow-motion revelation forming in his own mind. "I'm beginning to see the way forward," he said in Mosaic terms, often between the long dramatic pauses he favors during his radio monologues. "It's coming together in my head. The time is approaching when I will share the way out with you." True to cult leader form, Beck even prophesied his own martyrdom, echoing the final speech made one hot Memphis night in 1968 by the last American Moses. "You may not save my life, but you'll save the republic," he told his radio audience on August 29. "They need to destroy me because I'm a threat."

For months Beck talked as if he had been to the metaphorical mountaintop. With five number one *New York Times* best sellers of his own already on his shelf, and the power to catapult other conservative authors up that list with a single word of praise, Beck was being hailed as the conservative Oprah. But the conservative Moses? No one should have found the idea shocking. The audacity at the heart of the plan—Beck as Martin Luther King—represents a crowning and predictable synthesis of all that is brilliant, effective, and foul about Glenn Beck.

First is the oceanic audacity of his self-serving ignorance. As a professional "progressive hunter," Beck should have known that Martin Luther King was the enemy whose most famous anniversary should be avoided like that Bolshevik birthday, October 25, 1917. But that is expecting too much. For a man who never tires of screaming "Know your enemy!" Beck knows precious little about anything. For much of 2009, Beck flashed King's face and words at the beginning of each episode of *Glenn Beck* along with those of Washington and Jefferson. But had they been contemporaries, Beck would have been King's most rabid critic. He would have called King a traitor for opposing the Vietnam War and criticizing American militarism ("A nation that continues to spend more money on military defense than on programs of social uplift is approaching spiritual death," said King). Beck would have called King an enemy of the Constitution for supporting health-care reform ("Of all the forms of inequality, injustice in health care is the most shocking and inhumane," King declared). Had they met as men on the stage of history, Beck would have falsely labeled the civil rights leader a "convicted felon" who fraternizes with radicals. He would have demanded answers about his connections to leading Democratic politicians, all the while asking, "When did we lose our country?" Beck would have called King a progressive "cockroach" spreading the "viruses" of economic and social justice. He would have shrieked "mob rule" and "thugocracy" at the Poor People's March that King died planning. He would have called him a communist, or a willing tool of the communists, for daring to criticize the official racism in the country and in Beck's adopted Mormon Church.

We know Beck would have done these things because that is what the right-wing Mormons who he says inspire his politics spent the 1960s doing. It is also how Beck has built his empire. But if Beck would have despised King in 1967, he is more than happy to use him in 2009. King is revered, after all, and he is remembered. Standing in King's shadow also retroactively puts Beck on the right side of history, a place he never would have been a half century ago.

For Beck, August 28, 2010, has been a long time coming. He has waited years for his spotlight on the National Mall. In the winter of 2003, Clear Channel's D.C. affiliate, WTNT, declined to host Beck's traveling Rally for America prowar road show. "We support Glenn wholeheartedly," said the station's marketing director at the time, "but does D.C. really need another rally?" Beck marched on, eyes on the prize.

Six years later, he organized a massive rally for himself on the National Mall, but the Fox News brass kept Beck in New York on September 12, 2009, so he was forced to watch his nine-twelvers scream his name live by satellite. The multiple frustrations didn't stop Beck from broadcasting the occasional Lincoln Memorial dress rehearsal. "I have a dream," Beck exclaimed without irony, and not for the first time, in April 2009, "that we can stop playing not just the blame-the-messenger game. I have a dream that we can stop playing the game of blame."[3]

A few months later, in a fit of typically unaware projection, Beck blithely accused Barack Obama of possessing a "deep-seated hatred for white people."

If Beck merits a comparison to any American legend, it is certainly not Martin Luther King Jr. Nor is it Johnny Carson or Orson Welles, Beck's boyhood heroes. It is neither George Washington nor Thomas Paine, whose wigs and breeches Beck has donned while speaking of a second American revolution. The only apt comparison to greatness, if one has been earned, is to a nineteenth-century Connecticut Yankee who amassed an empire much like Beck's own in his day, built with solid blocks of what the press called "humbug," cunningly cemented by a mortar of disgust, amusement, and dismay.

Phineas Taylor Barnum earned his place in the American pantheon for his pioneering publicity and marketing instincts. But even Barnum had a mentor. That man was Jacksonian America's most famous circus owner, Aaron Turner, who briefly employed the young Barnum as a ticket seller and secretary in the mid-1830s. In his autobiography, Barnum recounts the day in 1836 that Turner taught him that the only bad press is your own obituary.

Turner's traveling circus had just rolled its wagons into a small town in Maryland, and much to the owner's chagrin, local excitement was slack.

Unwilling to accept the prospect of empty bench space in his tent, Turner took action. His ratings strategy was to spread rumors around town that his young ticket seller, who favored all-black suits, was a disgraced clergyman just recently acquitted of murder. As word spread, an angry mob surrounded Barnum, who knew nothing about the rumors. The townsfolk harassed him and began making noises about forcing him to "ride the rail," a painful public punishment held over from colonial times in which the victim is paraded atop a thin plank of hard wood.

Barnum's colleagues rescued him at the last minute. Rattled, Barnum located his boss and demanded an explanation. Turner could only chuckle at his young secretary's innocence. "Remember," he told Barnum, "all we need to ensure success is *notoriety*. You will see that this will be noised all about town, and our pavilion will be crammed tomorrow night."[4]

Today, few pavilions are as crammed as Glenn Beck's, whose hokum-filled programs on radio and television draw more than ten million each weekday. However grand and public-spirited his rhetoric, however earnest and enormous his pretensions, Beck is above all an entertainer and a huckster. To put it more charitably: he is a businessman out to make a nickel. He is the founder and president of a wildly successful media startup, Mercury Radio Arts, whose principals meet each morning to discuss present projects and future growth.* That growth—though accompanied by professions of selflessness and higher callings—is the realization of a dream Beck has been chasing since long before he found God at the bottom of a bottle and George Washington in the ashes of 9/11.

In recent years, Beck has increasingly become a narcissistic demagogue huffing delusions of grandeur, but his ego and his narcissism feed, and have always fed, directly into a larger business plan. They are one and the same. Beck's narcissism and demagoguery cannot be separated from his business success any more than that success can be separated from the spiraling madness we see on Fox News and in Washington, D.C.

Beck's political grandstanding is, at bottom, little more than a circus entertainer's love of an audience, matched with a fine appreciation for

---

*Beck sometimes winks at the dramatic entertainment roots of his broadcasting success. In an interview with *GQ*, a reporter challenged him directly on the issue of authenticity. His answer was uncharacteristically coy. "You know, the name of my company is Mercury, named after Orson Welles's Mercury Theatre. Orson Welles was a brilliant businessman, he was a brilliant stage actor, he was a brilliant filmmaker, he was a brilliant actor—all of those," said Beck. "What was he?"

the uses of notoriety, spectacle, and shamelessness. Like Barnum's great museums and traveling freak shows, Beck's twice-daily performances, one on radio and and one on television, trade in light amusement, canny deceit, and titillating monstrosity.

To Beck's fans, the monstrosities are the black nationalists and communists who, Beck tells them, are plotting from inside the bestiary of Obama's White House, which Beck invites his listeners and viewers to step right up and inspect themselves. To his critics, the only monstrosity on display is Beck himself. Put them together, and you have a pavilion crammed to capacity, night after night, around which endless debate about humbug swirls without cease.

To highlight Beck's business savvy and showman's instinct is not the same as saying that everything that comes out of his mouth is part of an act. There are no inherent conflicts between Beck the born entertainer, Beck the ambitious mogul, and Beck the touched-in-the-head far-right agitator. Indeed, it is hard to escape the conclusion that Beck's politics are deeply held. Barnum, too, genuinely believed in what he saw as his publicly beneficial crusade to inform and entertain a nation.

Beck may be a corporate shill and a dollar-a-holler goldbug with skyscraper offices in Manhattan. But he is dead serious when he recommends his three-G survivalist system of God, guns, and gold, which is nothing but the logical endgame of his paranoid and deeply religious politics whose hubs are the Mormon bastions of the Intermountain west, Beck's favorite region of the country. Beck's genius is not in fooling a nation of suckers, then kicking back with a cigar and laughing behind the scenes. It is in forging an empire out of his personal and political pathologies. He is our very own crackpot capitalist Che Guevara: fueling his legend and pushing his ideology with one hand, selling the T-shirt—millions of them—with the other.

There is also an undeniable innocence at work in Beck's profitable panic. His pawing of facts and logic may be ogrelike, but he possesses the honest curiosity of a young ogre exploring the forest on his own for the first time. Beck's shows are more than just manipulative entertainment. They are nationally broadcast exercises in adult remedial self-education, which draw much of their energy from the host's genuinely exuded sense of discovery. This can be seen in everything from his wide-eyed fear of labor unions ("Andy Stern has visited the White House a bunch of times!")

to his introductory-level documentaries about Stalin's infamous role in orchestrating the Ukrainian famine ("Nobody knows this stuff!"). Until his political awakening in 2001, Beck was really just an FM morning radio clown playing with toys. For much of the next seven years, he coasted along mainly on pro-Bush party lines, dabbling in libertarianism and conspiracism, as described in the Mormon coloring books he used to train for the mental rigors of Conservative Book Club membership.

With the election of Barack Obama, Beck was confronted with a Democratic administration for the first time since he had become a politically sentient adult. It is partly because he possesses a child's understanding of U.S. history and Democratic coalition politics that to him everything seems so shocking and new. This is why his rants about the "tree of radicalism" have the same feel as a freshman-year bong session devoted to the possibility that the universe is really just an atom, and within each atom another entire universe.

Showman, opportunist, manipulator, cuckoo bird, and innocent—Glenn Beck contains a multitude. If he were easy to unlock with any one key, any single defining characteristic, he wouldn't be where he is. He'd be no fun at all.

Years before his stardom as a cable news tent-show revivalist, Beck mastered the arts of the media stunt and the calculated outrage while working as an itinerant showman in the clownish and cutthroat world of Top 40 morning radio. As early as the mid-1980s, Beck was known for the same qualities and talents with which he has earned his more recent and much greater fame. His colleagues remember him as pompous, talented, ambitious, and possessing a vicious mean streak.

"Everything about him now was evident twenty years ago," says Tim Hattrick, Beck's radio partner during the mid-1980s. "He was sort of a caricature of the egotistical take-charge leader. The first time I heard Rush Limbaugh, I thought, 'This guy sounds like what Glenn wanted to be.' He was the same dramatic showman back then he is today."

This deejay-inflected showmanship gives Beck the appearance of something uniquely contemporary. The plastic toy props; the game show gimmicks; the sudden and unconvincing shifts between flamboyant sarcasm, desperate sincerity, and schoolgirl hysteria—all are fresh to cable news, all are owned by Beck. However, his trademark style is but a neon sports stripe sprayed onto a jalopy built from old and rusted parts rescued from the slag heap of American history. He did not invent paranoia, race and red baiting, or the conservative distrust of government that often borders on hatred. Beck is just an eye-catching twenty-first-century hybrid carrying timeless right-wing cargo into the age of Fox News, PlayStation, and Adderall.

That the past is Beck's prologue can be seen in the cultural touch-stones that dominate discussions of his unexpected rise. Beck is most often compared not to the weeping commentator of the futuristic 2005 film *V for Vendetta* but the aw-shucks faux populist Lonesome Rhodes of Elia Kazan's 1957 film *A Face in the Crowd.*

So it is with Beck's religious antigovernment politics. In analy-ses of Beck and the Tea Party movement he both shapes and embodies,* it has become a journalistic cliché to reference Richard Hofstadter's 1964 collection of historical essays, *The Paranoid Style in American Politics.* This is because the paranoid "pseudo-conservatism" that Hofstadter explores is so easily recognizable in the right-wing movement that has bubbled up since the election of Barack Obama. The same hysterics that define today's Tea Party scene also arose in response to alleged witches at Salem, Catholic immigration, Mormonism, the rise of modern finance, communism, and civil rights. As with previous herpetic outbreaks of the paranoid style, today's is defined by what Hofstadter identified as a recipe of "heated exaggeration, suspiciousness, and conspiratorial fantasy."[5]

Yesterday's pamphleteers against papal plots and antifluoridation activists now warn of government death panels and FEMA concentra-tion camps. Whereas previous practitioners of the paranoid style relied on speaking tours, mass mailings, and the occasional hour of community-access cable, Beck declares there are brown shirts under AmeriCorps windbreakers with the megaphones of cable news and AM radio.

Beyond an irrational fear of creeping totalitarianism and a triple obsession with ACORN, health-care reform, and the deficit, what defines the new pseudo-conservatism? It's hard to say. No conglomera-tion of specific policy positions can quite explain the sudden explosion of pseudo-conservative activism symbolized and fueled by Beck. "The

---

*Beck has done his best to claim the movement as his own, and he often refers to Tea Party protests as "nine-twelve tea parties," adding the name of the 9.12 Project, his trademarked initiative.

ideology of pseudo-conservatism can be characterized but not defined," noted Hofstadter, "because the pseudo-conservative tends to be more than ordinarily incoherent about politics." Anyone who has visited a Tea Party—where T-shirts sing the praises of red-nosed Joe McCarthy, protesters shout that government should "stay out of Medicare," and placards decry the nonexistent czars of Soviet Russia—will understand that this fundamental insight still applies.

Hofstadter began writing *The Paranoid Style* in the mid-1950s in an attempt to understand and explain the anticommunist hysteria of that era as embodied by Wisconsin senator Joe McCarthy. After McCarthy's ignominious fall during Senate hearings in 1954, the paranoid style did not disappear with him; rather, it continued to mutate and quickly regrouped under the banner of the John Birch Society. It is no coincidence that the same family that funded the Birchers, Koch Enterprises, today funds the groups that are feeding Beck many of his favorite and most popular scripts, most notably Americans for Prosperity. Just as fitting, Beck has led a revival of the most famous Mormon practitioner of the paranoid style, Willard Cleon Skousen, a Bircher whose three-stage intellectual odyssey from McCarthyism to the New World Order to Christian Constitutionalism has had a deep and formative impact on Beck. Skousen, too, was a born entertainer who loved an audience and understood that nothing keeps them coming back for more like promises of participatory revelation and hidden structures explained. Like Beck, Skousen was often accused of playing a few Jacks short of a full deck.

Rivaled only by his friend and ally Sarah Palin, Beck is the googly-eyed face of today's pseudo-conservatism. His fake populism is at once broadly grounded in reality (the federal deficit is a problem, both parties are corrupt) and in crazed flight from it (just about everything else). Once you get into the details, Beck's worldview collapses under the weight of its own discombobulation.

Beck professes love of the little guy but openly worships the superrich while inveighing against programs and institutions that help the average American. He is obsessed with the federal deficit and issues constant pleas to think of "our children," but he supports massive tax cuts, greater military spending, and remains dumb to non-debt-related measures of the intergenerational balance sheet. He claims to live and let live but moralizes about drugs and sex. He sees a burning Apocalypse in everything from Mexican drug cartels to civil liberties lawsuits but denies the reality of man-made climate change. He claims to cherish the freedoms, values, and institutions that are enshrined by the Constitution, yet defends torture, legal "black holes" like Guantanamo, and illegal wiretapping. And when his professed America-first principles come into conflict with the business of building his brand, the victor is never in doubt. He describes the United Nations as part of the New World Order threat to American sovereignty, but when Beck wanted a satirical Web site banished from the Internet, he immediately ran squealing to the UN's World Intellectual Property Organization, knowing he would lose in a U.S. court committed to the First Amendment.*

Beck likes to think his schizophrenic hard-right politics—which include advocacy for the distinctly nonlibertarian idea of militarizing the U.S.-Mexican border—add up to a pure and robust libertarianism. Whatever makes him happy. When asked if anyone at the libertarian monthly *Reason* thinks that Beck understands the philosophical club in which he claims membership, a ranking editor at the magazine was quick to reply, "No, though some of us are starting to think of him as one of the great intuitive surrealists."

It is now clear that Beck's surrealist take on antigovernment conservatism is having an effect on the real world in which most Americans live. In this world, Hitler was not "a man of the Left," Barack Obama is not a Marxist-Leninist, and clocks don't melt according to the laws of the fourth dimension. But it is a place where Beck has a monthly media footprint of thirty million and growing. As evidenced by his love of black-boards and spectacles, he relishes the role of teacher most of all and sees this massive audience as his student body. That so many Americans have willingly entered into this bizarre role play has consequences that cannot be parodied away. The only questions about Beck's influence are two: what form will it take, and will it last?

Some maintain that Beck is nothing more than a harmless jester, that he's nothing to worry about and not worthy of serious attention. Until recently, Beck himself said as much. In this view, he can no more control the direction of conservative politics than he can drive the price of his precious gold. The GOP strategist David Frum describes Beck's success as representative of "the collapse of conservatism as an organized politi-cal force, and the rise of conservatism as an alienated cultural sensibility."[6]

---

*He lost anyway.

And what's the worst a sensibility can do, after all? David Brooks of the *New York Times* has compared Beck and Limbaugh to the Wizard of Oz, capable of "remarkable volume" that hides "utter weakness."[7] Let Beck huff and puff into the ether and twirl his Dali mustache on TV, say members of this camp. Like a crew-cut Freddy Krueger who haunts our dreams, he can't hurt you if you refuse to believe in him.

The midterm elections of 2010 should help to clarify the value of this view. Under Beck's influence, Frum's "alienated cultural sensibility" could well result in more politicians on the national stage like Minnesota's Michele Bachmann and Sarah Palin. Beck may yet emerge as a kingmaker for the Tea Party–era GOP, able to crown up-and-coming representatives and senators the way he currently crowns authors of canned patriotic thrillers. Just as the Republican "class of 1994" bestowed honorary membership on Rush Limbaugh, Beck may yet receive a similar reward should enough of his refounders be swept to power on a tide of Beck-fueled pseudo-conservative activism. Beck's shows have already become mandatory stops for rising Tea Party–approved stars like Florida's Marco Rubio.[8] Will Beck's vaunted "independence" survive the temptation to curry favor with power should the GOP retake Congress and the White House? It is too early to tell. But as 2009 came to a close, the Republican Party was tracking closer and closer to Beck's Tea Party politics in rhetoric, policy, and intolerance of moderation. There is no clearer sign of this than the GOP's 2008 candidate for president. Less than a year after losing the election, John McCain had begun to sound like his former running mate, Sarah Palin, not to mention Beck's favorite senator and the sole senatorial darling of the Tea Party movement, South Carolina's Jim DeMint.

Constant primary season pressure from the Tea Party grassroots, accompanied by rhetoric labeling Democrats communists and fascists, makes bipartisan cooperation, and hence governance, impossible. When the president addressed his concern over this trend in a speech to congressional Republicans in January 2010, he spoke directly to a major toxic byproduct of Beck's success. "The fact of the matter is that many of you, if you voted with the administration on something, are politically vulnerable in your own base, in your own party," Obama said. "You've given yourselves very little room to work in a bipartisan fashion because what you've been telling your constituents is, 'This guy's doing all kinds of crazy stuff that is going to destroy America.'"

There are other concerns raised by Beck's rising influence. Some worry that Beck threatens more than the further retardation of an already dysfunctional two-party system. They warn that Beck's fearmongering and message of ticking-clock urgency can only lead to violence.

This is surely the prospect that most terrifies Beck. He knows his audience and understands better than anyone that the game he's playing could backfire. A common refrain in his books and broadcasts is a plea to fans to "leave your rifles at home." And usually they do. But as one popular sign read at the September 12, 2009, march on Washington, WE LEFT OUR GUNS AT HOME—THIS TIME.

Violence does not come only in the form of fertilizer truck bombs and hollow-point bullets. Even if none of his fans ever decides that the time has come to, in the words of Thomas Jefferson, "refresh the tree of liberty with the blood of patriots and tyrants," Beck has racked up a killed-in-action count in his war against history and reason that is worthy of John Rambo. The wasteland that has resulted from this mindless one-man rampage was on view on the afternoon of November 5, 2009. That was the day the GOP House leadership spoke on Capitol Hill before five thousand Tea Party activists. In turn, the ranking Republicans took to the podium to rail against Democratic health-care reform legislation. None took issue with the giant banner before them depicting a pile of Holocaust victims above the words NATIONAL SOCIALIST HEALTHCARE, DACHAU, GERMANY, 1945.

During the last outbreak of pseudo-conservatism, in the 1950s, the head of the Republican Party led the army that liberated Dachau. Fast-forward to the era of Beck, and the Nazi camps are just another Fox News ratings chit, useful in firing up the grassroots. For the Right's recent accomplishment of draining language and history pale and rehydrating them with propagandistic nonsense, Beck deserves much of the credit. During his rapid rise from Top 40 tool bag to Fox News scaremonger in chief, Beck has never hesitated to employ everything at his disposal: the death of his own mother, the physical handicap of his first child, and the millions murdered by Adolf Hitler and Joseph Stalin. He does it all to fill bench space in his tent show. The fact that we've seen his kind before, and will again, doesn't make him any easier to swallow. Perhaps this is Beck's greatest achievement. As familiar as apple pie, he nonetheless feels like something new and uniquely repulsive in American life.

1

Portrait of a Young Deejay

G lenn Lee Beck was born in Mount Vernon, Washington, on February 10, 1964. The third child and only son of William and Mary Beck, he remained in the idyllic farm town of fifteen thousand for most of his childhood. In terms of the scenery that surrounded him, he enjoyed a charmed youth. Framed by the snowcapped Cascade Mountains, Mount Vernon bleeds out into the rolling tulip meadows celebrated each spring during the Skagit County Tulip Festival. When Beck was a teenager, the area was also known for its bountiful high-grade marijuana harvests. After going clean in the 1990s, he would claim that he'd gotten high every day for fifteen years, starting at age fifteen.

Young Glenn's stoner apprenticeship aside, the Becks were never part of the local hippie scene, which swelled throughout the 1970s with northern California replants, among them the countercultural novelist Tom Robbins. The face-to-face community of Mount Vernon and the watercolor backdrop of Skagit Valley remain the soft-focus template for Beck's adult evocations of conservative "real" America. He has also pointed to the area's old-stock white demographic—largely made up of descendants of Swedish, German, and Dutch settlers—as the source of his lingering discomfort around religious Jews and ethnic minorities. "I'm the whitest guy you will ever meet," Beck never tires of saying. "The first time I saw an African American, my dad had to tell me to stop staring."

The Becks were best known around Mount Vernon for William's downtown family business, the City Bakery. Growing up, Glenn would sometimes wake before dawn and help his father to prepare the day's cakes and cookies. From the bakery, it was a short walk to one of Beck's favorite childhood hangouts, an old-time ice cream parlor called the Big Scoop. William Beck was the last of several generations of Beck bakers. Before moving into talk radio in the 1990s, Glenn would briefly consider reviving the family tradition.

The Becks had a reputation as a patriotic family with an eccentric streak. Mary Beck fancied herself something of a modern-day Martha Washington, hand-sewing Revolutionary War uniforms for her husband and children, which they dutifully wore for local parades. When a mall moved into the area in 1973, threatening local small businesses, the Becks helped to spearhead an attempt to save Mount Vernon's downtown by rebranding it as a West Coast "colonial village."

Playing on the town's shared name with Mount Vernon, Virginia, a few stores went along with the plan, adding fake brick facades and hanging lanterns next to their doors. As part of the campaign, Beck donned his Revolutionary War costume and played the part of a flag bearer on Mount Vernon's streets, marching alongside a friend dressed as a Revolutionary drummer boy. "One of their cars had a bumper sticker that said, 'This country is a Republic, not a Democracy,'" remembers Mike Kamb, a childhood friend of Glenn's. "The family definitely leaned to the right."

The Beck family was active at the Immaculate Conception Catholic Church, whose school Glenn and his older sisters attended from first through sixth grades. The family attended Sunday Mass, but their enthusiasm for religion was not strong. This was especially true of Beck's father. Just as Glenn would later convert to Mormonism while in his thirties, William Beck had adopted Catholicism as an adult; it was Mary's precondition for marriage.

Before meeting his future wife, William had adhered to a modern form of spirituality known as Religious Science. Developed by Ernest Shurtleff Holmes, the "science of mind" philosophy combined a Unitarian belief in God with a humanistic belief that we ultimately determine our destinies through our thoughts and actions. Holmes is considered a prototheorist of the modern self-help movement; he was the chief inspiration behind Norman Vincent Peale's 1952 best seller, *The Power of Positive Thinking*.

These ideas trickled down to the young Glenn. Holmes has graced Beck's recommended-reading lists, and a dime-store version of the science of mind philosophy appears just two pages into his 2003 memoir-cum-manifesto, *The Real America*. "I have found there are four steps to change," writes Beck. "1. You must want it. 2. You must believe it. 3. You must live it. 4. You will become it."

As Beck likes to tell it, his destiny in radio was sealed on February 10, 1972, his eighth birthday. That was when Mary Beck presented her son with the gift that would change his life: a double-record collection of comedic and dramatic radio productions from the Depression and war years. Beck credits these records, titled *The Golden Years of Radio*, with sparking his initial fascination with the medium. "[I was] mesmerized by the magic [that] radio was, how it could create pictures in my head," Beck later wrote.[1] One program in particular caught the boy's interest and launched his imagination in the direction of radio: Orson Welles's infamous faux news report rendering of H. G. Wells's *The War of the Worlds*. Welles's production would become a recurring motif in Beck's career.[2]

A tall and gangly child, Beck avoided sports. "He wasn't very graceful," says a childhood friend. Instead, Beck spent much of his time inside, where he recorded his voice and attempted to mimic the famous radio voices of yesteryear. He also practiced magic. During junior high he appeared on small local stages dressed in a tuxedo. At talent shows and at Mount Vernon's country club, he conquered a fear of audiences. He even had his own corporate logo by the time he was eleven. Behind him onstage, during each performance, a stylized hand-painted sign announced, NOW SHOWING THE MAGICIAN GLENN BECK.

Driving his interest in dramatic radio and magic was a general enthrallment with show-business heavyweights. When friends spent the night, they knew that Glenn would make them stay up and watch his childhood hero, Johnny Carson. "He was very aware that Carson got his start in radio," says Mike Kamb. "He always had a fascination with the big names in entertainment. He loved Welles, Groucho Marx. He was sure that's what he wanted to do from the beginning. He liked being at the center of attention."

Beck landed his first radio gig in 1977 at the age of thirteen. When Mount Vernon's local AM station, KBRC, held a contest for an hour on the air, there was never much question that Beck would win. For years, he had been practicing the art of the after-school bedroom deejay. Still, he was green. "My voice hadn't even changed," he has said of those first efforts. "I was sounding out words."

This early adolescent triumph in radio came against the backdrop of an increasingly troubled home life. As the local economy entered a downturn in the late 1970s, William's bakery struggled. The financial stress took its toll on the Becks' marriage, and in 1977, William and Mary divorced. Glenn, thirteen, and his sister Michelle, seventeen, moved south with their mother to the Tacoma suburb of Sumner.

Early one morning in May 1979, almost two years after her divorce, Mary Beck went fishing in Washington's Puget Sound. Her companions on the expedition were a retired papermaker named Orean Carroll, whose twenty-four-foot leisure boat she boarded near the Tacoma suburb of Puyallup, and her pet dachshund. Exactly what happened next remains shrouded in the morning mist, but only the dog would survive the day. The boat was recovered late that afternoon, adrift near Vashon Island, just north of Tacoma. It was empty except for a few personal items, the dog, and an empty pint of Gordon's vodka. Mary Beck's lifeless body was discovered floating nearby. Carroll's corpse washed ashore at the Vashon ferry terminal later that afternoon.

The county coroner found no evidence of violence on either body. The police investigators told Tacoma's *News Tribune* that the double drowning appeared to be a classic man-overboard mishap: a failed rescue attempt in which both parties perished.

Over the course of many retellings, the tragedy of Mary Beck would become the cornerstone event in her son's personal narrative of redemption. But state records and newspaper accounts tell a different story from the one that Beck has often recounted about his mother's death. Beck has always described his mother's drowning as a suicide that occurred when he was thirteen. Yet newspaper accounts and government records confirm that a forty-one-year-old woman named Mary Beck died "a classic drowning victim" in Puyallup in May 1979, when Beck was fifteen. "Everyone at the time viewed it as a terrible accident," remembers Mike Kamb, who was a pallbearer at Mary Beck's funeral. That Mary Beck killed herself surprised even Glenn Beck's first wife,

Claire, who had never heard of the alleged suicide until she heard her husband discussing it live on the radio.[3]

Whatever the circumstances surrounding his mother's death, the event brought Beck back under the roof of his father, who was living in the northern Washington suburb of Bellingham. There the fifteen-year-old Beck enrolled at Seahome High School and deepened his involvement in the world of radio. Among the courses offered at Seahome was a drama class whose teacher shared Beck's love of Golden Age broadcasting. One of the class projects involved visiting the studios of the local station WGMI, where Beck and his peers produced Orson Welles's "The War of the Worlds," complete with live scripts and sound effects.

As he entered his middle teenage years, Beck developed a technical love of sound, which he joined with conventional tastes in pop music. "Beck and his crew were devoted audiophiles," remembers a family friend. "Glenn was big into stereophonics, home-stereo stuff like turntables, equalizers, the newest speakers." The teenage Beck and his friends would get high and listen to bands like Cheap Trick, Supertramp, and the Electric Light Orchestra.

Beck wasn't just an average kid playing records and dreaming of becoming a famous deejay. At fifteen, he was already reading the local trade publications and charting a practical course to get there. It was in one of these publications that he saw a help-wanted ad for KUBE-93, Seattle's newly launched FM station. A high school junior at the time, he was hired on the basis of an audition tape that station managers assumed was the polished work of an older man. Beck's radio voice had already matured. "When he showed up, he didn't even have a driver's license and wasn't eligible for a worker's permit, but we hired him anyway," says Michael O'Shea, Beck's manager at the station.

From his father's home in Bellingham, Beck took a series of buses every Friday after school to KUBE's Seattle studio complex. There he spent entire weekends, sleeping between shifts on the conference-room floor. "He had a love of radio that reminded me of myself at his age, so I sort of became his mentor," remembers O'Shea. "We'd listen to his show and critique it in the studio. We took him under our wing as a bright young guy."

At KUBE, Beck befriended radio pros twice his age and learned about the multiple revolutions then transforming radio on both frequencies—revolutions that would make his future career possible.

First among these was the abandonment of AM frequencies by music stations for the richer sound quality of FM. Out of this void emerged hundreds of AM stations organized around the format known as news-talk. Across the country, a new generation of talk hosts emerged, some of them emulating New York's right-wing talk pioneer Bob Grant, who catered to white males who were confused and threatened by the cultural shifts of the 1960s and 1970s. On the technical side of the changes sweeping the industry, the introduction of satellite technology in 1978 marked the beginning of radio's syndication revolution.

When Beck graduated from high school in 1982, he was more familiar with these changes than were most eighteen-year-olds. He had five years of on-air experience on his résumé and no doubts about what he wanted to do with his life. Since no one in his family had ever attended college, it was not a rebellious act when he chose to pursue a career in radio. Working, Beck reasoned, was the quickest way to fulfill his childhood dream of reaching Rockefeller Center's Radio City Studios. Although Beck had never been east of Iowa, he had taken serious note of the mysterious midtown Manhattan castle mentioned in the liner notes of *The Golden Years of Radio.* In the late summer of 1982, Beck began a winding and unlikely quest to reach that storied address.

Provo, Utah, was not what the young disc jockey had in mind when he left Washington state to find fame and fortune. Just south of Salt Lake City, Provo might be the least fun city of its size in the United States. It hosts both Brigham Young University and Utah's missionary training center. With its 90 percent Mormon population, the town would have been a disappointment for any ambitious teenager. And Beck, not yet a religious conservative, was a partyer. He smoked pot and drank beer at home; he smoked clove cigarettes and drank coffee at work.

Beck was sent to Provo by First Media, a Mormon company based in Washington, D.C., which also owned his Seattle station. Run by the hotel-empire scion Dick Marriott, First Media had a growing portfolio of FM frequencies at the time, including KAYK, better known as K-96, a small adult-contemporary station in Provo.

The K-96 studios offered no refuge from the surrounding Mormon culture. The station played religious music on Sundays and maintained a G-rated playlist. Worse, the Mormons who staffed the station openly sniffed at Beck's coffee and cigarette habits. Faced with the condescension of his colleagues, he happily returned fire. "The first day I went to the radio station, I pulled out a cigarette and everybody said, 'Oh. I thought you were Mormon,'" Beck later wrote. "And I said, 'Oh. I thought you were normal.'" Beck called his Mormon colleagues "freaks," which quickly soured his relationships with everyone around him. Years later, Beck politely told the Salt Lake City *Deseret News*, "I lived in Provo for six months [and] didn't fit in." The short stint would set the pattern for the next decade of Beck's career.

The shining Mormon city may have been a young gentile's purgatory, but there was career logic to paying dues at K-96. First Media's other properties included WPGC, a respected Top 40 AM/FM powerhouse that served Greater Washington, D.C. The station had "blowtorch" tower power, defined as fifty thousand watts or higher, and in 1983 it was famous in the industry for being among the last of the big old-style Top 40 stations to resist format fragmentation. As niche formats became the norm, WPGC stayed relatively free-form and inclusive, a last bastion of rock 'n' roll, broadly defined, past and present.

When a job opened up at WPGC in February 1983, Beck seized it. More than just an escape from Utah, the transfer was a professional leap forward. The station didn't look like much—the cramped predigital studio was housed in a dingy building by the Baltimore-Washington Parkway—but the transmitter reached a large urban market, crisp and clear. Just as important, it was staffed by hip, ambitious young radio pros. There was even a tinge of celebrity glamour at the station. Among the members of the WPGC morning team was Joe Theismann, then an active All-Pro quarterback for the Washington Redskins, fresh off a Super Bowl victory.

Beck quickly gained a reputation at WPGC for three things: punctuality, a serious demeanor streaked with mordant wit, and a closet full of skinny ties. "Glenn had a very dark sense of humor. And he sort of lurked. You often got the sense that he was observing us, soaking everything up, trying to learn the craft of radio," remembers Dave Foxx, a morning colleague of Beck's. "He never talked politics back then. He even used to chide Theismann for his political rants, telling him, 'Well, don't sugarcoat it, Joe.'" This isn't to say that the young Beck was mousy. "He was a brash, outspoken guy off the air," remembers a former member of the WPGC news team. "He was always smoking these really funky-smelling foreign cigarettes."

Beck often says that he ran with a "bad crew" during his time at WPGC. It's a strange judgment, considering that the center of his social life in Washington was Claire, a pretty redhead from WPGC accounting who would become his wife and the mother of his first two children. The other major figure in Beck's social circle was a hard-living young deejay named Bruce Kelly. Arriving at WPGC from Miami around the same time as Beck, Kelly also met his first wife at the station. The four frequently double-dated and remained friends for years after leaving D.C.

The close friendship between Beck and Kelly began during a massive blizzard on Valentine's Day weekend. Both new to the station, they were the only two people working an overnight shift. To kill time, they passed joints back and forth in the office of the station president, Glenn Potter, a strict Mormon. Throughout the night, the two struggled to keep from laughing on the air and warned drivers to be careful on the roads. "When Jeane Oats, the manager, came in that morning, she thought we were laughing out of exhaustion, but we were just really stoned," says Kelly. "She told us to go home and get some sleep."

Like Beck, Bruce Kelly was precocious. Unlike Beck, Kelly had already mastered both the art of the publicity stunt and the marketing side of the business. As a twenty-year-old deejay in Virginia, Kelly had donned a white tuxedo and dived into a twenty-thousand-gallon tank of Jell-O. During the late 1970s, he had flown on private jets, toured Europe with Led Zeppelin, and partied with Bob Marley. In short, he was Beck's first hip radio friend. It was at Kelly's side that Beck began his decade-long relationship with cocaine.

As their bond deepened, the two started thinking aloud about hitting the big time together. While cutting up lines in Beck's D.C. apartment, the pair talked about teaming up to do a show. Fame. The big money. "Glenn clearly had it," says Kelly. "I wanted to work with him, and we started making plans."

It was not to be. Before the end of 1983, Beck's biggest booster within First Media, a rough-edged Mormon and former Marine named Jim Sumpter, became vice president of the Malkan radio chain in Texas. Among Sumpter's first moves was to lure Beck southwest with the promise of his own morning show at KZFM, Corpus Christi's leading

Top 40 station. It was there, in southern Texas between 1983 and 1985, that Glenn Beck fought his first ratings war. In the process, a new Glenn Beck was born. It was a person Bruce Kelly would not recognize when the two friends were reunited in Phoenix in 1987.

Beck rolled into Texas in late 1983 driving a blue two-seater Datsun 280Z sports coupe. On the bumper was a REAGAN-BUSH '84 reelection sticker. At his side was his wife, Claire. And taking form in Beck's mind was an invisible character with a high-pitched voice named Clydie Clyde, who would accompany Beck throughout his Top 40 career.

Beck's arrival in Corpus Christi coincided with a sea change in morning radio. It was known as the morning zoo revolution, and it is the key to understanding Glenn Beck's career, both in Top 40 radio and beyond. Before the X-rated in-studio antics of the shock jocks, there were the skit-writing schlock jocks of the zoo. The zoo's fast-paced approach to morning radio is perhaps best captured by two words that were practically invented to describe the format: *wacky* and *zany*. In its purest form, the zoo formula consisted of an ensemble cast that employed fake voices, loosely scripted skits, adolescent pranks, short topical rants, and spoof songs, backed by a Top 40 soundtrack and peppered with news and traffic reports. Beck was not a pioneer of zoo radio, but he was a member of the founding generation. The influence on his approach to broadcasting endures.

If the zoo revolution had a Lenin and a Trotsky, they were Scott Shannon and Cleveland Wheeler. The formula, as envisioned by the two Tampa, Florida, deejays, was a mixture of *Saturday Night Live, The Tonight Show, The Gong Show*, and outrageous talk radio. The idea was not completely original. During the late 1970s, the "Ross and Wilson" morning team on Atlanta's WZGC had built a reputation by performing pranks and acting out skits between songs and news reports. But Shannon and Wheeler sped up and built on the Ross and Wilson template. In the weeks before its first show, the duo formed a high-powered ensemble cast of the funniest, most creative people in Tampa.

"I was broadcasting my sports show live at a bar, and Shannon came up to me and tells me I'm going to quit my job and work for him," remembers Tedd Webb, an alumnus of Shannon's original zoo crew. "When I balked, he doubled my salary on the spot and told me it was going to be something very hot."

It was. Within four months of launching the *Q-Zoo*, Shannon and Wheeler owned every demographic in Tampa Bay. The show was a phenomenon: number one across the board, it produced unheard-of numbers and became the most talked-about development in radio. Within a year, the *Q-Zoo* was drawing the biggest share of adult listeners of any station in the country. The success was so complete and unprecedented that the impact was global. Deejays from Australia and Europe made pilgrimages to observe Shannon and Wheeler live in-studio and take notes. They returned home to spawn copycat zoo shows.

It is appropriate that the zoo was born in the age of cocaine. The essence of successful zoo radio was speed and rapid-fire creativity, creating a nonstop on-air party. Even when deejays were talking, Top 40 hits continued playing in the background. Zoo deejays, often fueled by that decade's iconic powder, pushed morning radio from peppy to manic.

"We'd be out all night partying, then go straight to the studio at dawn, cut up some lines, and start brainstorming skits based on news clippings from the early edition," remembers Webb. "It was a blast, but you had to be fast and you had to perform. Sometimes we'd sketch out a four-hour show in thirty minutes on no sleep."

Another part of zoo culture that reflected the ethos of the era was the deejay as high-flying and hard-partying local celebrity. Promotional events that featured morning zoo teams grew extravagant as the decade progressed. Bloated salaries and gilded perks fed egos. By the early 1980s, it was common for morning deejays to appear at promotional events in stretch limousines.

There is no understanding Beck's present-day shtick without first understanding the zoo revolution that transformed morning radio in the 1980s. Many of the audio and visual tropes that Beck employs today—the Muppet voices, the outrageous statements, the props, the stunts, the often fawning and giggling supporting cast—can be traced to the zoo and postzoo radio culture that sustained him professionally for years.

"You can see the influence in everything Beck does," says zoo pioneer Scott Shannon, who is now boss jock at New York's WPLJ and the official voice of *The Sean Hannity Show*. "The timing, the voices, the inflections, the whole approach—so much of it is from the old Top 40 morning style."

Brian Wilson (not the Beach Boy), a radio personality who was one of Shannon's original inspirations for the zoo idea, likewise notes Beck's successful adaptation and carryover from 1980s morning radio. "His performance in talk radio and television is full of hangover of basic Top 40 elements, formats, and principles," says Wilson, now a libertarian talk-show host. "The sound drops, the effects, the 'wackiness'—he's doing the same thing, minus the music."

"The first time I heard him do talk radio, I knew he was updating what [Rush] Limbaugh did when he brought Top 40 tricks into talk," says Barry Kaye, who competed with Beck in Corpus Christi and Houston in the 1980s. "Everything he does is basically a morning show. He was always great at it."

When Glenn Beck assumed morning-show duties at KZFM in Corpus Christi in 1983, the zoo model was ascendant. It was the year that Scott Shannon moved to New York to found WHTZ, better known as Z100, where Shannon's Z *Morning Zoo* took the station to number one in the market in under three months of its birth. Closer to Beck's new home, John Lander had just launched what would be a long-running and heavily syndicated morning zoo on Houston's KKBQ.

Like the shows on dozens of stations that were beginning to broadcast generic zoos around the country, Beck's first morning show was titled simply *The Morning Zoo*. It wasn't a playbook zoo, because it lacked an ensemble, but it had a zoo spirit. It was fast paced, and it featured skits and fake characters voiced by Beck. Beck's main cartoon character was named Clydie Clyde, a Muppet-voiced alter ego based on the most widely imitated character of that type at the time, Mr. Leonard from Shannon and Wheeler's original zoo team. Beck was not alone among zoo deejays who were imitating some version of Mr. Leonard, but his imitation was especially brazen.

"Radio is the only medium I know of where plagiarism is acceptable," says zoo pioneer Cleveland Wheeler. "It is a real unattractive form of flattery for which TV, print, and film have zero tolerance. For some reason, all levels of the [radio] business seem to consider any content, idea, or performance to be public domain and ripe for taking."

Beck's Corpus Christi show consisted of Beck, Clydie Clyde, and a newsreader. It was immediately clear to his colleagues that Beck was a young man on the move. "He was extremely talented, and he knew it," says Tod Tucker, who hosted the slot after Beck's at KZFM. "At first we didn't get along because he was so arrogant, but we became friends. He always talked about going to New York City and making it big. That was his dream."

He didn't advertise it, but at nineteen, Beck was the youngest morning zoo host and program director in the country. "At the time I thought he was in his mid- to late twenties," says Barry Kaye, former program director at KITE, a rival station. "He was an incredible talent to be working at that level at that age."

⌐ "Glenn was a young preppy kid with a bit of an attitude," remembers Meryl Uranga, a program and music director at KZFM. "I had never smelled clove cigarettes before I met him. Hanging out with Beck was also the first time I ever saw certain drugs. He partied a lot."

Along with giving Beck the space to develop creatively, Corpus Christi offered a crash course in the business side of radio. As a manager and programmer, Beck was responsible for tailoring KZFM's appeal to Corpus Christi's complicated market, a diverse population of Hispanics, whites, blacks, and active military personnel. And there was enormous pressure to get the formula right. At the time, KZFM was engaged in a heated ratings war with its rival, KITE.

In the studio, the early 1980s were the age of the zoo. In the back office, they were the age of federal deregulation. In 1982, the Federal Communications Commission (FCC) began removing the constraints on radio ownership across a range of areas, from public-service content quotas to filing requirements. Among the most consequential changes was the revocation of an antitrafficking rule that barred investors from quickly flipping stations for profit. The result was a radio bubble fueled by a newly feverish market for properties. To pick just one example from Beck's career, his future employer, WKCI in Connecticut, sold for $6 million in 1983. Three years later it went for $30 million. Between 1982 and 1990, almost half of the country's radio stations would change hands at least once.

This new quick-sell culture affected radio pros in numerous ways. As owners came and went, experimenting with staff and formulas, turnover rates increased. The result was a caste of radio vagabonds like Beck, who in effect wore a sign that declared, "Have mouth, will travel."

Increasingly, deejays did not know where they'd be at the end of the next Arbitron ratings quarter.

The new economics of radio ushered in a new golden age of ratings wars. As station values and salaries ballooned, so did pressure for market share and media attention. Because morning shows were the biggest and most personality-driven piece of Top 40 programming, rival morning teams in the 1980s fought wars with entertaining, and occasionally bloody, ferocity.

"Some radio people remember the radio battles of the 1980s for the off-air ugliness in the station parking lot," says Sean Ross, who tracks the radio industry for Edison Research. "It was a heady era in morning radio."

KZFM hired Beck as part of a stationwide blood infusion to replenish a staff that was being picked apart by rival KITE. The owner of the station and Beck's new boss was Arnold Malkan, a conservative Republican and an attorney known for his hot temper and his litigiousness. As Malkan hurled legal threats across town, the two stations' morning teams did battle on the air and off. This war often involved a heavy dose of camp. The military metaphor of a ratings war became literal when KITE's morning-zoo team christened itself the KITE Killers and began attending promotional events dressed in army surplus camouflage fatigues and berets. "They'd roll up to promotional gigs and jump out of the limo in uniform, waving plastic machine guns," remembers Barry Kaye.

Beck manned the KZFM war room in his civvies, but he had a military bent of mind. His hard-nosed mentor and recruiter, Jim Sumpter, instructed Beck and his fellow deejays to fight to win.

"Sumpter was one of the most vicious managers I ever competed against," remembers Chuck Dunaway, a KITE staffer who arrived in Corpus Christi around the same time as Beck. "Our two stations would have bombed each other if we could have done it legally."

"Jim Sumpter was a master at guerrilla war," says Tod Tucker, Beck's fellow deejay at KZFM. "I like to say that God gave Beck his talent, and Sumpter taught him how to use it." Sumpter, now a prominent "birther"—a member of the movement of people who question the validity of Barack Obama's birth certificate and thus his presidency—and a syndicated right-wing talk-show host, continued to work with Beck in various capacities until the early 1990s.

The morning mischief between the rival stations escalated after Beck's arrival in Corpus Christi. Chuck Dunaway, Beck's now retired former rival, recalls that early in his tenure he showed up at the KITE studio and found the station's front doors—the only exit in a converted storefront building—glued shut. A demolition crew had to knock the front doors down so that the KITE Killers could get inside in time to start their show. Then there were other pranks, which posed less of a fire hazard. Throughout 1983, Dunaway and his staff were anonymously placed on dozens of mailing lists for magazines and books sent cash on delivery. The sound track for it all was a Beck-written *Ghostbusters* spoof song, called "KITE-Busters," which became a local hit during Beck's morning show.

"We were the 'good guys' and didn't do any vandalism," says Dunaway. "In fifty years of broadcasting, I have never been in a market where those kinds of things were done. Who was behind the mischief I cannot identify, but it was during the time Beck was the morning competition."

In pursuing a career in Top 40, Beck opted out of a college education—at least, the academic part of a college education. In the *Animal House*–inspired world of 1980s morning radio, Beck found a real-world corollary to fraternity high jinks.

Beck's one-man zoo at KZFM held firm against the KITE Killers, and he won his first ratings war. By 1985, he was a polished morning deejay in the zoo mold. He had programming experience and two years' worth of tapes demonstrating wacky morning chops to broadcasters across a nation that was newly hungry for them.

One station that was looking to modernize was WRKA in Louisville, Kentucky. In mid-1985, the station tapped Beck—who at twenty-one now had eight years of radio experience—to headline the station's morning-drive slot. Although the station had been number one in morning drive for four years, Beck's new bosses thought it was only a matter of time before the cultural curve came around to clobber them.

The station had reason to worry. At the time of Beck's arrival, its on-air personalities and playlists were staid, bordering on geriatric, as captured in the WRKA slogan, "Between Rock and the Rocking Chair." Like Beck's future bosses at Clear Channel Communications and CNN,

WRKA saw Beck as the bright new thing capable of drawing a younger audience. A $70,000 salary made Beck the largest investment in the station's makeover. As a signing bonus, he received a gold Rolex.

Beck's first full-scale zoo show was known as *Captain Beck and the A-Team*. For four hours every weekday morning, Beck sat in WRKA's small, dimly lighted studio across from his producer and sidekick, Bob Dries. Dries was to Beck what Ed McMahon was to Johnny Carson and Artie Lange is to Howard Stern; he cackled like a hen every time Beck made a wisecrack. "It was Dries's job to punch buttons to launch sound effects and laugh like he'd just won the lottery at every single limp Glenn Beck joke," remembers a former WRKA colleague of Beck's.

With Dries across the console, Beck directed a rotating ensemble cast and wrote or cowrote daily gags and skits. Among the show's regular characters was Beck's zoo alter ego, Clydie Clyde. But Clyde was just one of Beck's unseen radio ventriloquist dolls.

"He was amazing to watch when he was doing his cast of voices," remembers Kathi Lincoln, Beck's former newsreader. "Sometimes he'd prerecord different voices and talk back to the tape, or turn his head side to side while speaking them live on the air. He used to do a funny 'black guy' character, really over the top."

"Black guy" impersonations were just one sign of the young Beck's racial hang-ups. Among the few recordings of *Captain Beck and the A-Team* that are archived online is a show from February 1986 in which Beck discusses that night's prime-time television schedule. When the subject turns to Peter Strauss, an actor known for starring in television's first miniseries, Beck wryly observes, "They say [that] without [Strauss's early work,] the miniseries *Roots* would never have happened." Clydie Clyde then chimes in with an exaggerated and ironic "Oh, darn." The throwaway dig at *Roots*, which chronicled the life of a slave family, wins knowing chuckles from Beck's cohosts.

Beck's real broadcasting innovation during his stay in Kentucky was in the realm of vicious personal assaults on fellow radio hosts. A frequent target of Beck's in Louisville was Liz Curtis, the host of an afternoon advice show on WHAS, a local AM news-talk station. It was no secret that Curtis, whom Beck had never met and with whom he did not compete for ratings, was overweight. And Beck never let anyone forget it. For two years, he used "the big blond" as fodder for drive-time fat jokes, often employing Godzilla sound effects to simulate Curtis walking across the city or crushing a rocking chair. Days before Curtis's marriage, Beck penned a skit featuring a stolen menu card for the wedding reception. "The caterer says that instead of throwing rice after the ceremony, they are going to throw hot buttered popcorn," explains Beck's fictional spy.

Despite the constant goading, Curtis never responded. But being ignored only seemed to fuel Beck's hunger for a response. As his attacks escalated and grew more unhinged, a WHAS colleague of Curtis's named Terry Meiners decided to intervene. He appeared unannounced one morning at Beck's small office, which was filled with plaques, letters, and news clippings—"a shrine to all that is Glenn Beck," remembers Meiners. He told Beck to lay off Curtis, suggesting that he instead attack a morning deejay like himself, who could return the fire.

"Beck told me, 'Sorry, all's fair in love and war,'" says Meiners. "He continued with the fat jokes, which were exceedingly cruel, pointless, and aimed at one of the nicest people in radio. Glenn Beck was over-the-top childish from day one, a punk who tried to make a name for himself by being disruptive and vengeful."

Louisville is where Beck began experimenting with another streak that would become more pronounced in later years: militaristic patriot-ism and calls for the indiscriminate bombing of Muslims.

The birth of Glenn Beck as radio superpatriot can be traced to the morning of April 15, 1986. It was the morning after Ronald Reagan ordered U.S. warplanes to bomb Libyan president Moammar Qaddafi's Tripoli palace in response to the bombing of a Berlin nightclub frequented by U.S. servicemen. Beck sounded stoned during the show—and given his later claim to have smoked pot every day for fifteen years, he might have been—but even then his politics were anything but tie-dyed.

After opening with a prayer and Lee Greenwood's "God Bless the USA," Beck played patriotic music throughout the morning. The only track receiving multiple plays was a New Wave–like spoof titled "Qaddafi Sucks." The song was a huge hit with listeners, dozens of whom called Beck to tell him how inspired they were by his patriotism. Caller after caller applauded him for "standing up for America." When someone argued that Reagan should have dropped more bombs, Beck agreed. "I personally don't think we did enough," he said. "We should've went [sic] over there and bombed the hell out of 'em."

What's most notable about this early version of Glenn Beck as superpatriot is his near listlessness. There are none of the fire-breathing, teary-eyed histrionics that would define Beck's future radio and TV persona. Even while offering up star-spangled red meat, Beck sounded as if he would rather have been smacking Liz Curtis around. When a young male caller suggested kidnapping Libyan agents and then torturing them by sliding them down razor blades into waiting pools of alcohol, Beck simply replied, "Thanks for the call. Buh-bye."

Whether Beck was tired or stoned that day, he was almost certainly depressed. Despite his creative freedom, his local star status, and his high salary, Beck's mental state was on a slide. By his own telling, he was drinking heavily, snorting coke, and entertaining thoughts of suicide. "There was a bridge abutment in Louisville, Kentucky, that had my name on it," Beck later wrote. "Every day I prayed for the strength to be able to drive my car at 70 mph into that bridge abutment. I'm only alive today because (a) I'm too cowardly to kill myself, and (b) I'm too stupid."

Beck left Louisville at the end of 1986 a defeated man. His signature mix of Qaddafi songs, fat jokes, and racial impersonations had made waves but had failed to produce numbers. With Beck at the helm during morning drive, WRKA slipped to third in the market. He was fired, and the station brought its youth experiment to an end. As Beck and his wife packed their bags for Phoenix in early 1987, WRKA switched to an oldies format.[4]

Beck was hired once again as a strategic youth injection. This time the channel in need of fresh energy was the Phoenix Top 40 powerhouse KOY-FM, known as Y95. The station brought in Beck to fill the morning shoes of a middle-aged deejay named Bill Heywood, whose mellow persona and long career made him a Phoenix institution, yet one out of step with the times. Heywood may have interviewed John F. Kennedy and Frank Sinatra, but he lacked the zany chops required to keep up with Beck's old friend from D.C., Bruce Kelly, who was then hosting the market's leading morning show on rival station KZZP. As usual, Kelly was respected as a flamboyant master of publicity stunts as well as a top-rated morning jock. Since parting ways with Beck in D.C., he had completed the Boston Marathon on a custom pogo stick and convinced Senator John McCain to dive into a pool of liquid chocolate. To compete with Kelly, Y95 needed someone who could make a lot of noise. Beck was their man.

At first, Kelly was happy to have his old friend in the same town. "My wife and I were excited when Glenn and Claire told us they were moving to Phoenix," says Kelly. But these warm feelings didn't last long. Something had changed in Beck. In Phoenix, Beck became known as an outsized and mischievous ego—a reputation that would dog him for the rest of his Top 40 career. This new Beck was symbolized by the cars that stocked the garage of his Phoenix ranch house: a navy blue Cadillac and that symbol of 1980s egomaniacal excess, a DeLorean.

The station partnered Beck with a twenty-six-year-old Arizona native named Tim Hattrick. More relaxed by nature than Beck, Hattrick expected that the two would share duties on the show as partners. But Beck had other ideas. On his first day in the studio, Beck called Hattrick into his office and laid down the law.

"I remember Glenn sat me down and pulled out a notepad on which he had drawn a planet being orbited by satellites," says Hattrick. "On the big planet, he wrote 'Me.' Then he pointed to the orbiting satellites and wrote names on them, such as 'Tim,' 'News,' and 'Clydie Clyde.' I'll never forget Glenn telling me I was a satellite. He was younger than me but carried himself like he was thirty-five or forty."

Dispelling any doubts about the station's new direction, Y95 also rented a mascot monkey named Zippy the Chimp. The station managers flew Beck and Hattrick to New York, where they watched Scott Shannon run his zoo at Z100. Back in Phoenix, the Beck-Hattrick show was announced in a local television ad that marks the twenty-three-year-old Beck's TV debut. In the thirty-second spot, Beck appears puffy-faced in a brown leather jacket. Next to him is the slimmer Hattrick in a satin Phoenix Suns warmer. The two young deejays are sitting in the studio stirring each other's coffee when an announcer's voice declares: "The new Y95 morning zookeepers: Glenn Beck and Tim Hattrick!"

> *Beck*: We told our bosses right up front, "We don't need *gimmicks* to sell the new Y95."
> *Hattrick*: We've got a better mix of music, great deejays who don't *yack* too much—

Beck: Plenty of easy contests for you to win *lots* of free money—
Hattrick: Plus more continuous music, Y95 Airborne traffic reports,
    and special guests!
Beck: With all that, who needs *gimmicks*?

As Beck delivers this last line, balloons and cash fall from the ceiling, model airplanes zip by, and a loud cuckoo clock goes off, sight unseen. A chimpanzee named Zippy the Chimp then jumps onto the table wearing a yellow Y MORNING ZOO T-shirt. The ad summarizes in thirty seconds most of what you need to know about the first fifteen years of Beck's radio career.

Beck never grew close to Hattrick, who thought that his new partner was talented but full of himself and incapable of thinking of anything but radio and ratings. "Beck lived, ate, drank, and breathed radio," says Hattrick, who still works as a deejay in Phoenix. "It was impossible to talk to him about anything without reference to how to bring it into the show. I never once saw any evidence that he could turn it off. In that sense he was a one-dimensional person. But he was great at being a grandstanding, pompous idiot and shaking the brushes for attention."

Beck and Hattrick began their show far behind Kelly's market-leading show on KZZP. As they continued to get clobbered, Beck grew obsessed with getting his name on the leading station. His first attempt to get Kelly to mention him on the air came shortly after his arrival.

"I walked out to get the paper one Saturday morning," remembers Kelly. "When I turned around, I saw that my entire house was covered in Y95 bumper stickers. The windows, the garage doors, the locks—everything. But I refused to mention Beck's name on the air, which drove him nuts."

Beck kept trying. When KZZP's music director held his wedding at a Phoenix church, Beck loaded up Y95's two Jeeps with boxes of bumper stickers and drove to the ceremony.[5] As the service was coming to a close, Beck and his team ran, crouching, from car to car, slapping bumper stickers on anything with a fender. The service ended while Beck was running amok, and the KZZP morning team appeared just in time to see Beck jump into his getaway car.

"Beck saw me standing in the way of the exit and gunned right for me," says Kelly. "I threw a landscaping rock on his windshield and blocked him." When his old friend demanded that he roll down the window, Beck reluctantly obliged. Kelly then unloaded a mouthful of spit in his face.[6]

"Glenn Beck was the king of dirty tricks," says Guy Zapoleon, KZZP's program director. "It may seem mild in retrospect, but at the time, that wedding prank was nasty and over the line. Beck was always desperate for ratings and attention."

The animosity between Beck and Kelly continued to deepen. When Beck and Hattrick produced a local version of Orson Welles's "The War of the Worlds" for Halloween, Kelly told a local reporter that the bit was a stupid rip-off of a syndicated gag. The slight outraged Beck, who got his revenge with what may rank as one of the cruelest events in the history of morning radio.

"A couple days after Kelly's wife, Terry, had a miscarriage, Beck called her live on the air and says, 'We hear you had a miscarriage,'" remembers Brad Miller, a former Y95 deejay and Clear Channel programmer. "When Terry said yes, Beck proceeded to joke about how Bruce [Kelly] apparently can't do anything right—he can't even have a baby. It was low class," adds Miller, who is now president of Open Stream Broadcasting. "There are certain places you just don't go."

"Beck turned Y95 into a guerrilla station," says Kelly. "It was an example of the zoo thing getting out of control. It became just about pissing people off, part of the culture shift that gave us [the MTV series] *Jackass*." Among those who were appalled by Beck's prank call was Beck's own wife, Claire, who had been friends with Kelly's wife since the two had worked together at WPGC.

Even after his friendship with Kelly had soured beyond repair, and Beck continued with the stunts, some of which won the competition's begrudging admiration. The most elaborate and successful of these neatly throws a double spotlight on both the juvenile nature of morning-radio competition and the culture of pop cheese in which Beck wallowed for twenty years.

Toward the end of Beck's time in Phoenix, KZZP sponsored a free Richard Marx concert at the Tempe El Diablo stadium in downtown Phoenix. Marx was, at the time, riding high on a triple-platinum album, and the show was a monster publicity coup for Beck's rival. But Beck was in no mood to let KZZP bask in the concert's glow without a fight. He and Hattrick arrived at the stadium early on the night of the show and gave the sound technician $500 to play a prerecorded Y95 promo moments before KZZP's Bruce Kelly was scheduled to announce the concert.

As an audience of nearly ten thousand waited for the show to begin, the KZZP mics were cut, and Beck's voice suddenly boomed out of the stadium's sound system, "The Y95 zoo team is proud to present: Richard Marx!" As soon as he heard his name, an oblivious Marx walked onto the stage and began to play. As the KZZP crew stood stunned offstage, scattered Y95 agents popped up and began throwing Y95 ZOO T-shirts in every direction to a cheering crowd.

"It was brilliant," remembers Kelly. "Totally brilliant. He nailed us."

In December 1987, downtown Phoenix went without Christmas decorations because of budget problems. Y95 was asked by the mayor to lead a fundraising effort to replace them. Beck and Hattrick came up with the idea to steal decorations from the city of Scottsdale. In the process of doing just that, the pair was arrested. "It didn't quite go as planned, but it resulted in a lot of news coverage and contributed to a successful fundraiser," says Mike Horne, the station's general manager.

The stunt was a textbook case of media marketing 101: Attention is good; controversy is better. Outrage is the gift that keeps on giving. By his midtwenties, Beck had become a canny and mature publicity hound. This is seen most clearly in his first move to gain national notice. In September 1988, Beck and Hattrick invited Jessica Hahn onto the show. That month, *Playboy* magazine was featuring a pictorial of the former church secretary, who had become famous for her affair with televangelist Jim Bakker.

"That evening, we took Jessica out to dinner," remembers Mike Horne. "I got up to go to the men's room and quickly found myself surrounded at the urinal by Glenn and Tim, who began lobbying me to hire Jessica as a permanent fixture of the morning show. They negotiated the deal, which was a rental car, an apartment, and two thousand dollars a month."

One is reminded of P. T. Barnum's famous arrangement with his longtime prize midget, Tom Thumb, who received $4 a week plus board. Beck's showman instincts were indeed worthy of Barnum: The hiring of Hahn as the zoo team's "prize-and-weather bunny" became an international story. Johnny Carson and David Letterman joked about it, editorial writers debated it, and as a result Y95 received a much-needed ratings jolt. When *People* magazine visited the station looking for a quote, Beck described Hahn's radio debut as "awesome" and explained that she filled the void of a "prize bunny for our zoo." The trio was short-lived, however. After a few weeks on the job, Hahn asked to be transferred to a nighttime slot.

Toward the end of his time in Phoenix, Beck's wife, Claire, gave birth to a daughter. As with the rest of his life, Beck had incorporated his wife's pregnancy into his radio show. He asked listeners to guess when his wife would go into labor and the sex of the child. When Beck came back on the air after the birth, he announced that the delivery had been problematic and that there would be no more games around the subject. The baby girl had suffered from a series of strokes at birth, resulting in cerebral palsy. Beck named her Mary, after his mother.

"After the public buildup about the baby, it was all very awkward and sad," remembers Hattrick. "I thought it was a good lesson in being careful about personal issues on the air."

Beck would later make his national name by turning that lesson on its head. But not yet. Shortly after the birth of his daughter, Beck resigned from Y95 to accept a job in Houston. Another also-ran Top 40 station needed a buzz generator. Beck and his young family headed east, back to Texas.

Beck arrived in Houston early in 1989. After he had spent years moving forward professionally, the oil city proved to be his Waterloo. Fueled by booze and cocaine, Beck produced some of the worst radio of his life here and tarnished his reputation in what one former colleague calls an "epic meltdown."

In a reprise of Phoenix, the number two Top 40 station had hired him to compete with the market's leading morning show. His new employer, KRBE, aka Power 104, brought him on board at a salary well above that usually paid by its parent company, Susquehanna.

"There was a lot expected of him," remembers his program director, Gary Wheeler. Beck's salary, said to be around $300,000, reflected the scale of his task, which was something like the morning-radio equivalent of a kamikaze mission. Beck was up against KKBQ's *Q-Zoo*, hosted by nationally syndicated zoo superstar John Lander. The mismatch was so great that nobody expected Beck to cut deeply into Lander's royal ratings. It was enough that he generate buzz while going down in sacrificial flames.

"KRBE brought Beck in to make some noise and to create public awareness through promotions," says Ed Shane, a Houston-based radio consultant. "They just wanted Beck to be Beck, because John Lander had cornered the zoo market."

For the first time in four years, Beck was working without a supporting cast. He would succeed or fail on the strength of his own personality and his box of cartoon voices. Alone in the studio, he struggled from the start. Defined by regular back-and-forth with Clydie Clyde, the show fell flat with listeners and industry pros. Guy Zapoleon, who as a program director competed with Beck in Phoenix and Houston, remembers marveling at how awful Beck sounded. "It was horrible," says Zapoleon. "It was just Beck and Clyde talking to each other. No one could believe it was the same guy as in Phoenix."

Beck doesn't argue with this assessment. "It was the worst time in my broadcasting career, and I wish people would stop bringing it up," Beck told the *Houston Chronicle*. "It's the most embarrassing thing I ever did on radio. If I could make everybody forget about my time in Houston, it would be good."

"Glenn took risks and was able to generate talk, but he never took off in ratings," says Gary Wheeler. "The thinking at the time was [that] Glenn was misplaced as a Top 40 morning host. He was not very hip and tended to sway in content toward things that might appeal to an older or non-music listener."

Among the lame stunts that Beck would like everyone to forget is his "breakfast meat" moment. On his first show, Clydie Clyde asked listeners to compete for cash prizes by mailing a slab of breakfast meat and a raw egg to the studio in standard issue envelopes. As Beck explained at the time to a *Houston Chronicle* reporter: "See, Wednesday was our first day and before that we had been running around like chickens with our heads cut off around here. And I had mentioned at one point that I wanted to meet the listeners at local malls. But Clyde took it in a completely different direction."

It wasn't just Beck who spoke to Clydie Clyde as though he were real. Beck's conversations with the Muppet-voiced creature were so seamless and regular that listeners showed up at promotional events asking to meet the character. "People would arrive and ask, 'Where's Clydie?'" remembers Mark Schecterle, KRBE's marketing director. "We'd always tell them [that] Clyde just left the building but would be at the next event. Beck was a creative, totally nonpolitical disc jockey back then."

That judgment depends on how you define *nonpolitical*. It was in Houston, whose adopted son George H. W. Bush was about to become president, that something began stirring in Beck, hinting of ambitions that could not be contained on the platform of local FM radio.

In Kentucky, Beck's idea of supporting the military had been looping the phrase "Qaddafi sucks" over a Duran Duran beat. Three years later, just a month into his new solo gig, Beck was playing phone tag with A-list publicists in New York and Los Angeles, laying the groundwork for a military-themed patriotic extravaganza.

There was nothing zoo about it. During one week in February 1989, Beck broadcast his morning show from the deck of the USS *Theodore Roosevelt*, an aircraft carrier patrolling the Mediterranean off the Libyan coast. After receiving clearance from the Sixth Fleet, Beck began lining up prerecorded celebrity greetings and scheduled phone-in interviews with more than a dozen celebrities, which he then wove into the morning show, along with interviews with the *Roosevelt*'s crew.

Beck's handpicked celebrity guest list presents a family snapshot of 1980s American pop culture. Beck's broadcasts from sea included voice cameos by Jon Bon Jovi, Eddie Money, LaToya Jackson, Joan Jett, Cheap Trick, Martin Landau, Wil Wheaton, Kathleen Turner, Brooke Shields, Lesley Ann Warren, Tina Yothers, Bob Hope, Mickey Mouse, Pat Sajak, and Ronald Reagan. Rounding things out was a middling Houston Astros left fielder named Billy Hatcher, a famous bat corker.

No doubt the crew of the *Roosevelt* appreciated the free morning entertainment. The same could not be said for Houston's radio audience. Not even Ronald Reagan could generate enough excitement around Beck's show to justify his enormous salary.

"Radio is about numbers, and Beck didn't produce them," says Mark Schecterle, Beck's KRBE colleague. "So they fired him."

It was not an amicable split. Beck had been working under a multiyear contract and fought hard for the maximum severance package. "His spent his last weeks in Houston battling on the payout with the corporate programmer," says Gary Wheeler. The battle was so drawn out that it caught the attention of potential employers in the clubby world of Top 40 radio. According to a veteran morning-radio hand, word spread that Beck was hard to work with and prone to wild behavioral swings. In industry terms, he had become "damaged goods." He was still only twenty-six years old.

It was 1990, the midpoint of Beck's career in FM morning radio. The morning-zoo craze had peaked, and the economy had stalled. Eight years after leaving Washington state with a suitcase full of skinny ties and dreams of working in Rockefeller Center's Radio City Studios, Beck was now a morning-drive journeyman with a family to feed and a reputation to rebuild. Despite having broken quickly out of the gate at age eighteen, Beck did not enter the new decade within sight of the industry's front ranks. New York's Z100, the leading station in his world, was not calling him. Neither were program directors in Los Angeles or Chicago. There were no syndication offers to compete with national zookeepers like John Lander and Scott Shannon.

After his personal and professional meltdown in Houston, Beck was lucky to find work in Baltimore at the city's leading Top 40 station, WBSB, aka B104. This time, however, he wanted a partner.

He found one in the form of a highly regarded New York morning deejay, writer, and producer named Mike Opelka. Over a series of phone conversations, Beck and Opelka crafted a morning-show concept and penned some skits to debut on B104. But *The Glenn & Mike Show* died in the crib. Four days before it was set to air, Opelka backed out, forcing Beck to find a last-minute replacement.

On the recommendation of a friend, he settled on a twenty-seven-year-old morning jock named Pat Gray. Although Gray and Beck had worked in Houston at the same time, they had never met. As Beck likes to tell it, it was deejay love at first sight, with the two bonding within minutes of meeting at the Baltimore-Washington airport.

Beck and Gray were unlikely bosom buddies. Gray was a Mormon who homeschooled his kids; Beck was a bong-ripping nihilist who on some days could barely remember his kids' names. But they shared a sense of humor and a love of morning-radio mischief. They also shared similar if inchoate politics. After their partnership ended 1994, both men would pursue careers in conservative talk radio. They now work together on Beck's nationally broadcast radio show, *The Glenn Beck Program.*

Beck wanted a new mascot along with a new partner. Early in his B104 tenure he spent two weeks calling veterinarians and pet stores live on the air, getting advice on gerbils. After choosing one, he announced that he was going to train the world's first bank-tube astronaut. Every day Beck would announce an update, some new detail about the gerbil's first mission. One day, he made a little cape; the next, he named the animal Gerry the Gerbil. Each development was accompanied by a press release. When all the pieces were in place, Beck and Gray visited a local bank and sent the animal to a teller with a known fear of rodents.

"The buildup was amazing, masterful," says a former programmer at the station. "PETA [People for the Ethical Treatment of Animals] was flipping out, picketing the station every day. Beck's on the local news. He took a stupid stunt and turned it into weeks of compelling high-publicity radio. He always knew how to get attention, how to get people talking about him."

The gag didn't end with the gerbil's bank-tube adventure. Weeks later, Gerry returned to the show and was supposedly eaten by a snake live on the air. As the snake swallowed the rodent, Beck pretended to rescue Gerry by banging the snake against a counter until Gerry flew out of its mouth, safe and sound. The faked death of a snake prompted another round of PETA protests. When forty animal-rights activists gathered in the station parking lot, a colleague asked Beck whether he wasn't concerned. Beck just laughed. "He told me, 'If you can get the freaks protesting you in the news, the normals will be on your side, because they hate the freaks,'" remembers the colleague. "It was a revelation to me at the time. Beck had thought the whole thing through."

Beck became known at B104 for his marketing acumen. After his show, he could sometimes be found in the office of programming director Steve Perun, playing Nerf basketball and talking marketing theory with senior staff. According to colleagues, Beck was introduced to the world of modern marketing during a weekend seminar that was popular at the time. Known as the War College, the course was developed and taught by Bob Hughes, chief of Ragan Henry Broadcasting.

"Beck was very familiar with all of the most famous marketing books, especially the 'positioning' series by [Al] Ries and [Jack] Trout," remembers the music programmer. "He once told me [that] so much of marketing today was just 'warmed-over [Nazi propagandist Joseph] Goebbels.'"

Beck's marketing instinct was put to its most memorable service in an elaborate prank built around a nonexistent theme park. The concept wasn't his own—it was a direct rip-off of a 1984 stunt scripted by Cincinnati deejay Jay Gilbert—but the execution was vintage Beck. The idea was to run a promotional campaign for the fictional grand opening of the world's first air-conditioned underground amusement park, called Magicland. Beck and Gray explained to listeners that it was being completed just outside Baltimore.

During the buildup, the two created an intricate and convincing radio world of theme-park jingles and promotions, which were rolled out in a slow buildup to the nonexistent park's grand opening. They then went to Kings Island in Cincinnati to record their voices over the sounds of a real theme park. On the day that air-conditioned Magicland was supposed to throw open its doors, Beck and Gray took calls from enraged listeners who tried to find the park and failed. Among the disappointed and enraged was a woman who had canceled a no-refund cruise to attend the event.

"They never told a soul what they were doing," says Sean Hall, a B104 newsman. "I didn't know until the morning it aired. People just drove around in circles on the Beltway for hours trying to find the place. And that was exactly what it was supposed to elicit."

Beck was known at B104 as a pro's pro in the studio but was becoming increasingly unraveled when not working. "Beck used to get hammered after every show at this little bar-café down the street," remembers the music programmer who worked closely with Beck. "At first we thought he was going to get lunch." The extent to which Beck was struggling to keep it together is highlighted by his arrest one afternoon just outside Baltimore. He was speeding in his DeLorean with one of the car's gull-wing doors wide open when the cops pulled him over. According to the programmer, Beck was "completely out of it" when B104's locally influential owner, Jim Fox, went down to the precinct office to "make the charges disappear."

In his 2003 book, *The Real America*, Beck refers to himself as a "borderline schizophrenic." Whether that statement reflects a diagnosis or is intended for effect, Beck's coworkers at B104 believed him to be taking prescription medication for some kind of psychological illness. "He used to complain that his medication made him feel like he was 'under wet blankets,'" remembers the former music programmer. "I'm fairly certain he was diagnosed as bipolar and was on lithium at the time. Everything pointed to it. [Program director Steve] Perun used to remind him to take his pills."

Beck's off-air problems found reflection in mounting professional frustration. Despite their on-air synergy and the praise of industry colleagues, Beck and Gray never took off in Baltimore. They had created Magicland out of thin air, but they couldn't summon enough ratings magic to revive B104 or win the full confidence of the station's impatient managers. Shortly after the birth of his second daughter in early 1991, Beck found himself working alone when Gray's contract was canceled. When Beck was fired later that year, the two men spent six months in Baltimore living off their severance pay, unemployed and plotting their next move.

2

Last Stop on the Top 40 Train

In early 1992, *The Glenn and Pat Show* found a second life further down the radio food chain at the New Haven, Connecticut, Top 40 station WKCI, commonly known as KC101. For Beck, coming from Top 20 markets like Houston and Baltimore, the southern Connecticut station, which was barely flirting with the Top 100, was a sign of serious professional decline. And even though New Haven was the closest Beck had ever come, in geographical terms, to his boyhood dream of working in Rockefeller Center, the Manhattan skyline had never been further from his grasp. Now approaching thirty, Beck was no longer a boy wonder destined for greatness. He was staring failure in the face.

"There's nothing like being 18 years old in the fifth largest market in America, and then spending the next dozen years dropping 97 spots," Beck later wrote. Even if he had wanted to, Beck could not have ignored the daily reminder of professional free fall represented by New Haven's morning commuter rail service to Grand Central Station in midtown Manhattan. A New York complex was even woven into KC101's public identity. A station promo mockingly bragged about its outsized fifty-thousand-watt signal: "Five states and the world's greatest cities—from a dumpy little building in North Haven."

Beck and Gray arrived at KC101's dumpy little building as morning-show bounty hunters, brought to town to capture the scalps of the

46

dominant morning team in the market: the "bad boy" duo of Brian Smith and Bruce Barber of WPLR, which had established a lock on the prized demographic of eighteen- to thirty-four-year-olds. Beck and Gray were famished for the success that had eluded them in Baltimore. A profile for the *New Haven Register* quoted their new boss, Faith Zila, marveling that the two spent up to eight hours prepping for every show. "I haven't seen anyone spend that kind of time," Zila said. "These guys would kill for a ratings win and I'm the same way."

Shortly after Beck's arrival in Connecticut in early 1992, KC101 was purchased by Clear Channel. Although it was not immediately obvious, this would prove to be a momentous development in Beck's career. At the time, Clear Channel was still a small player in radio, with just sixteen radio stations nationally. This began to change the year after Beck's arrival, when Congress further relaxed the ownership rules that regulated the radio industry. By the year 2000, thanks to the passage of the Telecommunications Act of 1996, Clear Channel had become a behemoth of twelve hundred stations.

In the winter of 1992–1993, Beck was practically in on the ground floor of Clear Channel's national growth. Clear Channel's appearance also ensured a level of security that was new in Beck's career. Clear Channel CEO Mark Mays told the *New Haven Register* that February that he had entered the market as a long-term "broadcasting operator, as opposed to just an investor" and stressed that he had "never sold a station." As one of the company's most experienced morning deejays, Beck got to know Mays, who was on his way to becoming the most powerful man in radio.

Along with the purchase of KC101, Clear Channel picked up New Haven's leading news and talk station, WELI. Having this sister station would prove crucial to Beck's early start in talk radio. Before the end of the decade, a melding of the two stations' content would create what the country would come to know as *The Glenn Beck Program*.

As Beck's post–Top 40 career started to take shape, his personal life was increasingly disintegrating. During his first two years in Connecticut, Beck slid further toward the abyss. He was drinking and mixing recreational and prescription drugs. Once again, he earned a reputation with his coworkers for being erratic and moody. "When Beck was not taking certain medications he was supposed to be taking, he could act very bizarre," remembers Kelly Nash, who managed Beck in New Haven.

"He didn't want anyone questioning his authority," Nash continued. "I remember he fired our consultant and brought in his old friend Jim Sumpter. The two of them created and launched an in-house research project that made absolutely no sense. When I confronted him on the absurdity of his approach, he said, 'This is above your head.' Then he locked the door to his office. I thought, 'This guy is out of control. He's insane.'"

Within a year, Beck's behavior would frustrate Sumpter as well, bringing an end to a decade of friendship that began in Washington, D.C. "It got to the point where Faith [Zila] and I had no idea what Beck was up to," says Sumpter. "He just completely unraveled. His programming decisions and management style alienated everyone, sent them into a panic, and I didn't want to be a part of it."

Some former employees in New Haven remember Beck for his mean streak. Today, when Beck wants to illustrate the jerk he used to be, he tells the story of the time in Baltimore he fired an employee for bringing him the wrong pen during a promotional event. According to former colleagues in New Haven, Beck didn't just fire people in fits of rage, he did so slowly and publicly.

"He used to tell employees that he wanted to take them for lunch. They knew what it meant, but he'd say it with a smile," says a former KC101 colleague. "Then he'd take them to a restaurant or bar and sit them down and just humiliate them in public. He was a sadist, the kind of guy who rips wings off of flies."

In 1994, Beck was made operations manager of Clear Channel's New Haven stations. The added responsibilities only worsened his mental state. That same year, he became suicidal. He imagined putting a gun inside his mouth and squeezing the trigger to the music of his fellow Washingtonian Kurt Cobain, who had recently killed himself.

Everywhere Beck turned, things were falling apart. His marriage was failing. Pat Gray, his best friend and creative partner, was sick of Beck's sadism and drama and was about to move his family to Salt Lake City. (Years later, Gray described the station under Beck as "a pretty cancerous place to be.") Beck saw his daughters only through a pot haze and in between blackouts. Twisting the multiple knives in Beck's gut was the regular humiliation of Top 40 promotional stunts imposed on him by management. In a typical KC101 event, Beck dressed up as a banana and dove into a pool full of Styrofoam.

Whatever indignities he suffered, Orson Welles never wore a banana suit.

Nor was Orson Welles ever called a racist. In October 1995, toward the end of their partnership, Beck and Gray found themselves at the center of a minor Connecticut scandal when they ridiculed an Asian American caller on the air after he called to complain about a racially tinged comedy segment. As a result, four local Asian American groups formed the Connecticut Asian American Coalition Against KC101 Racism. The *Hartford Courant* reported as follows:

> The negotiations between the station and the groups began as the result of a call to the station in August from Zhihan Tong, a 28-year-old computer network technician. Tong was driving from his New Haven–area home to his job in Danbury when he tuned in to the station, commonly known as KC101, for a traffic report. Instead, he heard Alf Papineau, the morning show's executive producer, pretending to speak Chinese to a bewildered Asian-American owner of a Chinese restaurant supposedly for sale. When Tong telephoned WKCI-FM to protest the broadcast as a racial slur, disc jockeys Glenn Beck and Pat Gray made fun of him. The two played a gong in the background several times, and Papineau, the executive producer, mocked a Chinese accent.[1]

The matter was settled when the station agreed to apologize on the air and to ensure Asian representation on a newly formed community advisory committee.

After Gray's departure, Beck and his wife, Claire, divorced, and he found himself alone and peering over the ledge. Slowly he began to inch back from it. In November 1994, he attended his first Alcoholics Anonymous meeting. Around the same time, he stopped smoking weed and chopped off his ponytail. As he struggled to stay sober, Beck began imagining a future outside Top 40 radio.

These transition years were accompanied by what Beck has often described as a spiritual quest. No longer seeking religious advice from the mouth of Jack Daniels, he sought it in churches and bookstores instead. Joe Amarante, a local New Haven reporter, remembers Beck wandering into his Catholic church during Mass looking "puzzled."

A similar confusion is reflected in Beck's reading list from the period. As Beck has recounted in his books and his stage performances, his first attempt at self-education involved works by six figures that formed a strange sort of Great Books program: Alan Dershowitz, Pope John Paul II, Adolf Hitler, Billy Graham, Carl Sagan, and Friedrich Nietzsche. As he surrounded himself with this brain trust, his friend and former partner Pat Gray argued in favor of the comprehensive worldview offered by the Church of Jesus Christ of Latter-Day Saints. Beck rejected Gray's overtures, teasingly calling him "freak boy."

Concurrent with Beck's mid- and late-1990s spiritual journey was his growing interest and self-education in talk radio. The culture was newly abuzz with the format. In early 1995, *Time* magazine published a cover story tackling one of the questions raised by the previous November's midterm elections, in which talk radio helped fuel Newt Gingrich's GOP insurgency. "Is Rush Limbaugh Good for America?" asked the magazine. "Electronic populism threatens to short-circuit representative democracy. Talk radio is only the beginning."[2]

By then, Beck was paying attention. "Beck was a close student of talk radio for years," says Sue Treccase, who was his first manager in talk radio. "Before he thought he was ready [to do it himself], Beck paid close attention to successful practitioners of the craft." After finishing his morning show in New Haven, Beck would often tune into WABC-77 AM, the nation's biggest news and talk station, which broadcast from Manhattan. In addition to Rush Limbaugh, Beck listened to Bob Grant, to whom he continues to pay daily homage by greeting listeners as "sick twisted freaks," a famous Grant catchphrase.

In the spring of 1997, a colleague of Beck's suggested he do some bits with a local music columnist named Vinnie Penn. A fast-talking future stand-up comedian with a bit of a goombah shtick, Penn was Beck's first partner in radio who was more ethnic than Wonder Bread. Beck never clicked with Penn the way he had with Gray, but the two got along well enough to produce four hours of morning radio every day.

Beck hadn't yet given up on making it big in Top 40 radio. Within a month of teaming up with Penn, he began musing about the chances of syndicating their show.

"Beck saw the syndication trend coming a mile away, I gotta give it to him," says Penn. "But he came to realize that talk was the easier route for him and the better fit. When I got there he was already wondering how he was going to sustain a career in Top 40 radio when his heart wasn't in it. He was like 'Where am I headed?' At one point I remember him talking about joining the ministry."

Beck wasn't the only one beginning to chafe under the limits of a morning show based around raffling off boy-band concert tickets to teenagers. In 1998, Beck and Penn were getting memos from management urging them to talk more about reality TV and pop culture as a way to attract young listeners. Penn, whom a local paper had dubbed the "Connecticut King of All Media," wanted to do edgier stuff. As his partner began thinking about talk radio, Penn began exploring comedy, eventually landing some guest spots on *The Howard Stern Show*. Beck and Penn's morning show became a microcosm of these midcareer tensions, with both men straining against the format: Beck talking politics, Penn working blue.

The more Beck dragged politics into the morning show, the more the station managers grew alarmed. They told Penn it was his job to stop Beck from getting too deep with callers. Chastened by orders, Beck and Penn plotted ways to try to make politics entertaining. The attempt failed. By 1998, Beck realized he'd never be able to do what he wanted to do on FM radio; he was limited to talking fluff in between Britney Spears songs. Out of this failed experiment with Penn was born Beck's idea of fusing morning radio wackiness and political debate.

His talk-radio identity still larval, Beck was already displaying the skills that one day would make him a lightning rod. "He always knew how to work people and situations for attention," says Penn. "He could pick the most pointless story in the news that day and find a way to approach it to get phones lit up. That was his strong point—pissing people off. He was very shrewd on both the business and entertainment sides of radio. He's built his empire on very calculated button pushing."

Not that this empire was imaginable back then. Most people who noticed the button pushing wanted nothing to do with it.

"Anyone in Connecticut who says they knew Beck was destined to run an entertainment empire is full of shit," says Penn. "The guy had dozens of enemies. People thought he was an annoying, washed-up has-been. When I see people today bragging that they knew him back then, I'm like, 'But you fucking *hated* him!'"

Among those who didn't hate Beck at the time was a young radio initiate named Steve Burguiere. Better known as "Stu" on *The Glenn Beck Program*, Burguiere began as one of Beck's interns on KC101 in 1997 and later became Beck's chief writer, producer, and creative partner.

The longer Beck stayed sober, the more his work depressed him. The high-flying zoo days were over, and he had no desire to compete with the new breed of shock jocks inspired by Howard Stern. If there were flashes of comedic brilliance on his show, they were not daily occurrences. With four hours to fill every day, he was mostly doing the radio equivalent of babysitting.

Beck did what he had to do, but his growing interest in talk radio was no secret to his colleagues and his listeners. He wasn't just talking about talk radio, he was trying to practice it on his morning show, despite Vinnie Penn's best efforts to rein him in. Among those who spotted the problem was Scott Shannon, the legendary zoo deejay who in the late 1990s consulted on morning programs for Clear Channel. Part of Shannon's beat was monitoring morning programming at Beck's station, KC101. Whenever he visited the studio, Shannon noticed that Beck was veering further away from traditional Top 40 morning radio. By 1999, Beck's desire to talk politics was seriously affecting his performance as a deejay.

"He'd get into these long, opinionated conversations with callers," says Shannon. "I had to tell him to cut out the long raps, which were not at all appropriate to the format." Beck acknowledged the problem and on Shannon's advice cut a compromise deal with Clear Channel: Beck would be allowed to host a weekday talk show on WELI, one of Clear Channel's AM stations. In exchange, he promised to end the confessionals and politics on his morning show and get back to bubble gum–flavored Top 40 radio. "We needed to find a way for him to scratch his talk radio itch and do FM mornings at the same time," says Shannon.

Launched around the time of President Bill Clinton's impeachment hearings, Beck titled his show *The Impeachment of Character.* During the show's short run, Beck followed his morning show on KC101 with three hours on WELI. According to a report on the show's cancellation in the *New Haven Register*, "WELI's program director reports it wasn't good business to have Beck do both shows because it was draining him."

The double duty may also have contributed to Beck's relapse in the effort to become a better person. "He was on everybody's nerves at the time and hated by the engineers," says Vinnie Penn. "The exceptions were myself and Burguiere."

His show may have ended in failure, but the experience only fueled his desire to succeed. The more talk radio Beck did, the more he wanted to do. With help from Scott Shannon, Beck landed some guest slots on *The Weekend* at New York's WABC, home to Rush Limbaugh, Sean Hannity, and (until 1996) Bob Grant.

Beck's first test in real-time topical talk radio came on August 22, 1998, his second show on WABC. The broadcast aired two days after the United States launched cruise missiles at suspected terrorist facilities in Afghanistan and Sudan. Beck has archived the show on his Web site, and it is the earliest recording still publicly available of Beck doing political "hot talk" radio.

It is not a pretty sound. From start to finish, Beck seems unpolished and green as he limps through an attempt to put current events into context. Although the show is technically amateurish, Beck displays, even at this early stage in his crossover period, a surprisingly mature command of being both obstinate and uninformed. Throughout the show's first hour, he manages to propagate dangerous myths about the Vietnam War and those who fought it, denigrate a major world religion, mock peace activists, and call for displays of air power against distant lands about which he knows nothing.

Beck begins with an ironic playing of Cat Stevens's "Peace Train." With the song playing softly in the background, he moves into a trope made famous by Bob Grant: loudly flipping through that morning's edition of the *New York Post*, the bible of New York conservative talk radio.

Without his booming Top 40 voice, Beck stumbles over his own words. His first sentence is inaudible, followed by a mumbling dismissal of what he calls "hate rallies" taking place across the country in protest of President Clinton's cruise missile attacks. Realizing that he has started off choking badly, Beck recovers with a long pause. He then riffs on the contents of the *Post*:

> The good news is, partial birth abortion is still legal. Sexual harassment is behind us. As long as they want it. I'm glad to know it's okay for the most powerful man in the world to prey on a lowly intern. Best news in the *Post* today: 53 percent of us have come together to support our military tactics. Quotes Arab press claiming bombings were a diversion. Protests all around the United States. Seventy-five losers in San Francisco. *Lo-sers.*

A story about the missile attacks catches Beck's attention. He stops to read the dispatch about the terrorist organization that's being targeted by the recent missile strikes. Encountering the name of its leader for obviously the first time, Beck attempts and fails to pronounce *Osama bin Laden*. Embarrassed, he launches into a kind of loopy scat:

> A paper in Pakistan received a letter from the spokesperson from, uh—Asma—Asma Bin Lay-deen? Is that his name? Bin Lay-deen? Bin Jelly Bean Green Bean? Mr. Clean? I love him. He's hot. He says he's ready for war with the U.S. Oh, yes. Thank you, Mr. Baked Bean. Loosen the turban! Mr. Clean, dig-my-scene. Oh, yes! Look at the latrine.

That settled, Beck introduces himself to his listeners. "I don't really consider myself a conservative," he says, echoing Bob Grant's self-description almost word-for-word. "I know I don't consider myself a liberal. I have a brain, and I like to use it sometimes."

With that, Beck is ready to take some calls.

Someone says, "The only message these people in the Middle East get is brute force." Beck agrees and likens that summer's African embassy attacks to the attack on Pearl Harbor.

Another caller says he doubts that Clinton would launch strikes just to deflect attention from the Monica Lewinsky scandal, considering that the action might cost lives. This confuses Beck, who asks, *"Lives? We used cruise missiles."* It doesn't occur to Beck that the caller is referring to the Sudanese who are working inside the medicine factory that is destroyed by the U.S. missiles.

The next caller supports the military action, adding that he "respects Jews, Catholics, and Muslims—everybody the same." To this Beck responds, "I can't go with you that far, Alan, but thanks for calling."

The next caller thinks that the United States needs to "take the fight to the enemy." Beck agrees. "War has changed; it's the way we have to fight it." To drive home the point that "war has changed" and that the United States has entered a new and dangerous period in its history, Beck segues to a commercial break with the chorus to "Danger Zone," the 1986 Kenny Loggins hit and *Top Gun* theme song. Further proving that you can take the man out of the 1980s but not the 1980s out of the man, Beck returns from the break with Toto's "Hold the Line."

Back on the air, Beck dives into the subject of dastardly peace protesters. He raises what will become one of his favorite subjects in a few years: the lessons of Vietnam. "The problem with Vietnam is we didn't fight to win," explains Beck. "When you declare a war, *there are no rules.* Have you learned the lesson of Vietnam that we can't fight it half-assed? We need to fight it to the last body."

Beck then goes for the emotional jugular for the first time. The move comes in the form of a story about an unnamed "friend" of Beck's. This friend returned from Vietnam only to endure the abuse of protesting peaceniks. "He got off the plane from Vietnam, and a woman spat in his face and called him 'baby killer,'" explains Beck. "Then he left his Medal of Honor in a trash can."

It is impossible to say whether Beck was aware that he was quoting almost verbatim from Sylvester Stallone's closing monologue in *First Blood*. But whatever its source, the story is dubious. As documented by Jerry Lembcke in his book *The Spitting Image*, stories of Vietnam vets being spat upon didn't gain currency until the 1980s. So many of those stories dissolved upon closer inspection that even after serious research efforts, not a single case of a Vietnam veteran being spat upon has ever been documented.

Beck's story about his veteran buddy sounds so pat that even his conservative listeners have to wonder. Within minutes, a caller asks, "About your friend who threw away his medal—did that *really* happen?" Beck mutters, "Yes, but he regrets it now," then changes the subject.

A few minutes later, toward the end of the first hour, Beck shifts gears. After expounding on war and peace with the certainty of someone who has spent a lifetime thinking about these things—rather than imitating Muppets between Bon Jovi songs—he swivels into a disarming Socratic stance of admitted ignorance. It is a move that would play a large role in his future appeal: the average guy who tells you the way it is, then shrugs innocently and says, "But what do I know?" The transition is obviously unpracticed, and it jars, but for the first time in the show, Beck's words ring true.

"I don't have a stinking answer to save my life," he admits. "I don't know what's going on."

At the end of 1998, Kelly Nash, Beck's boss, called his frustrated employee into his office and informed him that his contract would not be renewed when it expired at the end of the following year. "Glenn just couldn't function as a Top 40 deejay anymore," Nash says now. "I told him we'd try to help him get his talk career going, but he was no longer cutting it as a Top 40 morning guy."

As Beck honed his talk-radio chops during his final year of morning radio work, a new Beck came into focus. In 1998, he started dating Tania, the woman who would become his second wife. After they went on a church tour together, looking for a faith, they settled on Mormonism. In 1999, Pat Gray baptized his old friend in an emotional ceremony. That year, Tania and Beck were married.

As his contract wound down, Beck surprised his colleagues by convincing talk-radio superagent George Hiltzik to take him on as a client. A Democrat and a heavy hitter with New York's N. S. Bienstock agency, Hiltzik's clients at the time included Matt Drudge and Don Imus. (Years later, Beck would hire Hiltzik's son, Matt, to handle his PR.) "We were all shocked when he landed this big agent," remembers Nash. "It was like, 'Why is this guy with you?'"

There was just one piece missing: a job in talk radio.

In the autumn of 1999, Clear Channel's Atlanta-based director for talk-radio programming, Gabe Hobbs, received a phone call from the company's vice president for programming in the Northeast. "He told me they had this morning guy in New Haven who wanted to get into talk," recalls Hobbs. "I agreed to go up there and speak with him." During their first conversation, Beck impressed Hobbs with his intelligence and his determination. "Glenn told me he had simply outgrown the juvenile nature of Top 40 radio. He said he'd go wherever he had to for a talk show."

Hobbs immediately thought of Tampa, Florida, where liberal talk-radio legend Bob Lassiter was most likely approaching the end of his career at WFLA-970, Tampa Bay's leading news-talk station. Hobbs passed Beck's tapes to the managers at WFLA, who were intrigued enough to fly Beck down for an interview in early December. Beck was torn over the possibility of leaving his young daughters back in Connecticut with his ex-wife, Claire, but the chance was too good to pass up. Beck flew down. When the thirty-five-year-old returned from sunny Tampa to a snowy New Haven, he was holding a two-year contract to host an afternoon talk show on WFLA.

"To switch formats like Beck did, and take it immediately to a Top 20 market like Tampa, is almost unheard of," notes Nash, Beck's last boss in FM radio.

Although Nash didn't know it at the time, an equally unheard-of phenomenon was then transforming Tampa's airwaves: the steady, marketwide elimination of local talk radio.

But none of that was Beck's concern. He knew nothing of Tampa radio and had little time to learn. In December 1999, Beck had a house to sell, bags to pack, and a show concept to develop. At 3 p.m. on January 3, 2000, *The Glenn Beck Program* was scheduled to debut in Tampa Bay.

3

The Luckiest Loudmouth in Tampa

Beck arrived in Tampa during the final weeks of 1999 with a well-traveled bag of Top 40 radio tricks, a young second wife, and a guilty conscience. Accepting the job in Tampa meant leaving behind two young daughters in Connecticut, one of them severely disabled. It was a move that haunted Beck. During his first months on the air, he often told his listeners, "I may have made a huge mistake."

It wasn't long before his new bosses began having the same thought. The first sign of trouble came just minutes into his first show, when Beck cued the bumper music that links the program segments and the ads. "I'll never forget when Beck came on the air for the first time using Air Supply as his bumper," remembers Sue Treccase, then program director at WFLA. "It was like 'What the hell did we just get ourselves into?' We're a talk station trying to skew men twenty-five to fifty-four, and he's playing Air Supply?"

The Glenn Beck Program had bigger problems than corny soft rock interludes. As he attempted to introduce himself to his listeners, Beck often referenced his new Mormon faith, his newfound moral compass, and his life without alcohol or coffee. He also talked about waiting until marriage to have sex with the woman who became his second wife. "I called him into my office and told him he sounded like a weirdo," says Treccase. "I explained to him that his target

58

listeners are leaving work and thinking about two things: having a beer and getting laid. They really don't want to hear that you won't do either one."

Eighteen years after leaving Utah in disgust, Beck finally sounded as though he belonged there.

Beck has always struggled to find a comfort zone in discussing sex. Never was this more evident than in Tampa. In the first of many zigzags, Beck took Treccase's advice but overcompensated, veering wildly in the other direction. A few months into his tenure, his wife would complain to the *St. Petersburg Times* that she could do without her husband's "rants about coming home to me and what he plans to do."

That same article, Beck's first major treatment in the local media, also identified the host's on-air schizophrenia as the defining feature of his new show. From day to day, from hour to hour, marveled the *St. Petersburg Times* media critic, it was never clear who Beck was. Was he a born-again Mormon family man? Or was he a crass, vindictive jerk? The first newspaper article to explore the "tangle of contradictions that is Glenn Beck" offered the following:

> On the job at WFLA-AM 970 less than two months, Beck had rallied his listeners to donate $16,800 for a grieving family. Indeed, the family did need help paying for funeral expenses, but that wasn't why Beck talked about the story. There was something about it that touched him. "My gift is being able to emote and being able to have people feel what I feel," says Beck, 36. But on another day, listeners heard the other Glenn Beck, the one who joked about a Riverview woman who was trampled to death by an elephant. The one who skipped over tragedy for an on-air laugh. Good Glenn vs. Bad Beck. You never know which one will dominate The Glenn Beck Show [*sic*].[1]

Beck's ethical and emotional bipolarity, his discomfort with the subject of sex, and his general lack of a political worldview added up to more than just a mild case of rookie green. It was a daily on-air disaster. He had conservative gut instincts and voted Republican. But beyond that he seemed to know little and care even less about Tampa or the larger world. What knowledge he did possess he was unable to process in the systematic and consistent way expected of talk-show hosts.

After two decades of Top 40 morning-drive high jinks, Beck was still rooted in a nonintellectual radio culture of gimmicks and Muppet voices. This was obvious, despite the occasional family-values monologue that sounded as though it were stolen from the back of a Quaker Oats box. In its first year, *The Glenn Beck Program* was long on skits, parodies, and old FM-radio standby tricks like the small-donation listener fundraiser.

Anyone who tuned into Beck's show during those early days would have heard the host announcing that he would be broadcasting an abortion live on the air at 6 p.m. Then, at six, Beck would play a tape of *The Nancy and Mike Show*, a chatty morning program on a WFLA sister station. Tampa was not impressed. Bubba the Love Sponge, the FM shock jock who set the local stunt standard, would have broadcast the actual abortion.

"Beck talked to Satan a lot on-air in those early days when he was struggling," says Tedd Webb, then a host on WFLA's morning show. "He'd have Satan reporting from the scene of a bridge-jumping in progress and read Satan's correspondence with Hillary Clinton. Those were his two major characters: Satan and Hillary."

Then there was the Schlub Club. Upon his arrival in Tampa, Beck dusted off an old radio gag in which the host tells the listeners that later in the show he's going to endorse a crazy or offensive idea, such as chaining women to stoves. He then asks listeners to call in and support the notion. The payoff comes when those just tuning in are outraged and call in to excoriate the host. Those listeners then find themselves in Beck's Schlub Club. The gag perfectly captured Beck's content-free approach to talk radio. Bob Lassiter, Beck's predecessor at WFLA, used provocative and even polarizing opening monologues to draw calls, but these monologues involved real issues on which Lassiter had strong opinions. Beck performed the grade-school version.

Schlub Clubbers weren't the only ones confused by Beck's show. Listeners tuned out in droves. "People had no idea where Beck was coming from," remembers Jeff Liss, a marketing consultant at WFLA. "He wasn't conservative enough for fans of Rush [Limbaugh], who led into Beck's show. So [the] afternoon drive just turned into this cavernous ratings hole. His first months were atrocious. People were like 'Why is this on my radio?'"

If Beck didn't talk hard politics on the air during the first half of 2000, it was because he didn't seem to have any.

"When he started out, he wasn't really a conservative," remembers Mark Larsen, a former WFLA host and colleague of Beck's. "He had a lot of talent, but he wasn't connecting with listeners. The show was all bits and prerecorded voices. He seemed to have no convictions."

"When Beck first came down here, he was not very political at all," says a former Tampa talk-radio host named Rocky D. "He was a weenie with no idea where he was or who he was. He had zero understanding of Tampa. I mean, just completely tuned out of the city. I remember the day the mayor was involved in a drunk-driving accident. I switched on 970 and heard Beck talking about his favorite color of jelly bean. He had no clue. It was pretty clear he wanted to go national and get out of here as fast as he could."

When the first quarterly ratings came in reflecting these sentiments, it was hard to imagine that Beck would succeed at WFLA or any other AM station. A second and then third poor ratings report only seemed to confirm the obvious: a careerist carpetbagger with little interest in politics or his surroundings will not survive the cutthroat world of major-market local talk radio.

Unless, that is, the careerist carpetbagger in question happens to be the only game in town.

Glenn Beck's professional biography is an impressive thing. Listed on the Web sites of his affiliate stations and the Premiere Motivational Speakers Bureau, it tells the bullet-point version of his rise from teenage deejay to national media emperor. The bio sketches his Top 40 career, mentions his breakdown at thirty while "consumed by alcoholism and drug addiction," and pivots to the present with his Tampa triumph. "Despite inheriting the 18th placed position," reads the bio, "his new program landed the #1 position in his first year."

This is true, as far as it goes. But stated like this, the line conceals more than it explains. As Tampa radio hands like to joke, "If Beck was number one, who was number two?"

What the official biography does not mention is the peculiar context of Beck's success. Just prior to his arrival, Tampa became the talk-radio equivalent of a coral reef that had been artificially bleached. A steep man-made decline among his competition allowed Beck's talk-radio career, born prematurely and dangerously underweight, to incubate and eventually thrive.

It began with a megadeal. In October 1998, Clear Channel Communications emerged victorious in a bidding war with CBS radio for

Jacor Communications. Like Clear Channel, Jacor had been on a buying spree since the passage of the Telecommunications Act of 1996, swelling its acquisitions from 26 stations to more than 230 in fifty-five markets. By purchasing one of its main competitors for more than $4 billion in stock and debt, Clear Channel became instantly dominant in dozens of markets and strengthened its already dominant position in others.

The deal had profound implications for the country's AM and FM frequencies. On the AM side, the deal left Clear Channel in possession of a talk-radio empire in the form of two Jacor-owned syndication firms. One of these, Premiere Radio Networks, was home to a small army of national AM radio giants, including Rush Limbaugh and Dr. Laura Schlessinger.

Even under the loose ownership rules of the Telecommunications Act, Clear Channel now faced regulatory problems in certain markets. One of these was Tampa Bay, where the newly mammoth Clear Channel now owned fifteen stations, seven more than federal law allowed. Among these stations were five AM signals. Though the law required Clear Channel to spin off seven stations, the company was free to do so as it saw fit. As any company would have done, Clear Channel spun them off so as to best ensure the dominance of its remaining stations. For the AM side, this meant protecting WFLA-970. To accomplish this, the company sold 570 AM to a friendly broker in exchange for 620 AM, a stronger signal that was soon transformed into a sports station; 820 AM was spun off to a Spanish-language group, ensuring that it would stay out of competition for a decade; and 1380 AM was sold to Radio Disney, the children's network. When the dust settled, Clear Channel's Tampa jewel in its news-talk crown, 970, was safe.

And what a jewel it was. Within the industry, WFLA was legendary for its politically diverse and high-powered approach to local hot talk. When Clear Channel inherited WFLA in 1999, the station, though not what it once was, still featured more than a dozen hours of daily local programming: Tedd Webb and Jack Harris from 5 to 9 a.m.; Mark Larsen from 9 a.m. to noon; Bob Lassiter from 3 to 7 p.m.; and "Marvelous" Marvin Boone from 7 to 10 p.m. The station ran only one syndicated show, Rush Limbaugh between noon and 3 p.m.

Within months of the Clear Channel–Jacor deal, the ratio of local to syndicated programming on WFLA would be reversed. By the time Beck launched his show in January, WFLA had transformed from a diverse, local talk station to a heavily syndicated, overwhelmingly conservative one.

Nor was there much local talk radio found on the other Tampa stations.

"When Clear Channel came to Tampa, it was like Wal-Mart finally coming to town," says Marvin Boone, a former local host on WFLA. "It was only a matter of time before anything local died away. After Clear Channel swallowed Jacor, local talk and local radio in general became a thing of the past."

The one local competitor who survived the restructuring long enough to compete with Beck was Rocky D, a feisty Ted Nugent–style conservative who hosted a morning-drive show on Clear Channel's business-talk station, WHNZ-1250. No fan of Beck's, Rocky D taunted Beck as a fake and titled himself "the last man standing in Tampa talk."

At least, he did so for a little while. A few weeks after Beck's arrival, Rocky D was fired, leaving the newly arrived Beck as the last man standing. In December 1999, Beck would have struggled to find Tampa on a map. By March 2000, the local paper would marvel that this same man, this "tangle of contradictions," was Tampa Bay's "only local issue oriented radio host with a daily show."[2]

WFLA's move toward syndicated content reflected a national trend that accelerated after the Clear Channel–Jacor deal. If this trend has a face, it is that of Randy Michaels, a flamboyant Jacor executive who stayed on with the new company. While at Jacor, Michaels had developed a vision for the emerging economizing of scale in radio programming. He called it "hub and spoke." The strategy was simple. Develop a stable of prize talents and syndicate the hell out of them. Instead of paying salaries and benefits for a dozen local hosts, twelve stations could subscribe to any number of syndicated shows. The result would be dramatically reduced programming costs for stations. And the death of local talk radio.

When WFLA adopted the news and talk format in 1986, it joined two other full-time talk stations in town: WPLP-570 and WSUN-590. For the next decade, Tampa was a three-network AM free-fire zone. "Never before was there anything like the Tampa scene of the eighties and nineties," says Michael Lebron, aka Lionel, formerly of Air America. "Nor will anything like it ever exist again."

The city's famous eclecticism is apparent in WFLA's lineup of local hosts during the late 1980s: Dick Norman, a traditional conservative who mixed paeans to free enterprise with rants against corporate consolidation in radio; Tedd Webb, a politically independent stoner jock who fell into mutual belly-laughing marathons with callers; Jack Ellery, an old-school Connecticut liberal whose scuffles with Florida state officials became the subject of a *60 Minutes* segment; Liz Richards, a rabid Republican feminist who left the station under a blaze of sexual harassment lawsuits; Chuck Harder, an unpredictable hybrid anarchist-populist and self-made millionaire; and Jay Marvin, a published poet and 1960s academic radical turned broadcaster. The list goes on.

The hallmarks of Tampa's stations were tightly focused localism and extreme diversity. When Rush Limbaugh visited Tampa in 1989 as part of his "Rush to Excellence" tour, he guest-hosted a shift on WFLA. His cohost, Mark Larsen, marveled on-air over the strangeness of the occasion: it was the first time two conservatives had ever been in the WFLA studio at the same time.

The Pericles of Tampa's Golden Age was the man Beck replaced: a three-hundred-pound chain-smoking contrarian named Bob Lassiter. A bear of a man with a deep and creamy baritone that was sometimes compared to that of Barry White, Lassiter was born Robert Glodowski in the Philadelphia suburb of Camden, New Jersey, in 1945. A high school dropout, he spent his twenties as a roving deejay, working in the Caribbean and up and down the East Coast.

In his midthirties, he found himself in Miami, where he served a brief talk-radio apprenticeship under Neil Rogers, an early practitioner of urban combat radio (and future mentor to liberal talk host Randi Rhodes). Lassiter would later credit Rogers with teaching him the most important lesson in talk radio: the need to "bring a knife to the studio and cut your guts out onto the console every night." Lassiter might have learned the lesson too well. His first Miami talk gig ended after a few weeks when he told a caller, "You're so full of shit your eyes are brown!"

Lassiter arrived in Tampa in the mid-1980s, just as the scene was starting to hop. During stints at WPLP and WFLA, he developed the literary monologue skills that would become legend. During these years, he also discovered that thoughtful radio could be wildly entertaining. His eloquent opening monologues frequently took aim at sacred cows and often included elements that were designed to antagonize local rednecks.

"It dawned on me that if I talked for an hour and a half, by the time I stopped, these people weren't rational. And then I would just rip them to shreds," Lassiter explained in the mid-1990s. "I do a two-tier show. I do a show for half the audience that understands what I'm doing, so the half that doesn't can amuse the other half."

The industry had never heard anything like Lassiter's one-two punch of highbrow monologue and no-holds-barred phone brawls. No other host in the country was doing an angry shtick that was as smart or a smart shtick that was as angry. But at heart Lassiter was not nasty. Even when he was at his most acid, his fundamental decency was evident. Word of his unique genius spread, and in 1989, ABC radio offered Lassiter a seven-figure contract to take over the afternoon-drive slot at its Chicago flagship station, WLS. For Lassiter's fans in Tampa, the move was a logical and long-overdue ascent up the ladder. Some in the industry thought that national syndication would follow and that Lassiter would become the thinking man's Rush Limbaugh. The two portly hosts were occasionally paired on CNN to discuss current events.

It was not to be. Lassiter never had much patience with corporate types telling him how to run a talk show, and he spent his two years in Chicago clashing with station management. He often slyly messed with his bosses live on the air, a major industry no-no. When his contract was not renewed, he returned to Tampa and was promptly hired by WFLA.

Lassiter's politics were hard to pin down. Probably the most accurate description would be independent contrarian. Callers who tried to pick partisan political fights never lasted long. This was especially true of the dittoheads—people who agree with Rush Limbaugh on everything—who increasingly populated Lassiter's call lines as the 1990s progressed.

"Stop, sir!" Lassiter yelled at one WFLA caller in 1996. "Just stop! You're *boring* me. It's worse than boring. You're *depressing* me. It's people like you who are *killing* this format. Who are killing this *town*, this *country*. It's people like you who are killing *me*! It's just *bitch, bitch, bitch, bitch, bitch*! When is the last time you *laughed*? When you saw an old lady fall in the *mud*?"

And that was Lassiter in a good mood. "You're a typical talk-radio conservative," he told one caller toward the end of his tenure at WFLA. "You don't know what you're talking about. You're a parrot sitting in a cage and you want a cracker. You're *slime*. You hate yourself. You have no life." But then he would relax and tell a story about growing up in New Jersey that would mist the eyes of half his listeners.

"Bob was the greatest monologuist in the history of talk radio, period," says Gabe Hobbs, a former Jacor and later Clear Channel executive based at WFLA. "He succeeded in his art at levels not seen since."[3]

Tensions between Lassiter and management deepened in 1999. When the host requested a meeting to discuss his contract, which was set to expire at the end of the year, he received no answer. Seeing the writing on the wall, the host decided to say good-bye and take his parting shots. On December 1, 1999, a few weeks before his famous annual Christmas program, Lassiter tied his own noose by opening his show with a tirade against the new Clear Channel management. His assault on the station brass broadened into a meditation on slave psychology, labor-management relations, capitalism, and human dignity. "It's not what they're doing to me," he said about Clear Channel, "it's just the way things are done in this country."

Calls poured in from listeners who understood that they were listening to Lassiter's final show. After telling him how much he meant to them, the callers inevitably asked about Lassiter's replacement. Several expressed concerns about the trend in talk radio toward, in one caller's words, "lowering the collective listening intellect to the lowest common denominator." Would Lassiter, they wanted to know, be replaced by another right-wing buffoon? Lassiter replied that he had no idea, and he didn't care.

As for the chances of moving the show to another station in Tampa, Lassiter and his listeners understood that this was impossible in the Clear Channel–dominated market. "Doesn't matter if they fire me," said Lassiter. "There's nowhere for listeners to go. More important, there's nowhere for advertisers to go." Caller after caller expressed terror at the thought of Lassiter's voice disappearing from the already attenuated local talk scene. "Who are we supposed to listen to now?" one asked in anger. "There's no choice."

Lassiter appreciated the calls, but he was annoyed that nobody wanted to talk about the bloody protests then raging in the streets of Seattle, pitting young antiglobalization activists against the police and National Guard. "Not one word about what's going on in Seattle," said the host. Long pause. "That's why it's going on. Boss knows it, too."

That night, Bob Lassiter ended his final show with his trademark sign-off, "You be good." His comments in support of the Seattle protests marked the last time that a daily talk-show host expressed such politics on WFLA.

The following night, station managers hosted a show in which they took calls from Lassiter's irate fans. They assured them that they had good reasons for letting Lassiter go and that his replacement would not be another dull right-wing voice to those already crowding the ether.

Meanwhile, Glenn Beck oversaw the movers at his new home in the gated Tampa suburb of Valrico.

When Beck assumed Bob Lassiter's slot, the former host's loyalists called the show in droves to tell Beck how much they thought he sucked and how his arrival was the final "kick in the dead groin" of a once-great station. Beck had never encountered this kind of animosity before. "These [Lassiter] people came out of the woodwork with pitch-forks and torches," he complained to the *St. Petersburg Times*. "It's a radio show. Move on with your life."

Very few wanted to move on with Beck. Unable to keep Lassiter's fans and failing to develop a new audience in his disastrous first few months, Beck began to undergo a metamorphosis—from practical joker to social conservative. An early sign of this transformation was the start of what would become a running battle with Joe Reddner, a well-known local businessman whose interests include a legendary all-nude strip club, the Mons Venus.

Beck and Reddner first crossed paths a couple of months after Beck arrived in town. Reddner was listening to Beck's show and heard him discussing homosexuality in a way that Reddner, an outspoken champion of sexual freedom, found insulting. "He was spouting some antigay remarks, criticizing people who 'made the choice' to be gay," says Reddner. The strip-club owner called Beck's show and asked the host if he made a conscious choice not to have sexual relations with men. Beck responded, "Yes, it's a choice that I make." Reddner proceeded to inform him that he had just fulfilled the official definition of a bisexual, someone who could go either way. Beck became furious and ended the call.

Thus began Beck's running on-air vendetta against Reddner. Beck argued that clubs like Mons Venus were bad for children and hurt the local convention industry. "He talked about how he found my club degrad-ing during a visit," remembers Reddner. "He tried to pick a fight with me, and I wouldn't be drawn into it. Wrestling with a pig, and all that."

Beck pressed on. A few months after their initial clash, Reddner gave an interview to WFLA's morning show. During the conversation, he defended strip clubs as socially harmless and successful generators of economic growth. He also specifically rejected the charge that the clubs harmed children by noting that those under eighteen could not gain entrance.

Later that afternoon, while Reddner was sitting in his office, a friend called him and urged him to turn on WFLA. When he did, he heard his own voice smoothly elucidating how much he enjoyed molesting children. Beck and his producer had spliced Reddner's audio to make him sound like a proud sex offender.

"He moved my words around and presented it as my own speech," says Reddner. "When I called the show and demanded to defend myself on the air, they said, 'Tough shit, Joe. You're a public figure.' I thought about suing, but I knew I would never get a tape from the station. The next time they wanted me on the air, they apologized and promised to rein in Beck. I'd never heard anyone on radio as hung up on sex as that guy [was]. Those are always the weirdest ones in their private lives."

Beck would continue his crusade against Reddner and the local adult-entertainment industry until the day he left Tampa. By that time he had earned a reputation as a foe of not just strip clubs but all forms of pornography, especially that in which women dress up as young girls. "He used to really harp on that one," says Reddner. On his final local show, in December 2001, Beck replayed one of his favorite spoof songs, "Reddner Sucks, My Lord," sung to the tune of an old Negro spiritual.

The attacks on strip clubs and their owners failed to lift Beck's ratings. In the summer of 2000, six months into his tenure, there were growing rumblings within WFLA to fire Beck. Sue Treccase, the station manager, told Beck that if his show caused problems for her, she was "taking [him] down with me." Despite his two-year contract, Beck met with management in August and was informed that paperwork was being readied to put him on thirty days' notice, in case he failed to improve his ratings. "Had there been any competition left, he wouldn't have survived long enough to have that meeting," says a former WFLA employee. "Clear Channel's dominance in the market allowed them to be patient [and] bought Beck time he didn't deserve."

A nervous Beck appealed to Gabe Hobbs, who represented Clear Channel corporate. Hobbs expressed support but explained that he couldn't protect him forever. Deep down, Hobbs was beginning to suspect that Beck just didn't have enough to say about the world to make it as a talk-show host.

"I hired him because he was not overtly political," says Hobbs. "Still, Rush was his lead-in, and Glenn sounded juvenile, almost liberal. What did he believe? What were his politics? There is an expectation on the part of the talk-radio listener to hear something new, to learn something. He wasn't offering that. He had to start providing some meat with the cotton candy or he was finished."

With Beck staring down a short plank, Hobbs took the host to lunch. Over hamburgers, the talk-radio industry veteran gave the neophyte Beck a pep talk and some advice. The conversation centered on the career arc of a Denver talk-radio host named Peter Boyles. In 1997, Boyles went from being a relatively unknown figure to a national name through his advocacy reporting of two big local stories: the JonBenet Ramsey murder case and the Columbine High School massacre. In both cases, Hobbs explained to Beck, Boyles had seized on major news events and "made them his own" by mixing commentary and journalism.

Hobbs suggested that Beck find his own JonBenet Ramsey case and use it as a vehicle to take *The Glenn Beck Program* to another level. If he could learn to ride a fast news horse, he'd win over local listeners, deepen his skill set, and raise his profile nationally. Hobbs dangled before Beck that Boyles was now regularly appearing on cable news. The friendly message from his boss was urgent and clear: Up your pay grade, and soon, or you're done in Tampa. Just another gunslinger sent packing.

As summer 2000 drew to a close, Beck needed more than just an ordinary election-season ratings spike to save his fledgling talk-radio career. With the big day looming, Beck had failed to undergo the necessary transformation into a more serious host. Although he had grown too opinionated to work as a Top 40 deejay, he was not yet opinionated enough to meet even the low standards of conservative AM talk radio. His show still relied heavily on skits written by Steve "Stu" Burguiere, whom Beck brought down from New Haven to write and produce. Some of these skits were genuinely funny, such as a series of Ken Burns–style radio documentaries on Al Gore, George W. Bush, and Ralph Nader. But even the best material remained symptomatic of the problem that had driven Beck's ratings into the toilet: too much cotton candy and formless conservative politics. With less than two months to go in Beck's first year, no local story appeared on the horizon that offered the possibility of a Boyles-like break.

Then, on the evening of November 7, 2000, something happened—the only thing that could have saved Beck's talk-radio career.

After calling the state of Florida, and the presidency, for Al Gore, the major networks backtracked, describing the final count as too close to call. What followed was a gift from the talk-radio gods. The next morning, reports of voting-machine malfunctions and hanging chads began pouring in from Palm Beach County, where Pat Buchanan had received a suspiciously large chunk of the elderly Jewish vote. It was clear that something had gone terribly wrong in America's democracy. Within twenty-four hours, the global media were parachuting into southern Florida. Beck, the only daily talk-show host on Tampa's biggest news and talk station, suddenly found himself just across the peninsula from the political story of the century.

The prolonged recount drama that followed would have helped Beck simply by happening. The entire country was transfixed by events in the state, boosting ratings across the board for AM radio, public radio, and cable news. The walls that normally separated pop culture, news, and politics collapsed. The recount was all that anybody was talking about. And they were desperate to talk about it.

Beck recognized the opportunity he had been handed. He mastered the complexities of the legal conflict and positioned himself as a leading conservative voice on the story. He blasted the Democrats for cherry-picking the recount and mocked claims of voter suppression among black Florida voters. "During the recount madness, Glenn found his voice," says Sue Treccase. "Day in and day out, he went after what he considered stupid voters in southern Florida and the Democrats."

"Beck became the 'go-to' source for information and perspective on the biggest story of the year," says Gabe Hobbs. "Not only for the listeners but also local media. Television and newspapers were doing stories on Glenn. There wasn't a fact or development in that story that wasn't reported and discussed on his show. The public quickly caught on and became dependent on it. While the evening news might give it minutes per day in a thirty-minute broadcast, he was doing four hours a day on the subject."

Feeling the momentum, Beck took it to the next level toward the end of November. As his ratings surged on the back of the record public interest in the news, Beck invited listeners to gather after work in the WFLA parking lot, outside the boxy Clear Channel studio cluster on Gandy Boulevard. When Beck issued the call, the station managers expected a couple of dozen people to show up. They were shocked when hundreds of local Republicans, and new Beck fans, poured into the lot. Beck kept calling for rallies. Soon he was drawing up to a thousand people. No one at WFLA had ever seen anything like it.

It was around this time that Beck's rightward shift accelerated and deepened.

"Sometime around the election, Beck turned into a real conservative," remembers Rocky D. "Overnight, he went from making fun of rednecks to being this superconservative personality. It was noticeable from a Friday to a Monday. After his conversion, the big question was whether it was real or fake. The guy was suddenly diametrically opposed to his old self."

Whether the new Beck was authentic did not concern Clear Channel's management. Beck's audience was growing—and fast. The only question was how much.

The answer arrived on December 10, the morning after the Supreme Court stopped the recount. That was the day that Arbitron released its quarterly ratings report. The numbers told a story no one in Tampa radio ever expected to hear. Beck hadn't just climbed out of the ratings basement. *The Glenn Beck Program* was number one with adults twenty-five to fifty-four during the afternoon drive. "The recount lit the rocket, and Beck never looked back," says Gabe Hobbs. "After that he was number one in book after book after book."

Not that there was another local talk show to take second place. Tampa's conservatives had merely accepted Beck as one of their own. Instead of changing the channel or shutting the radio off after Rush, they now stuck around for more red meat.

After the election, Beck's newly conservative politics continued to harden and become more pronounced. The recount saga had been an epiphany for Beck, revealing the recipe for successful right-wing talk radio: Don't settle for easy jokes and shallow coverage. Believe in something. Pound away at your political opponents. Become an authority. Involve people. Create a stage for yourself off the air.

Meanwhile, in San Antonio, Texas, Clear Channel executives began contemplating something that was unthinkable two months earlier: a national rollout for their new star. In the corporate-radio lingo of the Clear Channel era, a "hub" had been born.

But he wasn't national yet. Beck began 2001 on the lookout for his next big local story. He found it in a long-running legal drama then on the cusp of exploding into a fiery new front in the Florida culture wars. The controversy involved the fate of a St. Petersburg woman named Terry Schiavo. After suffering a heart attack and brain injury in 1990, Schiavo was placed on life support and diagnosed as being in a persistent vegetative state. In 1998, her husband, Michael, sought to have her feeding tube removed. Terry's parents resisted these efforts, believing that their daughter maintained some level of awareness despite CAT scans indicating zero brain activity. The resulting legal battle became a microcosm of the national debate over right-to-die issues.

Shortly before Beck arrived at WFLA in January 2000, the Schiavo story had received a boost when Michael Schiavo took his petition to the Sixth Circuit Court of Florida. During Beck's first year on the air, before finding his conservative voice, Beck not only sided with Michael Schiavo but actually made light of Terry's condition. Years later, Beck would describe a Schiavo-themed gag he had produced as "probably the most insensitive bit of all time."[4]

In the early spring of 2001, Michael Schiavo succeeded in his efforts to have the feeding tube removed. By then, Beck had become a partisan. This time he sided forcefully with Terry Schiavo's parents. "After the recount, Beck felt an obligation to do a more serious conservative show," says a former colleague. "Schiavo was an early test."

Beck's idea of doing a serious show involved broadcasting live near Schiavo's hospital bed. He dove into a media circus that included everything from protesting biblical jugglers on unicycles to satellite vans from the major networks. Beck hosted Schiavo's parents on his show and sharpened his personal attacks on Michael Schiavo. Terry's husband, he declared, was a "murderer" who had remarried and sired two young "bastard" children.

Beck's local nemesis on the issue was a liberal *Tampa Tribune* columnist named Daniel Ruth. Ruth hosted a Saturday afternoon talk show on Beck's station, WFLA. As so often happens with Beck, what began as a political disagreement soon turned viciously personal. Beck accused both Daniel Ruth and Michael Schiavo of "attempted murder." During one show, Beck suggested that he'd like to "murder" Ruth in response to his columns.[5] Beck even gave out Ruth's personal phone number, office address, and e-mail address on the air.

"Beck was slandering Michael Schiavo every day, and his listeners were sending us both death threats," remembers Ruth. "You can imagine the kinds of messages I was getting from Beck's deranged fans."

It was just one of many examples of Beck working outside accepted professional boundaries. Even full-contact talk radio has its "war crimes," and Beck's attacks on Ruth constituted a brazen flouting of industry conventions. In 1996, WABC manager Phil Boyce had fired Alan Dershowitz on the spot for calling his colleague Bob Grant a "racist, bigot, and despicable talk-show host."

"Giving out a colleague's number on-air was beyond the pale," says Sue Treccase, the WFLA programmer. "They both worked here."

By September 2001, Clear Channel had made the decision to take Beck national. His seven-figure contract with the subsidiary, Premiere Radio Networks, would place the host on the company's roster alongside Rush Limbaugh and Dr. Laura. Impressed by his success with younger listeners, the executives considered rolling him out nationally at noon. This would set him up to compete with a rising star then being hyped by ABC Radio Networks: Sean Hannity, who was slated to go national on September 10, 2001.

On that day, Beck was still doing a local show. He spent much of his airtime that afternoon railing against two of his most shot-at targets: Jesse Jackson and the idea of reparations for slavery. You could practically hear the spittle hit the microphone as Beck hissed about Jackson, whom he called the "stinking . . . king of the race warlords."[6] The show found Beck digging deep into his box of imitation black voices to mock Jackson, Johnnie Cochran, and, in very short snippets, African Americans in general.

The same show includes a bit in which he pretends to claim responsibility for the murder of James Byrd, an African American man who was killed by white supremacists in Jasper, Texas; they chained him to the bumper of their pickup truck and dragged him down the road until his body was torn to pieces. Beck also mentioned an upcoming stunt in which he would dive into the shark tank of the Tampa aquarium. He was excited that the day marked his debut on XM satellite radio. There was no discussion of foreign policy or terrorism and no inkling of the world to come.

Beck awoke on the morning of September 11 with plans to riff on traffic disruptions caused by the presidential entourage of George W. Bush, who was in Florida at the time to promote an education initiative. Needless to say, those riffs never aired.

September 11 is the kind of day that broadcast professionals prepare for their entire lives. If the election recount was akin to the O. J. Simpson trial, 9/11 was Pearl Harbor. The news hunger it created was so powerful that it bordered on transformational. No news outlet could provide enough information or provide it fast enough. This explains the 9/11 birth of the television news phenomenon known as the news crawl.

As a student of classic radio, Beck understood that the attack and its immediate aftermath could be his Herbert Morrison moment. Morrison was the voice behind the famous broadcast of the *Hindenburg* crash in 1937; Beck later incorporated his dramatic gasp recorded during the event, "Oh, the humanity!", into his show's intro audio montage.

Beck was nothing if not dramatic on 9/11. He opened every hour of his show with a slow, martial, Germanic rendition of "The Star-Spangled Banner." He spoke in a reserved yet theatrical voice about the morning's events and the latest news. The calls he took consisted largely of people telling him what a great American he was. And he wept.

The first hour of Beck's 9/11 show culminated in a patriotic call for bombing the hell out of distant lands. He declared, "The man in me would *love* to drop a nuke on Palestine if they had anything to do with it. *Absolutely*. But before we drop it, before we pave over a country [*sic*] and make it a parking lot—because we *can*, and we have a *right* to—I think at this point, but [we should] know . . . that [it] could be the beginning of World War III."[7]

Throughout the show, Beck returned to the themes of total destruction and mindless revenge. He agreed with one caller that "our response, when we find out who harbored [the terrorists], should honestly make Desert Storm look like a picnic."

"We should absolutely release everything that we have," said Beck. "Let them see the fury of the United States when it is fully unleashed. You think we have enemies now? Wait until we take out Libya, Afghanistan, Palestine."

Just to make sure his listeners understood where "the man inside Glenn Beck" stood, he reiterated: "Any [country] with ties to Bin Laden I wouldn't mind turning into a giant glowing parking lot." Toward the end of the show, when news reports emerged of possible cruise missile attacks on Taliban-controlled Kabul, Beck expressed skepticism that the attacks were of U.S. origin.

"I would hope that when we found the people that were responsible and connected to the events of today, we use the full force and might of the United States of America and rain down fire like has never been seen before on planet Earth," he added.

During the show's second hour, Beck began organizing a candlelight vigil in the Clear Channel parking lot. He put out an all-points bulletin for a company to deliver American flags, in bulk, at cost. "I want everyone who wants a flag to have a flag," said Beck, "and if you can't afford a flag, *we will buy the flag for you*. I need five hundred candles by seven p.m. and a bunch of flags! And I need a ton of Americans that are not ashamed or afraid to get on bended knee." Later, he asked people who were driving to pull over to the side of the road and "pray to our Heavenly Father who gave us life."

Beck's calls for the massive aerial bombardment of Muslim populations were not just the outbursts of a distressed patriot driven mad by the events of the day. Beck had been a studio general since his days in Kentucky, when he had called for raining hell on Libya. Months before 9/11, Beck was ahead of the curve on Iraq. When most of the world was turning its attention to the misery inflicted on the Iraqi people by international sanctions, Beck was calling for tough unilateral military action. When the Bush administration launched pinprick bombings of Iraq early in its administration, Beck was livid.

"They're crying about three dead [in Baghdad]. *And your point?*" Beck said on February 16, 2001. "Bomb the living crap out of them until they have nothing but rocks. Why aren't we going into that country and just blowing the bat crap out of that country? Carpet bomb Iraq and Yemen."

Beck was hopeful that his advice would soon be heeded. Among the show's most popular spoof songs in 2001 was a warmongering tune,

"Who's in the White House?" sung to the tune of the Baha Men's "Who Let the Dogs Out?" It was actually an amazing accomplishment. Glenn Beck had taken what was arguably the most annoying song of the new millennium[8] and made it even more annoying by turning it into a gloating call for bombing runs on Baghdad. With George W. Bush and Dick Cheney in power, Beck was newly optimistic that the bombs would soon start falling in sufficient numbers.

"The good news is we're going to be a badass country again," Beck told his listeners one month after Bush took office. "You mess with us, and we bash your head in. We need a mob mentality. We need to pound Baghdad's face into the cement curb."

Beck's approach, part tough guy, part Top 40—call it Kermit LeMay—reappeared with new ferocity on 9/11, albeit poorly cloaked in half-hearted calls for a short "healing period." (Clear Channel had sent out a memo to all talk-show hosts calling for a modicum of "sensitivity.")

When he wasn't on the air, Beck wandered around the studio complex, sobbing. "He walked around here all day bawling his eyes out, up and down the hallway," remembers Sue Treccase. "That's all I remember. 'Oh, look, there's Glenn sniffling again.'"

The crying lasted all week. This wasn't Walter Cronkite taking off his glasses and getting choked up while announcing the time at which the president was pronounced dead. It was full-on bawling. The boards lit up with confused callers wondering why the hell a grown man was broadcasting his breakdown on the radio. "I tried repeatedly to get him to stop crying," says Gabe Hobbs. "It was a losing battle."

Thus were Beck's famous fake tears born of real sobs. In the previous year, he had hardened up his politics. Next he softened up his personality, a process that began on 9/11.

"It was after 9/11 that Beck found his stride and started to really open up and bare his soul," says Mark Larsen. "He backed off the comedy and Top 40 stuff, and conservative listeners began to think of him as a friend. Before 9/11, there was little of the emotion in his shtick that you see now."[9]

"Glenn is an emotional guy," says Treccase. "But he's not above using overwrought emotion for dramatic effect."

These tears weren't just for Tampa. While the twin towers of the World Trade Center in New York, the west side of the Pentagon in D.C., and a field in Pennsylvania smoldered, Glenn Beck suddenly found himself on radio stations across the United States.

On the morning of September 11, Gabe Hobbs was in Manhattan preparing for a day of negotiations with NBC. Clear Channel wanted to use the NBC name for its own in-house radio news network to compete with ABC News Radio. Both parties thought a deal was imminent, but the meetings never took place.

Shortly after the second plane hit the South Tower, the NBC negotiating rep, Joel Hollander, called Hobbs's team at its midtown hotel. "Boys, the price of news just went up," said Hollander. With people still jumping from the towers, the NBC representative doubled the original number up for discussion, putting a kibosh on the talks. Clear Channel would later sign a deal with Fox News.

At the time, Hobbs had more immediate concerns, such as coordinating talk-radio coverage for Clear Channel's twelve hundred stations. "We started looking for content and strategizing how to cover events after the initial shock," says Hobbs. "After a day or so of wall-to-wall news, people enter the 'we need to talk about it' cycle. They want to start venting. They want to hear other kinds of information. I wanted every show on point discussing the attacks."

But not everyone with a show wanted to talk about terrorism, Al Qaeda, and the Taliban. Among those who balked at the prospect was the host of *Dr. Laura*, Laura Schlessinger. Since most of Clear Channel's news-talk stations ran *Dr. Laura* from nine to noon, this posed a serious programming problem during the mother of all news events. The station needed to come up with an alternate feed during Schlessinger's time slot, and fast. The urgency to locate content was made greater by concerns that Rush Limbaugh would not have access to his midtown studio.

"I didn't have time to do a regional breakdown," says Hobbs. "Beck came to mind. I wasn't sure how long it would last, but it seemed a good stopgap." Hobbs called Beck and told him he needed him to do two shows a day. The first would replace *Dr. Laura* from nine to noon and be offered to all Clear Channel stations who wanted to stay on the attacks. The second would be his local afternoon-drive show for WFLA. Beck agreed, and a satellite uplink was set up in Tampa. Hobbs then sent word to station managers throughout Florida and the Southeast. He described Beck as a rising star who would discuss the attacks in a "fresh, appealing way." Beck's new morning show was branded with the rest of the Clear Channel's national coverage under the label "America under Attack."

Some of the affiliates reported a deluge of calls complaining about Beck's crying. But as the days stretched into weeks, more of them began requesting an extension of the Beck feed from nine to noon. To accommodate Beck, they said they'd be willing to drop or reschedule *Dr. Laura*. As word spread, requests from other non–Clear Channel stations started rolling in to syndicate the Tampa-based show.

Beck continued to do the two shows through the autumn of 2002. They were finally collapsed into each other in December, two weeks before his WFLA local contract was set to expire. On December 15, 2002, *The Glenn Beck Program* went national on a permanent basis from nine to noon.

The show officially rolled out on just under fifty stations. All were small and medium markets. There was no interest from stations in New York, Los Angeles, or Chicago. Wanting to be in a major market and closer to his kids, Beck let it be known that if a Top 20 station in the northeast took him on, he would move there and be "their guy." This eagerness to leave Tampa did not endear him to his colleagues, but it made professional and personal sense. With a little help from Premiere Radio Networks, Beck was hired by WPHT in Philadelphia.

Beck had become a star, but few of his colleagues at WFLA were sad to see him go. This was evident at his going-away party, held at the old Don Vicente hotel in downtown Ybor City, Tampa's historic cigar district.

"The station managers were begging people to go down so the party wouldn't be empty," remembers Roger Schulman, a former WFLA newsman. "It was an odd-feeling event. There wasn't any camaraderie or speeches. No roasts or humor. Nobody felt like they knew the guy."

Another member of the WFLA news team, Shayna Lance, says Beck was very aloof. "You never got the sense that he was comfortable hanging out with the little people," she says.

Perhaps the most telling symbol of Beck's alienation from colleagues was a box of pastries. On his last day in Tampa, Beck bought a dozen doughnuts for the WFLA newsroom. As far as the station's reporters were concerned, it might as well have been a bubbling vat of radioactive sludge. When the news team left the studio that night, there were still twelve doughnuts sitting in the box. "Usually news reporters are like cops with doughnuts," remembers Schulman. "But nobody touched them."

4

It's Always about Glenn

For Beck, the weeks and months that followed 9/11 offered a chance to indulge his flair for dramatic radio by tearing pages from the career playbooks of his old radio heroes. Channeling Edward Murrow at Trafalgar Square, he visited ground zero to report on a shell-shocked city. Assuming the mantle of Bob Hope, he held rallies for the troops stateside (but never visited the front). And hovering over Beck's increasingly dramatic post-9/11 persona was, as always, the ghost of Orson Welles.

Unlike his heroes, Beck only briefly enjoyed the sense of speaking to the entire nation. In December 2002, the numbed unity of the past year was quickly fading. In its place, a nation divided across the scorched ruins of Manhattan. On the right side of this rupture, Beck and his fellow conservatives embraced a crusading rhetoric of good, evil, and revenge. American liberals, meanwhile, began to express a growing dread over the likely shape of an open-ended "war on terror" directed by George W. Bush and Dick Cheney. One war had begun; the distant rumblings of another could already be heard by placing an ear on the political rails. Across the polarized spectrum, a general apocalyptic paranoia began to crystallize. The mood was dark.

It was against this shifting political landscape that Beck settled into his new base and his biggest market to date, Philadelphia. He was the star at his new station, WPHT-1210, Philly's "Big Talker." He arrived just before another rising star, Michael Smerconish, a lawyer-turned-talker who years later would substitute for Beck on CNN Headline News. But Beck didn't socialize much with Smerconish or other station colleagues.

"I don't hang out with a lot of people," Beck told *Philadelphia Magazine*. As for the city itself, Beck enjoyed the cheesesteaks but didn't bother himself with local politics. "Philadelphia always made me really sad," Beck said. "It is one of the greatest cities in America, but corruption is just destroying it."

Philadelphia put Beck on the same East Coast urban corridor as his New York–based talk show twin, Sean Hannity. Although both men launched their careers in the fires of 9/11, Hannity went further faster. Assisted by his nightly television perch on Fox News, the Long Island native, just three years Beck's senior, had launched on hundreds of stations to Beck's forty-seven. Unlike Beck, Hannity was immediately bracketed with the biggest names in the business. In 2002, Hannity had already begun work on the conservative talker's rite of passage, the patriotic manifesto. That book, *Let Freedom Ring*, included praise for dozens of conservative talk-show hosts around the country. Beck was noticeably absent from the list.

While Hannity's book sold well and helped to build his reputation as a serious new player on the scene, Beck remained a small- and medium-market phenomenon throughout his first year in Philadelphia. The man whom Clear Channel had declared "the future of talk radio" was still known only by industry pros and talk-radio listeners in small and rural markets (what the radio industry calls "flyover air" conservatives). Station managers in Los Angeles, Chicago, or New York were not interested in Beck's trademarked "fusion of entertainment and enlightenment."[1]

Although few people knew it at the time, Beck's ambitions in 2002 were bigger than just catching up with Sean Hannity. In fact, his dream had always been bigger than could be contained by any single medium. Going back to his years in Top 40, Beck imagined a production and content empire equal to his ego.

"He started talking about something like Mercury Radio Arts in New Haven," says Vinnie Penn, his former morning partner. "That's where he linked up with the early core of the company, [Chris] Balfe and Stu [Burguiere]."

Beck even had a model in mind, one improbably larger than life.

An early sign of Beck's post-9/11 self-image and ambition can be seen in the Web site he unveiled during his final year in Tampa. The site design features a black-clad Beck peering out from behind a heavy fan-style vintage radio microphone. He leers out of the shadows with furrowed brow, practically glowering behind the classic instrument. His lone visible eye is colored a piercing unnatural blue. The historical echo is clear: the pose is redolent of photos of the young Orson Welles fixing a shot with a camera or posing while hunched over scripts and storyboards in a dimly lit room.

Beck's Orson Welles complex was fully revealed in mid-2003, when he incorporated his production company, Mercury Radio Arts. At the time, the company consisted only of Beck and his closest collaborators: his intern-turned-producer, Steve "Stu" Burguiere, and writer-manager Chris Balfe. Today the Manhattan-based firm's staff of twenty produces Beck's stage shows, a radio program, *Fusion* magazine, videos, and books for print and audio.

The Mercury name is a respectful nod to Orson Welles's Mercury Theatre, which the precocious polymath founded in 1937 at age twenty-two. The homage was no shot out of the blue. The young Beck's love of radio can be traced back, appropriately enough, to a "Rosebud" moment in his youth, when his doomed mother gave him a collection of classic radio broadcasts that included Welles's "The War of the Worlds."

The effect was enduring. Welles's DNA is all over Beck's career. Even before Beck utters his first word on his program, Welles makes three appearances. The first, third, and fourth clips in *The Glenn Beck Program*'s introductory sound montage are taken from the 1938 radio production of "The War of the Worlds," including Welles's gloriously rotund first utterance, "Across an immense ethereal gulf . . ."

Like the company Beck envisioned for himself, Welles's Mercury Theatre was a multimedia production octopus, the first of its kind. The company produced for the stage, most notably modern adaptations of *Dr. Faustus* and *Macbeth*. The company's radio program, *The Mercury Theatre on the Air*, adapted novels and short fiction for CBS Radio, including the newscast rewrite of H. G. Wells's *The War of the Worlds*, which made Orson Welles a national name beyond the theater.

The company also had a Hollywood offshoot, Mercury Productions, through which Welles paid Herman Mankiewicz to write the screenplay for *Citizen Kane*. When Welles conducted lecture tours, it was under the Mercury banner. Although the firm employed a team of writers and technicians, the final products were always published and publicized under the name "Orson Welles." In a similar fashion, "Glenn Beck" is the face of all joint efforts produced by his own Mercury, even when he himself has little to do with the actual writing.[2]

As Beck began laying the groundwork for Mercury Radio Arts, George W. Bush was putting the finishing touches on plans to give Iraq the curbside face pounding that Beck had long advocated. The result of this war drumbeat was increased political polarization. This was a wave that Beck knew how to ride. Sure enough, before long the host found a way to put his stamp on the pregnant moment before the United States went to war. His tactic joined his natural instinct for self-promotion with his love of performance and his inability to feel shame.

As hundreds of thousands of people around the world protested the coming war, Glenn Beck hit the road with his Rally for America— the "real" America.

His Bob Hope moment had arrived.

Bob Hope looms large in Beck's personal pantheon of classic radio idols. If Welles provided the business model and early dramatic inspiration, Hope blazed the path for hokey conservative comedy and middle-American magnetism. In the sound collage that opens *The Glenn Beck Program*, a sample from Welles's "The War of the Worlds" is followed by a snippet from the April 4, 1947, broadcast of Bob Hope's radio program, *The Pepsodent Show*.[3]

Beck claims that he not only met Bob Hope but that he won the old comedian's admiration. The alleged contact came during preparations for Beck's 1987 broadcast from the USS *Theodore Roosevelt*. According to Beck, he spent two weeks writing Hope's recorded monologue for the aircraft-carrier show, after which Hope used the material and praised it as "good stuff." But it's unlikely that Hope would have favored the jokes of a twenty-five-year-old disc jockey over his own voluminous reserve of military-specific material. Indeed, the week that Hope died, Beck's comedy writer and on-air partner, "Stu" Burguiere, let it slip that Hope had actually rejected Beck's jokes. Not for the first time, Beck struggled to contain his annoyance with his partner.

Beck has monologued about Hope twice, once on the entertainer's centennial birthday and again a few months later, on the occasion of his death. In the birthday monologue, broadcast May 29, 2003, Beck mused:

> I was thinking the other day, "Where are the people like Bob Hope?" That really truly believe in something, something good and decent and American, who will actually take the time and spend it with the troops, who will stand up for the stereotypical corny stuff in America. Where are those Hollywood guys [today]? And then it hit me. Bob Hope didn't come from Hollywood. Bob Hope started in radio, was a radio star that crossed over.

This wasn't quite right. Hope leaped from stage and film to radio midcareer, and he continued to work across the wide range of show business. But Beck's larger point was clear. Today's Bob Hopes, tomorrow's legends, are found, like Beck, on the radio—specifically, on conservative talk radio. This is where people are still proud of "the corny stuff" and are unafraid to wear plaid pants and knit American flag sweaters. Beck was laying claim to Hope's legacy.

But Beck couldn't come out and say he's the new Bob Hope. Instead, he did something very sly: he pointed to Sean Hannity, the only man on the radio whose own fans would freely admit that his humor is about as funny as rectal cancer. Hannity and Beck are rivals who rarely mention each other on the air, and if the Hope reference felt painfully forced, that's because it was. Even while promoting a shared patriotic cause, Beck pads the Hannity reference with two mentions of their rivalry:

> [Bob Hopes] exist still. One of them is Sean Hannity. Sean Hannity is a competitor of mine. But I want to mention that he's doing something on Friday, July 11. He's welcoming the troops home with a concert. You see, Bob Hope still exists. It's not about radio competition. It's about doing what's right for America. Happy birthday, radio legend Bob Hope.[4]

If hosting military-related events marked a new generation of Bob Hopes, then Beck had beat Hannity to the punch. For months previous to Beck's "Happy Birthday, Bob Hope" monologue, he had toured the country as the host of his Rally for America road show. His mention of Hannity was actually a disparaging remark cloaked as a compliment. In anointing a Hope who wasn't really a Hope, Beck assumed the role of patriotic radio priest, allowing Hannity to wear the Hope crown by his grace.

But the role of priest didn't quite do justice to Beck's growing reach or his self-regard. In the weeks and months before his Hope monologues, Beck had regularly drawn audiences worthy of the pope.

It is tempting to drag out Leni Riefenstahl when discussing Beck's 2003 Rally for America. Flags, soldiers, and oaths to God, leader, and country dominated Beck's rallies, just as they did the political theater of Nazi Germany. The Rally for America also featured speakers who made threats against the Left, echoing the threats of violence that were routinely heard on Beck's radio show. Although Beck made much of keeping politicians out of his spotlight, some rallies featured Jumbotronic messages from President Bush, whom Beck declared in need of his nation's prayers. In general, the scene and tone of the rallies make a mockery of Beck's future allegations that the Democrats employ fascist stagecraft.

And then there was the rallies' star. Before the events, which took place between March and May, Beck often rode around the stadium standing atop buses adorned with his show's logo, propaganda posters from World War II, and the words FOLLOW US AND ... RALLY FOR AMERICA.[5] He often wore khakis and his favorite item of clothing: a blue knit sweater emblazoned with American flags and fire trucks.

If this was political theater with Riefenstahlian overtones, it was fascism on a picnic blanket. The events were a strange U.S. hybrid that combined Nurembergian expressions of power, blind allegiance to a divinely anointed leader, and TNN schmaltz.

Unlike USO performers in Iraq, Beck never sacrificed much personal comfort during the Rally for America tour. He frequently traveled between events in Clear Channel's corporate planes and limousines. Nor were his speeches wasted on the ostensible subject at hand; rather, they served as self-promotional talks that leaned heavily on biography and could be recycled for his future one-man stage shows and books.

The final rally was staged more than two months after the start of the Iraq War, on Saturday afternoon, May 24, inside the Marshall University Stadium in Huntington, West Virginia. The event was the climax of an extended self-promotional buildup, Beck's specialty. His logo-emblazoned bus had led a caravan from Dallas, Texas, to the stadium's parking lot; Beck arrived, waving from atop the bus, outlined against a clear blue sky, like some goofball Caesar. The weather was perfect.

It's worth revisiting that day in detail. The brazenness with which Beck wraps his personal-corporate brand in the nation's flag and dips it for flavor into family tragedy is nothing short of breathtaking. That his fans did not charge the stage and beat Beck to a pulp also tells us much about who they are and how little they understand their hero.

The event began at 3 p.m. with swelling patriotic tunes on the sound system and a montage of U.S. military heroes flashing on two Jumbotrons at opposite ends of the packed stadium. Vintage 1958 Thunderbird jets make two flyovers, followed by an echoing voice informing the crowd that the event is being beamed by satellite to every military base and navy ship on the planet. An Olympic-style torch is lit onstage as the announcer declares: "Let—freedom—*ring!*" This triggers wild applause, which hushes for the singing of the national anthem followed by "God Bless America."

A young girl is the first speaker of the day. She talks about how much she loves her dad, a soldier in Iraq. She leads the crowd in the Pledge of Allegiance. The crowd screams the phrase "under God" in defiance of those who prefer the pledge without it. (This group includes Francis Bellamy, who wrote the thing.)[6] A local school choir then sings "Grand Old Flag."

The next speaker is a woman named Cindy Whitmire from Duluth, Minnesota. After stepping to the microphone without introduction, she declares, "We are all proud to be Americans. No doubt. We live in the greatest country in the world, and we are darn proud of it." She salutes the nation's veterans, George W. Bush, and "American principles." This gives rise to a spontaneous chant of "U-S-A! U-S-A! U-S-A!"

Into this controlled fury strolls the day's first musical act. Daron Norwood is introduced as a "true patriot from Texas." He launches into a country music medley that begins with "Take Me Home, Country Roads" and ends with "Sweet Home Alabama." After the medley, Norwood informs the crowd that some people want God removed from the pledge. "I learned about it watching Fox News," says Norwood. He thanks the Christian Country Association, says, "God bless America," and walks off the stage.

With the crowd of twenty thousand now whipped up into a patriotic frenzy the announcer's voice returns. He calls everyone in the crowd "sick freaks." This is, of course, Beck's signature opening line at the time for every episode of *The Glenn Beck Program.* The crowd applauds in recognition of the signal. The full intro to Beck's radio show then rolls across the stadium. Beck's name is repeated four times over a heavy guitar riff. After the tension-building intro, the announcer shouts, *"Let's—get—going—with—Gle-e-e-enn Be-e-e-eck!"*

Beck runs onto the stage and waits for the applause to die down. He asks veterans to stand up and thanks them for their service. He then thanks "the commander in chief," who is "here in heart." With this, the face of George W. Bush appears on the Jumbotron behind Beck. The president thanks the troops as patriotic tunes play softly behind him. "God bless America," says Bush in closing.

Beck returns to the stage and acknowledges the presence of antiwar protesters outside the stadium. He dismisses the idea that Clear Channel is doing the bidding of the administration by organizing the rallies. Not that there is any daylight between the president and the Clear Channel personality. "I am so grateful to God in heaven that George W. Bush is our president," says Beck. He then introduces country musician Tracy Byrd.

Byrd walks on and screams, "God bless the U.S.A. and Glenn Beck!" He dedicates his first song to the protesters outside the stadium. It is a ditty based around a chorus hinting of violence. "When you're running down our country," sings Byrd, "you're walking on the fighting side of me."

Beck returns after the song to introduce a contingent of New York firemen who hold up some of the flags that were used to cover the dead firemen at ground zero. Beck then introduces musician Darryl Worley, who sings his 9/11 country music anthem, "Have You Forgotten?"

Beck returns and welcomes the parents of Private Jessica Lynch to the stage. (The true story of their daughter's rescue was not yet known.) A moment of silence is observed. The names of the war dead are read over the return of swelling patriotic tunes, which bleed into orchestra-backed singing of "America the Beautiful" by Daniel Rodriguez, the only noncountry musician on the program.

Beck next introduces Lee Greenwood, "the voice of the American spirit." Greenwood opens by leading the audience in another recitation of the Pledge of Allegiance. He next sings a song about the Pledge of Allegiance.

Beck then introduces his old friend and morning-radio partner, Pat Gray, now a conservative talk-show host in Houston. Here the program deviates from patriotic homily and gets down to nitty-gritty Beck brand building. Gray tells the crowd that he's known Beck for fourteen years. He explains his presence on the stage by saying that he's here in Huntington "as a proud American and best friend."

Gray then makes what can only be described as a product testimonial. A day for the troops here pivots into an infomercial for Glenn Beck, in which Gray offers a money-back guarantee on the rising-star conservative host. "He's the same person you know and love," says Gray. "He's honest, caring, open, sensitive. I used to wonder if Glenn was a woman. I tell people there are two women in my life: my wife and Glenn."

The weirdly gay joke falls flat on the conservative crowd, so Gray retreats to the safer ground of Beck's patriotic credentials. "This isn't a Johnny-come-lately patriot," Gray declares:

> He's felt this way his entire life. In Baltimore, our station was a music station. Then came Desert Shield. Glenn said, "We've got to talk about what's real. It's gonna kill us in the ratings, but we have to do what's right, make sure Vietnam is not repeated—ever." He is open, honest, shares his feelings. I know you feel that Glenn is your best friend. You wake up every morning and feel like Glenn Beck is your best friend. I wanna introduce to you your best friend: Glenn Beck.

It's worth pausing here to note the lie in Gray's homage to Glenn Beck's authenticity, which sticks out like a blue heartworm pill on a bowlful of canned dog food. The lie is that Beck would have done *anything* as a Top 40 deejay, if he thought it might hurt his ratings. At the time of the Persian Gulf War, Beck was, by his own admission, an ambitious, fiercely competitive, nonpolitical Top 40 jock. If he spouted yellow-ribbon rhetoric in Baltimore, it was because he knew it was safe and expected.

Beck had been reaping easy praise for generating patriotic fluff going back to his "Qaddafi Sucks" days in Louisville. The idea that Beck was willing to risk ratings in order to remember the lessons of Vietnam would be funny were it not so grotesque in the context of real war and peace.

When Gray finishes his windup, Beck grabs the microphone and immediately addresses Gray's homoerotic dud. "I know what you're thinking," says Beck, "and the answer is, no, I'm happily married." Left unsaid is the fact that Beck was rather unhappily married during the first years of his friendship with Gray, the intensity of which drew the notice of media reporters in New Haven.

Beck proceeds to tell a series of stories from his life that have no bearing on the military that the rally is supposed to be honoring, the war he helped to boost, or the war dead trickling into Dover Air Force Base under the cover of a White House–enforced media blackout.

Instead, Beck picks up on Gray's biographical testimonial and works it for everything it's worth.

He begins with a tale that would later recur in Beck's stage shows and first book, *The Real America.* It is a simple story, tailored to feed the vanity of Beck's fan base. In it, Beck meets a woman at a stoplight in Topeka, Kansas. After a brief exchange, Beck has a revelation. Americans, he realizes, are a friendly people. At least, they are in the "real" America. In places like Kansas. And Indiana.

"That's why we're here," Beck tells the crowd. "That's why we didn't go [to rally in] D.C. or New York. They have nothing to teach us. I saw my grandparents everywhere in Topeka. I was in *the real America.* The America of my grandmother and [grand]father, who came from Iowa. They had dirty hands, calluses, wore homemade clothes. They were Depression people."

It's tempting to read this as a sly dig at Sean Hannity, who was about to host his first Freedom Concert just outside New York City. But whatever the intent of the hammy red-state nationalism, Beck concludes the grandma and grandpa bit by aping Dana Carvey's "grumpy old man" character from *Saturday Night Live*, played completely straight. "And they *liked* it!" shouts Beck.

Beck then invites a group of veterans from World War II onstage. He asks all the vets present to rise and declares, "These men are not monsters, they are heroes!"

With the World War II veterans still onstage, Beck launches into a diatribe against Jimmy Carter, a navy veteran. Beck being Beck, he doesn't stop with an attack on a president who served six years in the military during a period of his life in which Beck was snorting cocaine off the dashboard of his DeLorean. Beck proceeds to run down the president in a way that also makes light of a deadly military operation. "Carter couldn't rescue our own soldiers out of the crap hole of Iran," Beck reminds his audience.

From Carter's iconic failure in the sands of Iran, Beck zooms ahead to the next major moment in his narrative of liberal decline. Under Bill Clinton, Beck explains, the "real" America kept slipping through our fingers. "It wasn't about the economy," he says. To illustrate the Clinton legacy, Beck creates a non sequitur by bringing up Jayson Blair, the *New York Times* reporter who was dismissed for inventing stories, including some concerning the family of Jessica Lynch. "This loser just signed a book deal! These are the forces keeping us from being who we really are," he says. (Beck was less vocal about these "forces" when Jessica Lynch's dramatic rescue from a hospital in Iraq was revealed to be a government lie.)

As inspiring as Lynch's story was at the time, and as ridiculous a character as Jayson Blair may be, Beck's examples of "real" America—white, military, West Virginia—and its counterpoint in "false" America—black, media, New York—suffer from the same problem: neither story has much to do with Glenn Beck. Nor do these subjects work very well as believable tear triggers. Beck had already choked up once that day, but it was just a minor catch in the throat. He needed something to send the crowd home with.

Beck had his grand finale. It was a teary closing speech that he had used at previous rallies and would use again during his 2006 Mid-Life Crisis stage tour. It is the story of Mary Beck, his first child, who was born with brain damage. He explains that the subject is painful for him. His voice breaks. "I don't usually do this," he says. He then brings his daughter onstage. The fragile lesson of Mary Beck is his gift to the world. "There is always hope," he says.

Beck knows that this is an odd way to close an event supposedly devoted to the U.S. military. So he tosses out another Jessica Lynch reference and reintroduces Lee Greenwood, who proceeds to sing "God Bless the USA." Beck had played this song in Louisville the day after Reagan bombed Tripoli. Now, seventeen years later, Beck introduces Greenwood to play the song live. A circle is closed.

Greenwood's performance is the last act of the day, but the applause is not followed by silence. As Beck makes his way backstage, the three-letter chant returns, louder this time. "*U-S-A!*" chants the crowd, both adoring and angry. "*U-S-A! U-S-A! U-S-A!*"

It was the sound of Glenn Beck Nation, in utero and in song.

In a much-discussed *New York Times* column published March 25, 2003, the sixth day of the Iraq War, Paul Krugman compared the Beck-emceed rallies to state-sponsored events in Nazi Germany. Just as Nazi rallies enjoyed corporate support and featured book burnings, the parking lots outside Beck's rallies sometimes featured tractors rolling over piles of Dixie Chicks albums. (The Dixie Chicks, an all-female country music band, were a target of right-wing hatred because the group's lead singer had announced onstage at a concert overseas that she was "ashamed" to be from the same state as George W. Bush.)

"Who has been organizing these rallies?" asked Krugman. "The answer . . . is that they are being promoted by key players in the radio industry—with close links to the Bush administration. The company appears to be using its clout to help one side in a political dispute that deeply divides the nation."

The allegations infuriated Beck. In the narrative painted by Krugman and other liberal critics, Beck's role was reduced to that of corporate pawn. It drew attention away from Beck and everything that made him great in his own eyes: his drawing power, his marketing sense, his authentic love of country, and his support for the troops. When the *Washington Post* called Beck for comment on the backlash, he huffed at the idea of a conspiracy.

"There is not one shred of evidence," Beck said. "They're only accusations and innuendo and insinuation, and it is absolutely outrageous they could make a claim like this and offer no proof whatsoever."[7] Translation: No one ever accused Bob Hope of being Richard Nixon's poodle!

Beck's own version of events was more mundane but ultimately more compelling than Krugman's. The Rally for America was less a historical sign of impending fascism than it was a touring monument to the genius of Beck's marketing instincts.

The first rally was held a month before the war, in February, in Dallas. The idea belonged to talk-radio host Daryl Ankarlo, who urged his listeners to come out and show their support for the troops. When Beck heard about the initiative, his antennae perked up. He asked Ankarlo to report back to him the next day. When Ankarlo called Beck in excitement with the news that a thousand people had showed up in the rain, Beck knew immediately what to do: make the rally idea his own.

As Reed Bunzel writes in *Clear Vision*, an official corporate history of Clear Channel, "Beck immediately realized that the rally had struck a chord with the audience, and invited Ankarlo to call his nationally syndicated show the next day to discuss the experience. As soon as Ankarlo was off the air, Beck decided he wanted to become involved with the rallies."

Of course he did. Beck instructed his listeners to call their local affiliates and support the idea of organizing similar events. The result was a flood of calls to stations on which Beck broadcast. Beck handpicked seventeen rallies he would headline and began putting his stamp on the efforts with a call for donations. He asked his listeners to each send in a dollar to show their support. He estimated that he would need $250,000 to put on a show. Striking a populist pose, Beck claimed that he was asking for small donations only because he didn't want the "fat cats" to underwrite the rallies.

No, getting the help of fat cats would have been too easy—and too quick. Where's the buildup? Not for the first time, Beck milked the fundraising drive for all he could. And the envelopes poured in, each containing worn dollar bills. This allowed Beck to dramatically announce the contents of the growing pot until he had raised $450,000. It was at least the fourth time that Beck had asked listeners to send in token donations in support of a Beck-branded cause.

When it comes to self-promotion and publicity, Beck is broadcasting's white shark, the industry's perfect predator. The rallies were preceded by more than twenty years of successful and increasingly shameless self-promotion. In Phoenix, he crashed Richard Marx concerts and hired Jessica Hahn. In New Haven, he drove a charity school bus and wore giant banana suits at malls. In Tampa, he protested the election recount and hosted parking-lot flag giveaways.

The Rally for America road show was part of this continuum. Only the scale had changed. A touring series of patriotic megaconcerts with stadium-quality sound systems blaring "Glenn Beck!" to cheering multitudes, the rallies constituted the mother of all advertisements for himself, a publicity coup that beat the hell out of anything that Bruce Kelly, his deejay friend from D.C., had ever done.

While Beck was leading the rallies, the number of affiliates that carried his show surpassed a hundred and continued to grow.

The audience donation drive like the one Beck used to hijack Ankarlo's rally idea has a long pedigree in populist broadcasting. And if such theatrical clarion calls for small donations sound cinematic, that's because they are. The practice is immortalized in Elia Kazan's 1957 film, *A Face in the Crowd.* Based partly on CBS radio host Arthur Godfrey, the film stars Andy Griffith as the radio and television huckster Lonesome Rhodes. On Rhodes's first show after he has made the leap from local radio to national television, Rhodes asks his audience to each send in a half-dollar to help a black member of the station's janitorial staff keep her home. The result is a torrent of silver coins, which Rhodes collects in a wheelbarrow and proudly displays to his audience. The stunt launches Rhodes's meteoric but short national career, which comes to an end when a rogue hot mic reveals the host to be a fraud.

If the rallies proved Beck worthy of Lonesome Rhodes's legacy, they also proved him unworthy of Bob Hope's. Beck's self-centered and unfunny performances offered no obvious echoes of the golfing comedian. The one exception might have been to remind crowds of Hope's famous line about playing before presidents: he had performed before many and entertained none.

No, Beck is not the new Bob Hope. He isn't mild-mannered. He doesn't write jokes. War zones frighten him. Still, Beck knew after the rallies that there was an enormous market for his brand. Because the core of that brand is biography, it was necessary to write a book, and it had to be much more personal than the best-selling talker manifestos by Limbaugh or Hannity. This book would chart Glenn Beck's search for the "real" Glenn Beck, a born-again voice for the "real" America. In such a book, Beck could develop his narrative, reinforce his brand, and put his pitch to his listeners in writing. The result would be a radio personality more "real" than any other: one that bleeds.

During downtime on the Rally for America tour, Beck could often be found pacing in a nearby trailer. It was there that he dictated his thoughts to a muscular, middle-aged man in thick-rimmed glasses named Mitchell Ivers. An editor with Simon & Schuster, Ivers had been tasked with getting Beck's first book out the door. The manuscript, written in what Beck called "record time" during early 2003, was published in September of that year. It was titled *The Real America: Messages from the Heart and Heartland.* The first hardback edition enjoyed a wide release on Simon & Schuster's Pocket Books, a mostly paperback imprint that counted Beck's hate-radio hero Bob Grant among its stable of talkers turned authors.[8]

With the release of *The Real America*, Beck completed what had become a mandatory and often profitable coming-of-age ritual for conservative talk radio hosts. At the time, Hannity was already at work on the sequel to his best-selling debut, *Let Freedom Ring.* That follow-up, *Deliver Us from Evil*, would eventually top the *New York Times* bestseller list.

Whereas the cover of Hannity's first book showed the native Long Islander standing before the Statue of Liberty, Beck's book positioned the author as Hannity's rural talk-radio twin. And as Beck knew well, this was his ace in the hole. The cover shows Beck standing in front of a (screen-projected) landscape of a farmhouse surrounded by fields of grain, with a faded American flag painted onto the roof. It could be Iowa, Wisconsin, or Kansas. The clean-cut Beck stands in the foreground in khakis and a dark denim button-down shirt, his hands on his hips. To anyone familiar with Beck's career, the mismatch between man and nature is jarring. Beck may have known farms as a boy in western Washington state, but his adult life had been spent in a string of exurbs and cities, working out of dumpy little windowless radio parks next to freeways. Beck seemed an odd messenger for notes from a corn-fed and corn-producing heartland.

But Beck's defiant appropriation of an idealized heartland made pitch-perfect marketing sense. The cover reflected the makeover in his broadcasting persona since his post-recount conversion and, especially, 9/11. As Victoria E. Johnson chronicles in her study of modern heartland-image appropriation, *Heartland TV*, the broadcasting era is marked by a sea change in popular representations of the Midwest. It is a transition away from radical populist traditions and toward a "heartland" of conservative values. This trend began to gain traction in the 1960s and has always become more pronounced during moments of national trauma. Beck understood intuitively that he was working in just such a moment since 9/11, well before the red state–blue state dichotomy gained mainstream currency.[9] The idealized Midwest was everywhere a broadcast personality wanted to be.

The post-9/11 shift was definitive, even affecting how the networks approached sitcoms:

> With regard to the development of new entertainment series, network executives have recently spoken of "not wanting shows that are aimed at people within 10 miles of the Atlantic and the Pacific," and imagining their core audience as "the 37-year-old woman from Topeka, Kansas."[10]

If one is thinking like a network executive, it is precisely this woman— middle-aged and living in Topeka—who delivers the payoff lesson in Beck's Rally for America stump speech. The Topeka woman reappears at the stoplight again in *The Real America*. The pleasant exchange tells Beck everything there is to know about the country. "That morning, I wasn't in Topeka, Kansas. I wasn't even in Kansas. I was in the Real America."[11]

In the words of a March 20 Clear Channel press release for the rallies, Beck was drawing tens of thousands of people like her: "reasonable, thoughtful, and prayerful people." Beck was their new champion, cutting a hero's figure amid the shaggy protesting hordes that populated Godless Gotham, where Beck would eventually base his heartland media empire.

Though a best-seller, *The Real America* undersold Hannity's first effort. But the book was ahead of its time. More than any of the dozens of books then offering post-9/11 conservative wisdom, Beck's book anticipated the neo-Nixonian rhetoric that five years later would find a champion in Sarah Palin. It didn't matter that Wasilla, Alaska, was really a festering suburban hive of teenage pregnancy and backyard meth labs, its economy anchored by strip malls, drive-thru restaurants, and liquor stores. Like Beck, Palin understood that she was trafficking in a heartland idea rooted not in reality but in fantasy and spite.

The split-screen country described in *The Real America* is a familiar place for listeners of conservative talk radio. On one side is the bad, fake, politically correct America, home to Hollywood elites, career-ist women with armpit hair, and Michael Moore. Beck harbors an especially profound hatred for Moore, whom he uses as the butt of a multipage joke.

Over the picket fence from this Gomorrah we find Beck's soft-focus "real" America, drenched in sunlight and filled with birdsong. In this country dwells a silent majority of decent, hardworking, family-oriented, pie-eating patriots who quietly suffer under the twin Big Brothers of political correctness and a godless culture. If Beck's real Americans could speak their hearts and their minds, what would they say? Although they themselves are "too terrified to speak out," their spokesman is not. If they had the power of speech, the oppressed would unite and declare, "I wish I could live in a neighborhood that's quiet and flag-lined, where the neighbors are all next door to one another [and] the air is filled with the sound of screen doors slamming shut as the kids run out to play." Beck concedes that the liberation of Real America to be itself is likely to result in the release of some hurtful language of the kind that is no longer tolerated on college campuses or among "elite" company. But the free expression of hate, he believes, is better than "people feigning bogus compassion by not noticing the difference between me and the guy who should be hanging from a tool belt."[12]

As usual, Beck struggles mightily in *The Real America* when talking about sex. A chapter on homosexuality opens with a long fantasy of an erotic encounter between Beck and his sister on a Ferris wheel. The message of the chapter, titled "Tolerance," is a not-so-subtle equation between incest and gay sex. "Why did I spend a whole chapter talking about a committed loving relationship with my sister?" asks Beck. "I did it because right now there is an organized ongoing effort to try to bend your values. To slowly shape your deepest beliefs into toleration and eventually acceptance."[13]

The author's journey takes him abroad. In order to truly find the Real America, he must leave it. Beck has never been much of a traveler—a couple of trips to Mexico and one trip to Italy—but he visited Israel the year before he went national. He shares the lessons of that trip in a chapter titled "Jesse Jackson *Is* Yasser Arafat." Here we see two new faces of Glenn Beck: travel writer and Middle East analyst. While in the Holy Land, Beck makes a brief excursion into Jerusalem's Old City. In *The Real America* he describes this transformative experience:

> It was dirty, dark and grimy, even the kids had filthy faces. You know how in a Disney movie, whenever there are orphans involved, there are always little English kids running around with soot on their faces who say, "Please, sir, if I only had a little bit o'chocolate . . ." That's the way it looked. But this wasn't Disney. This was real.

The Real Jerusalem! He then turns to the subject of Islam. Like many evangelical Christians, Beck has been very open about his struggle to understand and tolerate Islam, which has led him to visit mosques and personally question imams. In describing this quest, Beck almost succeeds in sounding reasonable. But even in print, he proves unable to control himself. A couple of paragraphs into his discourse on Islam, Beck collapses into a rant that sounds like something Michael Savage might say after losing both his legs in a suicide bombing.

"Hey, camel countries," he writes, "do you know why you guys are having rock sandwiches and washing them down with glasses of sand for lunch? Because . . . you are so busy terrorizing each other that you couldn't even build a Fiat . . . and Fiats suck."[14]

Five years later, when Fiat became part owner of General Motors, Beck's Real America would eat a different kind of sandwich. But by then Beck would have little love to spare for the failing heartland industry.

In another chapter, Beck returns to one of his favorite subjects: the painful lessons of the Vietnam War. As he had done so many times before, he parrots the Reagan-era myth that the war was lost by cowards in Washington who lacked the heart to "fight to win." The war's most pitiable victims, in his view, are the veterans who suffered abuse at the hands of America-hating antiwar protesters. Although most Vietnam War soldiers returned from Indochina with antiwar politics, Beck presents yet another of the book's many false dichotomies: evil protesters versus valiant vets.

One passage in particular illustrates Beck's champion-level combination of ignorance and smugness. In it, Beck mocks the outrage that greeted the publication of Nick Ut's famous photo of terrified

South Vietnamese children escaping a napalm attack on their village. As only Glenn Beck can do, he manages to get the basic facts wrong while digging around his ethical turd box for something to throw. Beck explains: "During the bombing of Cambodia, we bought into that 'evil America' stuff here at home: 'Oh, look . . . that poor little girl is running down the street naked . . . we can't do that to her . . .'"[15]

Many little girls did run scared from U.S. bombs in Cambodia, but the one in this picture was not one of them. The girl in the photo, Phan Kim Phúc, was Vietnamese, not Cambodian, and was burned in an attack carried out by the U.S.-supplied South Vietnamese Air Force. If Beck's readers didn't learn much about the Vietnam War, they could at least be thankful the author didn't subject them to the image of Beck and Kim Phúc making out on a Ferris wheel.

Even by the riding-helmet-and-training-wheels standards of its genre, *The Real America* is an embarrassing mess. It is less a conservative treatise than a pop-up book of shopworn far-right myths and canards. If its analysis is distinguished by anything, it is the breathtaking lack of knowledge that undergirds it. "For those who are crying that America is building an empire," Beck writes, "I ask you to point to the U.S. occupying forces in the former Axis power countries. You can't, because they don't exist."[16]

The Real America is most interesting when Beck stops talking politics and history and turns to something he actually knows and cares about: himself. Like *The Glenn Beck Program*, *The Real America* is mortared by biography. The whole inspirational story is here: from latchkey kid to high school deejay, from alcoholic cokehead clown to sober Mormon talk-radio superpatriot. In a chapter titled "Glenn Beck: Behind the Music," he speaks frankly about the business goals that drive everything he does. It is on the subject of wealth that Beck is forced to part ways with his hero Orson Welles, who died poor. Beck finds fresher inspiration in the form of two flamboyant Hollywood liberals, Ben Affleck and Matt Damon. After sketching the business architecture of Damon and Affleck's Live Planet Productions, Beck observes in near awe:

> That's four distinct forms of entertainment, four ways to reach their audience, four products that act as marketing and publicity for

each other and four sources of revenue. . . . This is what Mercury Radio Arts aspires to be. . . . We want to start with the Glenn Beck Program and find ways to . . . maximiz[e] its ratings and revenue.[17]

Like his target audience of heartlanders rooted in the Protestant ethic, Beck believes that the quest for riches is a divine pursuit. Here's Beck, part lay Mormon theologian, part discount Anthony Robbins:

> It's interesting to me that Jesus said, "Inside my Father's house there are many mansions." . . . That means that wealth and riches are not bad things. . . . God believes you deserve a mansion. Do you? . . . There is a universe full of money. There are riches beyond your wildest dreams. God doesn't give you a taste of ice cream unless he's willing for you to have the entire cone.[18]

As 2003 came to a close, Beck's career was cruising along according to the divine cone-growing plan. After the Rally for America tour and the publication of *The Real America, The Glenn Beck Program* continued to rack up affiliates. The national media were also starting to notice Beck's rise. In October 2003, Beck appeared with Chris Matthews on *Hardball* to discuss his new book. During the interview, Matthews admits to listening to Beck's show and praises its host as "amazingly smart" and a "great guy."

That camaraderie between Beck and Matthews would be impossible to imagine just a few years later. In the wake of the Iraq War, the tone of cable news would become increasingly bitter and partisan. As did his peers on both sides of the political divide, Beck helped fuel this change and reaped its rewards.

Beck spent the 2004 election in full elephant costume. Still nominally independent, he aligned himself strongly with the Real America, which was George W. Bush's America. In the January 2005 paperback edition of *The Real America*, the author praises Bush in gushing language, anticipating the cult of Obama that he would later decry.

"What lesson should Democrats take away from their defeat?" he asked. "You can't win on hate, Hollywood, or image. You can only win on leadership, values and vision. . . . Presidents bring us together by highlighting what we all have in common: Hope."[19]

Beck captured that unifying sense of hope on his broadcast the day after the election by playing an audio loop of himself laughing hysterically. The show was later made into a CD titled *Gloat Fest: 2004* and sold on his Web site.

A week after the election, Beck renewed his contract with Premiere Radio Networks. With Bush back in office and his own employment secure, Beck relaxed a bit and revisited some of his favorite perennial gags. In late April 2005, he spent a week building up a broadcast of a live abortion in progress. Then, in place of the audio from an abortion clinic, he played clips from *The Al Franken Show*, newly launched on a fledgling Air America. After the clip, he claimed that the real audio had been censored by some affiliates.

At the end of the show, Beck came clean and admitted that there was never any abortion audio. He defended the gag as a profound piece of radio in a long tradition, citing in particular one comedic genius. "Andy Kaufman was the kind of guy who wanted you to feel something, to know that you are alive," Beck explained. "That is kind of the premise of what we have done for the last week. I wanted you to feel it without actually having to hear [the abortion]."

Beck then asked his listeners to reflect on the important lessons offered by his genius. Among them were the need for adoption services and—this especially—the travesty of the trend of giving television personalities like Franken their own radio shows. "Stop putting television people on [the radio] and expecting that [television people] can paint pictures!" Beck said. "[They] don't understand that this is the most sensitive and expressive medium there is. This does take some talent."

As the Bush-era culture war intensified, Beck increasingly put his talents to use slamming critics of the Iraq War. Most notably, this included two activists whose children had been killed in action. When Cindy Sheehan began speaking out against the war in the name of her fallen son, Casey, Beck called her a "prostitute." When Michael Berg, the father of a U.S. civilian beheaded in Iraq, followed Sheehan in criticizing the Bush White House, Beck called him a "scumbag." Anyone who protested the Bush administration or questioned its honesty or motives became a target for his vitriol.

On the morning of September 9, 2005, three years into his syndicated career, Beck entered a new stage in his profession. This was the day that Beck registered his first audible blip on the radar of Media Matters for America, a media watchdog outfit founded by David Brock the previous year. The monologue that caught the attention of Media Matters was destined to become one of the most infamous of Beck's career, and it began innocently enough as part of a Clear Channel fundraiser for victims of Hurricane Katrina.

As Beck developed a riff on his reaction to those trapped in the city's Superdome, he began to seethe. Specifically, it was images of those struggling for government-issued emergency ATM cards that set him off. After comparing the Superdome situation to a casual-dining buffet, Beck declared that he was sick of seeing images of these "scumbags" who failed to escape the hurricane's path. It was a striking judgment—one that Beck, quite noticeably, did not pass on to the World Trade Center and Pentagon employees who failed to evacuate their respective burning buildings in an orderly fashion in time to save their lives on 9/11.

Beck's brain then made a classic and revealing leap of logic. His feeling of disgust at watching those trapped in the Superdome reminded him of his feelings toward some of the families of the 9/11 victims' families. Four years after that event, Beck still approached 9/11 as a child would. He wanted to keep it a simple morality play that ended with President Bush and his bullhorn at ground zero. He had no patience with anyone who was seeking an investigation into the intelligence bungles that preceded the attacks.

Beck would spend much energy on the air and in print trying to explain away his comments, but the transcript speaks for itself. Anyone with eyes can follow Beck's bouncing ball as it connects those trapped in New Orleans—contrasted with the Real America of rural Louisiana— and the outspoken 9/11 families:

> [After thinking of a buffet line] the second thought I had when I saw these people and they had to shut down the Astrodome [*sic*] and lock it down, I thought: I didn't think I could hate victims faster than the 9/11 victims. These guys—you know, it's really sad. We're not hearing anything about Mississippi. We're not hearing anything about Alabama. We're hearing about the victims in New Orleans. This is a 90,000-square-mile disaster site. New Orleans is 181 square miles. A hundred and—0.2 percent of the disaster area is New Orleans! And that's all we're hearing about, are the people in New Orleans. Those are the only ones we're seeing on television, are the scumbags—and again, it's not all the people in

New Orleans. Most of the people in New Orleans got out! It's just a small percentage of those who were left in New Orleans, or who decided to stay in New Orleans, and they're getting all the attention. It's exactly like the 9/11 victims' families. There's [sic] about 10 of them that are spoiling it for everybody.

From what source did Beck draw this precise fractional breakdown of the Gulf disaster zone, employed to highlight the "scumbags" trapped in New Orleans? And why call for geographical parity when New Orleans was the only city under water? Both remain mysteries. The critique was especially strange coming from a man who spent the first month of his talk-radio career raising awareness about a single backyard tree house in central Florida.

The providence of Beck's hatred for certain 9/11 widows is less of a mystery. Beck was actually a little late to that game. Criticizing the most outspoken families had been a right-wing media meme since the spring of the previous year. Rush Limbaugh and Bill O'Reilly had attacked the widows as "obsessed with rage and hatred" and "aligned with the far left."[20]

Beck would later argue that he couldn't have meant what he said, because, after all, he had raised funds for the hurricane victims. But his Philadelphia fundraising event was actually one of many around the country that had been organized by Clear Channel to benefit the Red Cross.[21] Unlike the Rally for America, it was not Beck's baby. Among the fifty items that were up for bidding on Beck's infamous September 9 show were "a new set of Callaway Big Bertha Golf Irons [and] two first-class accommodations to Philadelphia to watch *The Glenn Beck Program* and have lunch with the host and his radio crew."

When Katrina hit in August 2005, Beck could afford to buy lunch for whomever he wanted. *The Glenn Beck Program* had grown to become the third most listened-to radio show in America. His voice now reached three million listeners every day on almost two hundred stations. Though expanding in all directions, his affiliates still consisted mainly of small- and medium-size markets in the middle of the country. But not all of Beck's fans dwelled in the fabled heartland. At least a couple of them lived and worked in its geographic and psychic opposite, midtown Manhattan. Around the time of Beck's Katrina monologue, they began wondering what Glenn Beck might do with a nightly hour of national television.

5

This Is CNN?

As winter gave way to an unusually warm spring in New York in 2006, those living in the southern shadow of the Time Warner Center in midtown Manhattan began to notice a regular new visitor. A black stretch limousine could frequently be seen idling on West 58th Street, just around the corner from Columbus Circle. Out of the vehicle would always appear the same man, tall and blond, striding toward the stainless steel doors next to the Time Warner garage. Curious residents eventually came to recognize the man as Glenn Beck, host of an eponymous new evening program on CNN Headline News.

"Over the years, I've seen all of the CNN talking heads maybe once or twice," recalls a longtime resident of 333 West 57th Street. "But Beck was frequently parked right across from my rear door. He loved to sit in that limo before making grand exits toward the building. For weeks I wondered, 'Who the hell is this guy?'"

Around the world, millions were beginning to ask the same thing. How to answer that question—*Who the hell is this guy?*—is something that had been worrying CNN executives since the January 2006 announcement of Beck's hiring. When Headline News named Beck as the network's latest addition to a revamped evening lineup, the response from liberal quarters was ferocious. Within days, Moveon.org and Media Matters for America had collated and distributed samplers of Beck's recent radio bile.

The centerpiece of the campaign was Beck's infamous Katrina monologue. MSNBC host Keith Olbermann amplified the Internet campaigns by quoting the offending passages and naming Beck one of the "Worst People in the World." Also making Olbermann's list was Beck's new boss, CNN executive Ken Jautz. The bad press failed to derail the show, but it succeeded in coloring the coverage of Beck's transition to television.[1]

During the four months leading up to his Headline News debut, Beck's Katrina monologue was a magnet for liberal outrage. And Beck loved every minute of it. The campaigns not only drummed up interest in his new show, they signaled his arrival in the nation's ongoing cable news melodrama. As he always does, Beck used his radio show to stoke the controversy and reinforce his conservative bona fides. On the January 20 edition of *The Glenn Beck Program*, Beck discussed at length how "all these socialist organs . . . now think I'm the Antichrist. They hate me. They *really* hate me. It's kind of a nice thing."

His new bosses at CNN weren't so sure. As Beck's May debut loomed, e-mails poured in urging the network to reconsider Beck's hiring. CNN kept a poker face, but the campaign could only have rattled network nerves. The charges that Beck was mean-spirited and bigoted raised the specter of another failed experiment in bringing a right-wing radio personality to television: Michael Savage's brief and ill-fated 2003 stint on MSNBC. *The Savage Nation* was canceled amid public outrage after Savage told a gay caller, "Get AIDS and die, you pig."[2]

CNN finally addressed public concerns about Beck a month before his first show. In early April, Headline News chief Ken Jautz issued a defensive press release touting Beck's "incredibly engaging" on-air style and "his no-nonsense approach." Without mentioning Beck's politics or the multiple controversies swirling around his radio rants, Jautz maintained that Beck was "the perfect next step in the evolution of the Headline Prime line-up."

The backlash against Beck wasn't just coming from outside the network. Beck's hiring also sparked an internal revolt among CNN and Headline News staff. The more network employees learned about their new colleague, the more alarmed they became. CNN's famously diverse newsroom staff had just won a Peabody Award for the network's Katrina coverage. Now they were being asked to stack their shows with promos for a man whose voice took on a noticeable hiss when discussing the country's most prominent civil rights leaders and its "oppressive" regime of political correctness. As Beck's Katrina monologue made the rounds in Atlanta and New York, most people concluded that Beck had not been misquoted but had indeed looked at terrified, hungry people trapped in the Superdome and judged them "scumbags."

"Beck's hire caused a lot of staff complaints," remembers Herb Sierra, Headline News' former editorial manager. "The rank and file was like 'What the hell are we doing?' There was a lot of angry internal e-mail calling Beck a bigot. The complaints were channeled up to [CEO] Jim Walton. But that was the end of it."

Three days before *The Glenn Beck Program* debuted, CNN made a belated effort to reframe the identity of its new host. On May 5, Beck went on CNN's *American Morning*, where an openly antagonistic Soledad O'Brien asked him to explain his Katrina comments. The question unnerved Beck, who responded with the disjointed if not contradictory defense that his words had been taken out of context, and anyway, much of what he says is "just joking." Reflecting the general sentiment of her colleagues, O'Brien was unimpressed with Beck's explanation. She ended the segment with a curt "Good luck on your show."

Beck found a much friendlier reception later that night on *Nancy Grace*, hosted by his new colleague and the top-rated host on Headline News. Grace spent little effort trying to hide the purpose of Beck's appearance, immediately deflecting attention from his Katrina comments toward the specter of Mary Beck. The scripted verbal softball between Beck and Grace is a classic illustration of Beck using his embellished biography to build and defend his brand.

Right out of the gate, Grace lunges for the juiciest bits in Beck's biography:

> *Grace*: A lot of people don't realize where you're coming from with your life history, and I'm referring specifically to your mom and [your] brother.
>
> *Beck*: I mean, I've grown up—I've had a lot of experiences in my life. My mom committed suicide when I was thirteen. My brother has committed suicide. I'm an alcoholic in recovery, did drugs every day of my life for many, many years. I like to say I'm a work in progress. . . .
>
> *Grace*: Aren't we all?

With the viewers' sympathy glands fully activated, Grace then shifts the focus to Beck's response to Katrina. Along the way, she makes a verbal slip, showing familiarity with the problem that the interview is meant to solve: Beck's famous segue from hating Katrina victims to hating 9/11 victims' families.

> *Grace*: Is it true you threw a benefit somehow for 9/11—Katrina victims?
>
> *Beck*: Yeah—no, I threw a benefit for Katrina survivors. I didn't like to call them victims as much as survivors. I think there were some victims out there. And then there were those who were capitalizing on the event, and they were stealing televisions and shooting at helicopters. You know, those people, I didn't raise money for them. And we raised—I don't even remember what it was—$150,000 in an afternoon for them to try to help those people who were trying to be decent people and get back on their feet.

If viewers were left scratching their heads over Beck's compulsion to separate Katrina victims into "decent" and unworthy camps, they didn't have to wait long to see for themselves where he was coming from.

In crafting his new TV show, *Glenn Beck*, Beck used a lot of creative carryover from *The Glenn Beck Program*. There were also some strong additions to his team, most notably a former *Daily Show* producer named Evan Cutler and the comedian Brian Sack. At first, it seemed that *Glenn Beck* might more closely resemble a humor-based variety show than the kind of cable news showcase that Beck claimed to hate, full of preening blowhards spouting partisan talking points.

The show's studio set suggested something new in cable news. It featured faux-brick walls and neon signs in a massive space more closely resembling a boho artist loft than the antiseptic sets of *Hannity & Colmes* or *The O'Reilly Factor*. In a nod to his origins and previous generations of radio men–turned–TV hosts, Beck decorated his desk with two custom-made radio microphones dipped in chrome. Off-camera was a whiteboard listing the four ingredients of the show that Beck asked his staff never to forget: relevance, humor, self-deprecation, and entertainment.

After four months of simmering controversy, *Glenn Beck* debuted on May 8, 2006, at 7 p.m. Beck opened the show true to his white-board commandments, with a fireworks display of self-deprecation. *Glenn Beck* was just a "stupid little show," he declared, hosted by a "middle-age[d] recovering alcoholic with no fashion sense." As for the show's politics, Beck trotted out the routine about his independence and declared his new motto (not for the last time): "It isn't about left versus right, but right versus wrong."

The charade of political independence died during the first ten minutes of the first episode. The opening segment featured Beck mocking a University of California study that indicated that liberal children are happier and better adjusted than their conservative counterparts. Beck had not read the study, but he pointed to Ronald Reagan and Michael Moore as proof of its worthlessness.

Aside from his childlike rejection of an academic study by anecdote, Beck might have thought twice about evoking Moore in an attempt to defend the emotional balance of conservatives. For years, Beck had indulged in murderous fantasies about Moore, whom he once described as a "morbidly obese, violently grotesque, greasy, hair-covered, sweat-drenched Gila monster who is simultaneously both completely irrelevant to society and also a filthy, cancerous scourge on humanity."[3] Compared to Beck, Moore is just a heavier Mr. Rogers.

Beck then introduced his first guest, the journalist Eric Schlosser, who attempted to discuss his wide-ranging and best-selling exposé of the fast-food industry, *Fast Food Nation*. But like the California study, Schlosser was merely being trotted out as a prop. Beck made no pretense of having read *Fast Food Nation*, and he spent the segment mocking his guest. As Schlosser discussed by satellite the dangers of letting fast-food chains market to children, Beck winked at the camera and crammed a Big Mac into his mouth, giggling as he licked his fingers and wiped his chin. Had Beck read Schlosser's book, he would have known that he was making a literal ass out of himself on national television by smearing heavy traces of cow feces all over his smug face.

Arguably the most memorable moment of Beck's television debut came with Erica Hill, an Atlanta-based Headline News anchor. Beck treated Hill as if she were his new Jessica Hahn "prize bunny," telling her that she "looked hot in leather." It was not the last time that Beck would extend a public flirtation with Hill to the breaking point and beyond. Beck's on-air exchanges with Hill were a regular feature of the show until she was replaced later that year.

"It was always painful whenever Erica had to chat with Beck between segments," remembers Ben Arnold, a former Headline News staffer. "It was like watching a dumb frat guy hit on a girl who wasn't interested. She hated it. We'd all be cringing in the studio, screaming, 'Oh, God! Stop!'"[4]

But there was no stopping Glenn Beck. In the following weeks, he would set the pattern for his television career by spouting a panoply of conservative myths and lies, from junk climate science to claims that illegal immigrants were conspiring to "conquer our culture."

Beck's liberal critics watched dumbfounded, but the network brass in New York was pleased with Beck's performance. To boost his profile and bolster his credibility as an analyst, CNN cross-booked Beck on marquee shows like *The Situation Room* and *Anderson Cooper 360*. On the latter, Beck was asked weeks into his tenure to discuss border politics and illegal immigration. According to Cooper, Beck's expertise on the issues rested on the fact that as a talk-radio host he had his "finger on the pulse" of public opinion. Beck didn't have much to say about immigration other than to reiterate his call for a border fence. Fans of *The Glenn Beck Program*, however, knew that Beck considered Mexico a "dirtbag country" with an economy based on "beans and big hats."

To know Beck only through CNN was to see something considerably less than half of the man.

Missing on Beck's studio whiteboard of commandments was the show's dominant element: crackpot conservatism. But as *Glenn Beck* developed into 2006, that element was increasingly there in spirit. While Beck and his bosses publicly clung to the myth that Beck represented a "new kind" of postpartisan cable news host, the guests featured on the show told a different story. During the show's early weeks, Beck presented an industry-funded view on climate change, declared his affection for Ann Coulter, and identified signs of biblical prophecy in news from the Middle East. The result bore no resemblance to the postpartisan, libertarian-tinged conservatism promised by CNN press releases. Aside from occasional admissions of self-doubt and aw-shucks regular-guy confusion, Beck was just another conservative with a burning hatred of liberals. The only thing that made Beck a "unique voice" was the frequency with which he expressed this hatred in the form of violent fantasies, sometimes followed by sudden downward spirals into fetid pools of pathos.

The most distinguishing feature of the show was how Beck's hawkish views on foreign policy careened into apocalyptic ravings. By the summer, he had fully entered the mode for which he would become famous: dry-drunk harbinger of the apocalypse. Typical of this turn was a July 12 monologue that featured Beck's long-standing obsessions with Hollywood, Islamic terrorism, and concentration camps.

"Hollywood, clean the ears out and listen up," Beck intoned while looking directly at the camera. "You are the first in line for the gas chambers if they ever win. You're the ones who are producing a lot of the trash that's spilling out into their cave that's hacking them off. . . . It's the whole Western way of life that is in trouble. That's why we need to get on that World War III bandwagon."

By the end of the summer, Beck was talking politics through a permanently frothed mouth. On his radio show, Beck warned the world's "good Muslims" to start doing their part in World War III. "Muslims who have sat on your frickin' hands the whole time and have not been marching in the streets" should look out, said Beck. "Human beings are not strong enough, unfortunately, to restrain themselves from putting up razor wire and putting you on one side of it. . . . When people see that their way of life is on the edge of being over, they will put razor wire up and just based on the way you look or just based on your religion, they will round you up. . . . Is that wrong? Oh my gosh, it is Nazi, World War II wrong, but society has proved it time and time again—it will happen."

Was this a warning? A threat? A hope? It was hard to tell. Beck's obsession with the end of days and the existential threat of militant Islam became more pronounced as the anniversary of 9/11 approached. On September 12, Beck turned during his Headline News show to his recurring fantasy of turning the Middle East into an ocean of glass.

"The Middle East is being overrun by tenth-century barbarians," he told his growing and increasingly fascinated audience. "If they take over—the barbarians storm the gate and take over the Middle East—we're going to have to nuke the whole place."

Beck's joining of neoconservative swagger and blood-thirsty biblical imagination was not limited to his television and radio platforms.

In June 2006, Beck took his second one-man stage show on the road. The Mid-Life Crisis tour was largely a biographical hodgepodge of bits from *The Real America* and his Rally for America routine. The topical elements that Beck wove into the show were notably gruesome.

During a performance in Columbia, South Carolina, Beck revisited his desire to smash actor Tim Robbins over the head with a shovel, and he joked about "cutting the fingers off" of terrorists and watching their "butts shoot blood." He transitioned away from this gory ramble to tales of family life that culminated in an inspirational pep talk that was typically trite and self-serving.

The show ended with a slide-show dramatization of the lives of astronaut James Erwin and Beck's physically handicapped daughter. "Colonel Sanders was sixty-six when he opened the first Kentucky Fried Chicken," Beck told the crowd, before closing with words that could have been taken from a late-night infomercial for motivational DVDs.

"Never give up," said Beck. "Live the life you've always imagined."

Beck was clearly living the life he'd always imagined. During one week in November 2006, he enjoyed the two biggest publicity bonanzas of his career.

The first, more enduring moment came on the evening of November 14, shortly after the Democrats retook Congress in the midterm elections. Among those swept into Washington was the first Muslim ever sent to Congress, Minnesota representative-elect Keith Ellison. Beck asked Ellison onto the show and made a statement that he has never been able to live down. "Sir," said Beck, "prove to me that you are not working with our enemies."[5]

Although it was couched in more conciliatory language, the sound bite became a lightning rod for Beck's growing legions of dedicated critics, who now included comedian Jon Stewart. "Finally, someone who says what people who aren't thinking are thinking," Stewart quipped the night after Beck's remark. An adept practitioner of public relations aikido, Beck later splashed Stewart's crack across the back of his 2007 best-seller, *An Inconvenient Book*. (In the same book, Beck called the Ellison question "the most poorly worded question of all time.")

If Beck was feeling especially paranoid about congressional Islamofascist sleeper cells in Minneapolis, it was probably because he had spent most of that autumn preparing for the November 15 airing of *Exposed: The Extremist Agenda*. The first of four specials he would host during his time at Headline News, the show strung together sensational footage of radical clerics calling for the destruction of the United States and Israel. Though not exactly revelatory, the program struck ratings gold. The two airings, in the 7 p.m. and 9 p.m. time slots, drew a combined audience of almost two million.

Encouraged by the results, CNN rewarded Beck with the funds to produce four more specials. "Glenn's unique style works well for his everyday-show format, but giving him a full hour on just one topic really gives him the chance to delve deeper, in a way that clearly resonates with his viewers," said CNN executive Ken Jautz. "We look forward to hearing what Glenn has to say on these timely and provocative issues."

As his first year on television drew to a close, Beck continued to make a mockery of his regular professions of independence. He pointed to the Dow Jones Industrial Average as proof that the Bush economy was strong, heartily defended torture, and compared Republican senator Rick Santorum to Winston Churchill. Proving that he was ahead of the curve on GOP talking points, he also invoked the Holocaust in an early mention of health-care reform. For such cutting-edge analysis, Beck was rewarded at Christmas with a commentator gig on *Good Morning America*, ABC's lobotomized morning program. Despite attempts to stop this further legitimization of Beck's politics—the Arab American Institute called attention to Beck's "blatant anti-Arab, anti-Muslim bias"[6]—the deal went through, putting Beck back in the early-morning element of his youth. Compared to CNN, it was actually a pretty good fit.

If Beck's arrival at CNN made for weird pairings with straitlaced colleagues like Wolf Blitzer and Anderson Cooper, that awkwardness reflected larger tensions within the network. Beck arrived at CNN Headline News during a transitional year for both CNN networks. Jonathan Klein had just been hired as the new president and was charged with beating back the Fox News juggernaut. One of his first moves was the hiring of Joel Cheatwood to oversee development at CNN and Headline News.

A veteran TV news executive, Cheatwood had built a reputation in the industry as a ratings rainmaker and news sensationalist. Owners loved him, newsrooms not so much. In Miami and Boston, Cheatwood had perfected a formula that leaned on flashy design, gimmicks, and a gory, crime-heavy approach to local news. In Chicago, he famously hired tabloid talker Jerry Springer as a news commentator, causing the station's two star news anchors to resign in protest. When Cheatwood joined CNN in 2005, his ability to draw younger viewers by raising the pitch on tabloid accents was legendary. Among Cheatwood's first recruits were CNN's first stunt reporter, Rick Sanchez, and Headline News's first stunt commentator, Glenn Beck.

"Joel Cheatwood doesn't have a news philosophy," says Aaron Brown, a former CNN anchor who was fired soon after Cheatwood's arrival. "I think he has a TV philosophy that has nothing to do with journalism."

CNN hired Cheatwood precisely because of this TV philosophy. His talents were especially suited to the latest effort to revamp CNN's little brother, Headline News. In 2005, CNN was preparing for the most dramatic shake-up in the history of either channel. The face-lift of Headline News would involve every facet of its identity, including tone, politics, and formats. By the time it was over, it took the junior CNN network into territory that Ted Turner never imagined in his youth and found difficult to bear in old age. "Headline News used to be straight news anytime you wanted it," Turner lamented to a reporter in 2009. "It's unwatchable now. It's heartbreaking."[7]

Like the Laffer Curve and the lyrics to "Blowin' in the Wind," the idea for Headline News was first scratched out on a paper napkin. In 1980, Ted Turner drew a circle divided into half-hour segments, mirroring the dependability of all-news radio. Two years later, the station launched as CNN2, offering television's only nonstop "news wheel." For two decades, this thirty-minute wheel turned day and night, providing headlines in "get to the point" environments like airports and hotel bars.

A couple of decades later, thousands of bars and airports in the United States, Asia, and Latin America were broadcasting the Headline News wheel. But the world had changed since 1982. The rise of MSNBC and Fox News brought pressure on CNN, particularly during prime time. In response, Time Warner authorized a radical overhaul of Headline News in 2004. The water-mill predictability and faceless presentation of the old news wheel was out. In its place,

Headline News would create a kaleidoscope of feisty opinions, strong personalities, and candy-covered culture news. Overseeing this shift was a CNN executive named Ken Jautz.[8]

A former Associated Press reporter, Jautz had risen to vice president of CNN Worldwide by the time he was sent to Atlanta and tasked with transforming Headline News in early 2005. He arrived in Atlanta with a plan in hand that he called the Blue Sky initiative. He came as New York's man, inserted by Klein above veteran Headline News chief Rolando Santos. Facing a staff weary of rumored changes, Jautz gently presented Blue Sky as a trial balloon. He promised that CNN standards would not be diluted in the makeover and that soon-to-be hired Headline News personalities would not appear on traditional CNN news programming. He broke both promises.

"He told us he envisioned a CNN version of 'Nick at Night,' with daytime programming leading into something completely different," remembers a veteran Headline News staffer. "The reference didn't have the calming effect he intended."

When Jautz arrived in Atlanta, Time Warner was in the process of finalizing the purchase of Court TV. Although few in Atlanta knew it at the time, CNN executives in New York were already planning on building the new Headline News prime-time lineup around Court TV's biggest star, a pugnacious former prosecutor named Nancy Grace. When rumors of this plan started to circulate, many began to suspect that CNN was planning a double-team strategy aimed at containing Fox. According to this view, CNN would continue to lead on hard news while Headline News siphoned off Fox viewers with candy, conservatives, and cranks.

CNN had already shown it was not immune to the "Fox effect." In 2000, when Fox first threatened to overtake CNN, CNN news chief Walter Isaacson quietly met behind closed doors with Republican leaders in Washington. The meetings were seen by many as constituting an apology for past crimes of liberal bias, as well as a promise to make amends. Maureen Dowd criticized Isaacson in her *New York Times* column for "giving the impression that he will sacrifice objectivity to improve ratings."[9]

Five years later, CNN no longer worried about impressions. More than ever, it was worried about getting creamed by Fox.

Jautz finally unveiled his Blue Sky initiative at the end of February 2005. The new Headline News prime-time lineup included *Showbiz Tonight, Nancy Grace*, and *Prime News Tonight*, all bundled under the programming tag Headline Prime. Many veteran employees were apprehensive about the direction the network was taking. But the revamp succeeded quickly in drawing viewers. Less than a year after launching, *Nancy Grace* had nearly tripled Headline News' previous ratings at 8 p.m. It was the fastest growing cable news show of the year.

But the transformation of Headline News wasn't quite complete. In May 2005, Jautz held a network staff meeting to announce that there was still one "missing piece" in the Headline Prime puzzle. Screen tests, he said, were under way in New York to find that piece.

Among those who completed screen tests for CNN around the time of Jautz's announcement was Air America talk-radio personality Rachel Maddow. Originally brought in to audition for a new weekend show on CNN, the rising liberal star was also on the Headline News radar.

"There were a lot of names being thrown around for the new Headline News show, Maddow included," says Herb Sierra, the former editorial manager. Years after both CNN networks passed on Maddow, CNN chief Jon Klein explained the decision by saying that an "obviously liberal" host didn't fit with the mission of an objective news network. "It's like, you wouldn't put *The Sopranos* on Comedy Central."[10]

On January 17, 2006, Headline News announced that it was doing something even stranger. "Glenn Beck is the next step in the evolving Headline News strategy," said Ken Jautz in a press release. "We set out to find the best talk-show host we could."[11] Echoing Beck's previous bosses in Tampa, CNN went out of its way to reassure its staff and its listeners that Beck was not a raving right-wing nutcase. He was, rather, fiercely independent. A "unique voice."

When staff protests against the hiring of Beck's unique voice were ignored, some veteran staffers began polishing their résumés. "I knew I could no longer stay at a network that gives this kind of programming implicit endorsement," says Christine Boese, a former newswriter who left within a year of the Beck show's launching. "It is tempting to imagine an alternative universe in which [Headline News] embraced a show with Rachel Maddow instead of Glenn Beck."

Others were more resigned to Beck's arrival.

"Beck was part of a total transition in the industry toward a new dynamic media that incorporated the Internet, personalities, and infotainment," says Herb Sierra, the former editorial manager. "It was inevitable. Traditional journalism and news gathering was pushed down by the weight of the changes. And the fact is, in terms of ratings, it worked."

So it did. In a replay of the explosive growth achieved by *Nancy Grace, Glenn Beck* was the fastest growing cable news show of 2006.

When Beck revisits his start on television, he often makes a big deal of having refused the Headline News job when it was offered. According to the story he tells on the radio and on stage, Beck rebuffed CNN with force. Eventually, he says, he agreed to a meeting only as a favor to his agent. "First thing I said was, 'This is going to be the shortest meeting in TV history. I'm not interested.'" The two-sided debate structure of cable news programs, he maintains, annoyed and bored him.

Maybe it did. But it is hard to believe that the boy who grew up worshiping Johnny Carson had to be dragged kicking and screaming before a television camera. Nor was Beck blind to the boost that a national television platform might give his radio ratings. Although he was heard on two hundred stations at the end of 2006, he was still primarily a small-market name. This was true of red states as well as blue. When CNN approached him about doing a show, *The Glenn Beck Program* was heard in the Georgian cities of Macon, Savannah, and Columbus, but not Atlanta. The move to television was solid fuel for the next boost of *The Glenn Beck Program.* Radio was more than his first love; it was the base of the brand.

Beck had long been thinking of that brand as bigger than just radio, or even radio and TV combined. "I don't know how you can survive in today's media world just by being on radio, just being on television," Beck told *Broadcasting & Cable* after his first year on Headline News. "You've got to be ubiquitous."[12]

As 2007 loomed, he was well on his way.

6

A Rodeo Clown Goes Large

Those who had opposed CNN's hiring of Glenn Beck felt vindicated a year later. By any reasonable standard, *Glenn Beck* began 2007 as the new bottom-feeder in America's cable news aquarium. The same fatheaded viciousness that defined Beck's radio show had been transplanted to television. The host had merely added visual elements to his shopworn material. On the radio, Beck was limited to talking about his desire to nuke other countries. On television, he could fill the screen with the image of a letter he wished he could write to the president of Iran, in which Beck warns him that it could soon be "ten thousand degrees" in Tehran.

Among those who marked the first anniversary of Beck's CNN contract by saying "I told you so" was Arab American pollster John Zogby. "While the network may have hoped that Beck's flamboyant style would increase ratings," he wrote, "the cost to [its] integrity has been staggering."[1]

But if CNN had sold its soul, it received its asking price. The point of transforming Headline News was never to win Peabody Awards; it was to rack up eyeballs. Barbed charges of critically wounded integrity may have stung the network's news staff, but by the time they reached Ken Jautz's executive suite, they made no sound. The only measure that mattered to Jautz and his superiors was ratings. By that standard, they too were vindicated. Thanks to Nancy Grace and Beck, more Americans were watching Headline News in January 2007 than ever before. During his first eight months, Beck increased viewership of his 7 p.m. slot by 60 percent over the previous year. In the favored demographic of viewers ages twenty-five to fifty-four, that number was 84 percent. The Beck haters seethed; Cheatwood and Jautz toasted their success.

As with Beck's belated triumph in Tampa, however, his Headline News numbers are less impressive when viewed in context. In May 2006, Beck inherited a ratings moonscape. A new show hosted by a baby orangutan would have enjoyed some sort of bounce over the old news-wheel programming. All Beck had to do was keep from drooling too much and address topics sexier than oatmeal preparation, and he was all but guaranteed to attract new viewers.

And attract them he did. On that the ratings reports were clear. Less clear was audience motive. How many people were tuning in to *Glenn Beck* because they were genuine fans of the show, and how many watched out of an abject, slack-jawed fascination tinged with horror? There was something about Beck's show that tempted even fierce critics into wide-eyed nightly voyeurism. *Glenn Beck* wasn't just a more watery, sillier version of *Hardball* or *The O'Reilly Factor.*

Whatever one thought of Beck's politics, he was creating some of the strangest television since the psychedelic savantism of Paul Reubens's cult children's show of the early 1990s, *Pee Wee's Playhouse.* Like *Playhouse, Glenn Beck* was fast-paced, often driven by spectral logic, and hosted by a manic man-boy surrounded by vintage props. Just as Reubens found inspiration in classic children's programs like *Rocky and Bullwinkle* and *The Howdy Doody Show*, Beck showcased an apocalyptic ultraconservatism that borrowed heavily from the John Birch Society of the 1950s and 1960s. This facet of the show deepened throughout 2007, as Beck came under the increasing influence of a notorious Cold War conspiracy crank named Willard Cleon Skousen (more on him later).

Mainstream-media reporters were perplexed by the arrival of this odd duck on the scene. Previously, grown men who traded in emotional caprice and apocalyptic harangues had been relegated to street corners and local public access programming. But Beck was plying this routine on international cable. In the still young world of cable news, he was a mutant among mutants.

The reviews started rolling in toward the end of his first calendar year, after a CNN hype campaign touting *Glenn Beck* as "the fastest growing cable show of 2006." In its first in-depth look at Headline News' revamped lineup, the *New York Times* noted Beck's "brash . . . unfiltered approach" but skirted a detailed analysis of Beck in order to focus on the more familiar and easily digested character of Nancy Grace.[2]

It was left to the *Washington Post* to write Beck's first national profile. In a generally bemused and respectful piece, the *Post* touted Beck as a mellow new voice in cable news' blowhard cacophony—"more culture worrier than culture warrior." Echoing Beck's first newspaper chronicler in Tampa, the *Post* writer was dumbfounded by his subject's ability to "contradict himself without even noticing."[3]

That was one way of putting it. Those not bound by the strictures of daily newspaper writing were considerably less kind. In his television column for *Entertainment Weekly*, the novelist Stephen King described Beck as "Satan's mentally challenged younger brother."[4] Then there was the venomous bewilderment expressed by the Buffalo *Beast*, quoted by the *Post* as representing the ferocity of many Beck critics:

> If the dumbing down of political commentary continues along this trajectory, the next pundit to make the grade will be a hyena. Even the leather-winged shouting heads at Fox News look like intellectual giants next to this bleating, benighted Cassandra. It's like someone found a manic, doom-prophesying hobo in a sandwich board, shaved him, shot him full of Zoloft, and gave him a show. What makes Beck special, aside from appearing to have derived his entire geopolitical outlook from a five-minute segment about Iran on "The 700 Club," is the folksy "golly gee" manner in which he accuses his guests of collaborating with terrorists. At least Hannity and O'Reilly have the decency to act like bellicose pricks when they're engaging in breathtaking cheap shots.[5]

Of course, decency was never Beck's calling card. And differentiation from competitors like O'Reilly and Hannity was very much the point of Beck's shtick; its stock rose with each passing day.

As the liberal pile-on grew, Beck's conservative business boomed. The more the media bulls charged, the more Beck found his rodeo-clown barrel padded with gold. During his second and only full calendar year on Headline News, Beck wrote a number one seller, performed onstage to sellout crowds, and became one of the richest hosts in talk radio.

In November 2007, Premiere Radio Networks re-signed Beck to a five-year, $50 million deal. In the period between signing with Headline News and re-signing with Premiere, Beck added dozens of affiliates, including those in Los Angeles, Chicago, San Francisco, Dallas, Houston, and Atlanta. With a daily radio audience of three million people on three hundred stations, he was a flyover-market phenomenon no more.[6]

Nothing symbolized Beck's mainstream success like his embrace by the sunny pioneer of morning mush, ABC's *Good Morning America*. In January 2007, Beck was hired as an occasional "commentator," to share his thoughts on life and the news of the day. Once again, Arab American groups protested the announcement and were ignored.

Beck's appearances at America's broadcasting breakfast table did not signify an exhaustion of his deep and proven reserves of bile, despite the smile on his face. Two months into his contract with *Good Morning America*, Beck began hurling a series of physical insults at his new ABC colleague, Rosie O'Donnell. On the March 21 edition of *The Glenn Beck Program*, Beck called O'Donnell a "fat witch" who has "blubber just pouring out of her eyes." The dough-bodied Beck revisited the subject of O'Donnell's weight in April, saying that the only distinguishing characteristic between O'Donnell and Ellen DeGeneres is "about 400 pounds."

Beck's string of misogynist comments extended throughout the year. As the Democratic primary season began, Beck called Hillary Clinton a whiny-voiced "stereotypical bitch" and "a nag." Longtime listeners of *The Glenn Beck Program* knew that Beck's Hillary hatred ran deep. In Tampa, he once included the New York senator in a list of famous women who shouldn't be working outside the home.[7]

These comments and others were further evidence of the lie at the core of Beck's oft-repeated redemption narrative: that he had become a "better man" when he found God and that he had been cleansed of self-hatred and purged of the need to lash out. Eight years after accepting Jesus into his heart, Beck was the same punk who had mocked a fat Liz Curtis in Louisville. The only difference was a veneer of political argument.

Also evident by 2007 was the fraudulence of Beck's other self-serving myth: that he wasn't just another a GOP flack. As the Republican label became increasingly tainted in 2006, Beck joined a conservative trend in turning the volume up on his self-proclaimed independence, centered on a newfound sympathy with libertarianism. It was an act that many in the media continued to swallow.

In January 2007, National Public Radio's *All Things Considered* featured Beck in a series called "Crossing the Divide." In one episode, the NPR correspondent contrasts Beck's "bridge-building approach" with the more partisan tone of Rush Limbaugh, who has "absolutely no interest in crossing the divide." In a sign that nobody at NPR had ever watched or listened to Beck's shows, the reporter described Beck as a moderate conservative who believes that "severe rhetoric only drives people apart."

That spring, Beck would prove that NPR's description of him bore no resemblance to the flame-throwing reality. In April, Beck began one of the most deranged chapters of his brief television career by comparing Al Gore to Adolf Hitler and the work of the UN's climate scientists to Nazi eugenicists. CNN's Mr. Apocalypse saw the end of the world in everything from Mexican gang violence to Islamic extremism. But in climate change, Beck saw only media hype facilitating a fascistic liberal power grab that was pushing the world closer to the New World Order of his nightmares. Such was the psychological climate of fear that drove Beck's second one-hour special, *Exposed: Climate of Fear*.

On the afternoon of May 2, 2007, Beck appeared on *CNN Newsroom* to discuss his new special on climate politics, which was scheduled to air that night. When host Don Lemon asked his guest about the source of his interest in "the other side" of the climate debate, Beck took one of his wildest swings.

"The scientific consensus in Europe in the 1920s and '30s was that eugenics was a good idea," Beck explained. "I'm glad that a few people stood against eugenics." He continued by repeating something he had said many times on the radio but not yet on television. "You got to have an enemy to fight," Beck said. "And when you have an enemy to fight, then you can unite the entire world behind you, and you seize power.

That was Hitler's plan. His enemy: the Jew. Al Gore's enemy [and] the UN's enemy: global warming. Then you have to discredit the scientists who say, 'That's not right.' And you must silence all dissenting voices. That's what Hitler did."

Among those appalled by this freakish take on the climate debate was the Anti-Defamation League (ADL). Following Beck's *Newsroom* comments, ADL national director Abe Foxman joined the ever-growing list of ethnic and religious leaders to publicly rebuke Beck. "Glenn Beck's linkage of Hitler's plan to round up and exterminate Jews with Al Gore's efforts to raise awareness of global warming is outrageous, insensitive, and deeply offensive," said Foxman.

If Beck thought Al Gore was Hitler, then he must have considered his guests on *Climate of Fear* to be the leaders of a modern-day environmental reenactment of the Warsaw Ghetto uprising.[8] But unlike the Polish Jews who rose up against the Nazis, Beck's ragtag group of climate skeptics was backed by some very powerful allies. The guests who emerged from Beck's climate clown car included Patrick Moore, a mining industry consultant; David R. Legates, a Delaware climate scientist with ties to several ExxonMobil-funded think tanks; and Patrick J. Michaels, the editor of big coal's favorite climate-studies newsletter and the president of a consulting firm that represents major utilities such as the Intermountain Rural Electrical Association.

Also featured prominently in the special was Tim Ball, a consultant at the lobbying group Friends of Science, which receives at least one-third of its funding from the oil industry. At the time of his "expert" testimony in *Climate of Fear*, Ball had not published any climate research in a peer-reviewed journal in more than a decade.[9]

This was more than could be said for Beck's prize guest, Chris Horner, however; he was not a climate scientist at all but rather a law-yer with the Competitive Enterprise Institute. During his five minutes of uninterrupted screen time, Horner made two enormous false claims that went unchallenged by Beck. The first was that leading skeptics do not receive much funding from the oil and gas industry. The second involved the discredited theory that data from ice cores proved that temperature change drives carbon counts and not the other way around.[10]

Climate of Fear was also dusted with the New World Order con-spiracy theory that was becoming more pronounced in Beck's politics.

As presented by Beck, the climate melodrama pitted U.S. patriots against Eurocrats and the United Nations. On the April 30 edition of his radio show, Beck plugged the upcoming special by warning not just of Al Gore's closet Nazism but also of the one-world designs of the United Nations.

"Al Gore's not going to be rounding up Jews and exterminating them," Beck explained. "It is the same tactic, however. The goal is different. The goal is globalization. The goal is global carbon tax. The goal is the United Nations running the world."[11]

Unlike the film it was designed to debunk, *Climate of Fear* received scant critical attention. If noticed by science journalists at all, it was panned as a ludicrous response to *An Inconvenient Truth*. The working climate scientists at RealClimate.org dismissed it as "the usual cocktail of long debunked contrarian talking points."

Phil Plait, an astronomer and writer-blogger at *Discover* magazine, was less kind. After running down a few of Beck's more glaring errors, Plait marveled that Beck was even allowed on television, given that "his intellectual capacity is clearly such that he shouldn't even be allowed to rant in public parks to passing squirrels."[12]

Of more importance to Beck, the show also fell flat with viewers. Unlike his previous special on Islamic extremism, *Climate of Fear* flopped. Total viewership was less than one-third the number who tuned in for its predecessor. Beck's rejoinder to Al Gore placed dead last for the night, behind the regularly scheduled programming on Fox, CNN, and MSNBC.

The failure of *Climate of Fear* was not an isolated event. A year after his launch, Beck's ratings were stagnant and showing signs of decline. In what seemed a possible harbinger of Beck's own imminent departure, Joel Cheatwood jumped ship in April to Fox News, where he became vice president of development. The two friends kept in touch. Cheatwood would soon introduce Beck to his future boss, Roger Ailes.

With Beck threatening to flame out as primary season loomed, CNN sought to burnish its struggling host's image. Beck competed directly with Chris Matthews, and if he was going to hold his own covering presidential politics, it was important that viewers see him as more than just a rodeo clown. Toward this end, the network tapped Beck to guest-host *Paula Zahn Now* during the first week of July.

But Beck was less interested in playing journalist than he was in advertising his hard pivot away from the rapidly declining fortunes of the Republican Party. As Beck explained to his radio audience in June, "I have decided to do a theme all next week on both television shows of 'We the people declare our independence.' [It is] a good place and a good time to bring my theory to CNN that America is changing, that we are not Republicans and Democrats."

It was indeed a good time and a good place for Beck to position himself as a leading independent. The Republicans were no longer in control of Congress. Support for the president was below 30 percent. Three retired four-star generals had recently declined the post of "war czar." After seven years of toeing the GOP line on every major issue except immigration and prescription-drug benefits, Beck was eager to disentangle himself from the falling fortunes of his fellow conservatives.

Viewers were another story. They weren't moved by Beck's theory of a changing America or his claim to represent that change. Even though Paula Zahn was about to be fired for poor ratings, Beck underperformed her average by 23 percent.[13]

The following month, Beck received a chance to tell President Bush to his face what he thought of his party. Along with a select group of fellow conservative talk-show hosts, Beck was summoned to the White House for a personal meeting with the president in the Oval Office. How did America's leading voice of independent conservatism react to meeting the man who destroyed the Republican Party? When Beck discussed the meeting on the August 1 episode of *Glenn Beck*, Beck the angry libertarian was curiously AWOL. He had been replaced by the gung-ho Beck of 2000 and 2004. Despite all of the information that had come to light by August 2007, proving beyond a doubt that the Bush White House had misled the country into war, here is Beck's response to the "off-the-record" presidential meeting:

> Let me tell you the whole story on this. *He feels the pain of every wounded hero*, every lonely, grieving parent this war has caused.

He is a man who understands the heavy cost that we are paying,
but who believes with every ounce of his being that we are in the
fight for our very survival, a fight that's [*sic*] importance can only be
judged fairly decades from now, and I believe a fight he is willing
to be judged harshly for until that time comes, even if he's long
dead. . . . I can also tell you that he's—frustrated is not exactly
the right word—hopeful, yet frustrated. *He's so frustrated that so
many people are so myopic* that they have lost sight of the forest
through [*sic*] the trees.

The weekend after his sit-down with Bush, Beck headlined the thirty-
fifth annual Republican barbecue in Idaho Falls. There he repeated his
gushing report on Bush. "He's not the guy you see on TV," Beck told the
crowd. "He is the guy on the truck with the bullhorn."

Two years after his pep talk to Idaho Republicans, Beck would tell
Newsmax with a straight face that he "soured on George W. Bush pretty
quickly after 9/11."[14]

Beck's ratings funk continued into 2008, his final year on Headline
News. He began the election year with a nightly viewership of fewer
than three hundred thousand people ages twenty-five to fifty-four. He
also had a nasty case of hemorrhoids.

The first video footage of Beck to make its mark on YouTube was
filmed not on his television set but from his bed. In early January, Beck
posted a seven-minute home video clip in which he explained that his
recent surgery had gone "horribly awry." Lying in front of a tricornered
flag, an unshaven Beck talked about the pain cocktail administered by
the hospital that had resulted in "one of the darker experiences of my
life." Beck claimed that the combination of Toradol, fentanyl patches,
Percocet, and a synthetic morphine drip had made him wonder if life
had a point. Beck's critics, meanwhile, wondered if it wasn't the hemorrhoids that requested removal from Beck.

Back on his feet, Beck dove into the primaries. At first he seemed to
have a soft spot for Barack Obama. During a February 7, 2008, appearance on *Larry King Live*, Beck compared Obama to Reagan, calling
him "a person who's unafraid to say, 'I know you're gonna disagree, but
I believe it to the core of my being.' I want that in a president, and I
think most Americans want that."

The soft spot didn't last long. Throughout the winter and into spring, *Glenn Beck* functioned as a vehicle for GOP attack memes that painted the Illinois senator as the un-American "Other" of the campaign. On the March 19 episode of *Glenn Beck*, former Ohio secretary of state Ken Blackwell said, "Obama embraces [Nation of Islam leader Louis] Farrakhan." Beck let the comment slide, despite Obama's repeated and well-publicized denunciations of the controversial minister. On April 10, conservative journalist Mark Steyn appeared on *Glenn Beck* and called Michelle Obama "[North Korean dictator] Kim Jong-Il dressed up with a bit of Oprah Winfrey dressing." Later that month, on April 30, Ann Coulter appeared on the same show to introduce what would become a common conservative attack line by asking, "Is Obama a Manchurian candidate to normal Americans who love their country? [Do these normal Americans think he] secretly agrees with the Weathermen [*sic*] and the Reverend [Jeremiah] Wright faction?"

By the time Obama secured the Democratic nomination, Beck was part of a coordinated conservative blitz. "The thing that I do find about Barack Obama is that—and I think America is starting to catch on to this—this guy really is a Marxist."

But not a Marxist whom Beck would be attacking on Headline News.

On October 16, just a couple of weeks before Election Day, Fox News announced that it had signed Beck to a multiyear deal. The news did not come as a shock to anyone at CNN. Negotiations with Beck, whose contract expired in February, had been stalled for months. It was also public knowledge that Beck had struck up a friendship with Fox News president Roger Ailes. The two men not only shared politics, they also felt in their guts that the upcoming election was likely to result in a Democratic victory that would affect the country, and conservative politics, in profound ways. In his announcement of Beck's hiring, Ailes declared the United States was about to "embark on a new political landscape." Ailes understood that this new landscape would create space for new conservative icons.

Following the conclusion of Beck's final show on Headline News, broadcast just hours after the Fox deal became public, the host was escorted by security off his set and out of the building to his waiting limousine. He would cover the election from his studio in Radio City.

On the morning of October 31, 2008, Beck played for his radio audience a scratchy recording from the 1960s. He set up the clip by identifying the voice on the tape as belonging to Dwight Eisenhower's secretary of agriculture, Ezra Taft Benson. While serving in that position, Beck explained, Benson had met with Nikita Khrushchev during one of the Soviet premier's visits to the United States. In that meeting, Benson claimed to have gained valuable insight into the global communist conspiracy. Three days before the election, Beck was eager to share Benson's insight with his audience. "Listen carefully," said Beck. The voice on the tape began to speak:

> I have talked face-to-face with the godless communist leaders, though I still feel it was a mistake to welcome this atheistic murderer as a state visitor. As we talked face-to-face, [Khrushchev] said to me, "You Americans are so gullible. No, you won't accept communism outright. But we'll keep feeding you small doses of socialism until you wake up and find you already have communism. We don't have to fight you. We'll so weaken your economy until you fall like overripe fruit into our hands."

Beck stopped the tape there and asked, "Is that where we're headed?" He quickly answered his own question. "I contend we're already there, gang." In fact, Beck had proof that we were already there. He then played an audio clip of a giddy African American woman who had just left a Barack Obama campaign speech.

"It was the most memorable time of my life," she says. "It was a touching moment. I won't have to worry about gas or mortgage. If I help him, he's gonna help me."

In these words, Beck heard the fulfillment of Khrushchev's threat, as relayed by that grandfatherly seer, Ezra Taft Benson. "I never thought this day would happen," said Beck, as if extraterrestrials had just landed a spaceship in Central Park.

Beck's decision to feature Benson on his show was a revealing one. As Beck knew quite well, Benson was not just a member of

Eisenhower's cabinet. He was a notoriously illiberal Mormon Church president who helped pioneer Mormonism's apocalyptic hard-right strain, which Beck latched on to and appropriated following his conversion. Had Beck allowed the tape of Benson's lecture to continue, it is possible that listeners would have heard Benson ask, "When are we going to wake up? What do you know about the dangerous civil rights agitation in Mississippi?" Or they might have heard the sound of Benson's voice railing against "traitors within the church" who criticized the mixing of religion and extreme right-wing politics.[15]

They might have heard Benson speak about his attempts to build a third party, led by himself and South Carolina senator Strom Thurmond.[16] Or they might have been treated to snippets of Benson's wisdom as found in the foreword he penned to the 1967 tract of Mormon race hate, *Black Hammer: A Study of Black Power, Red Influence and White Alternatives*, which featured on its cover the severed, bloody head of an African American.[17]

Ezra Taft Benson was no ordinary agriculture secretary. Along with being a dedicated foe of the civil rights movement, which he thought was part of a communist plot to destroy the Mormon Church, he is also remembered for seeing U.S. politics through the prism of Mormon prophetic folklore. After being asked to join Eisenhower's administration in 1952, Benson told a Brigham Young University audience that his appointment was part of "the fulfillment of a prophecy of Joseph Smith, who said the Church would one day assume leadership in Washington."[18] According to Mormon legend, Smith prophesied shortly before his death that Mormons would assume power after a period of crisis in which the U.S. Constitution would "hang by a thread."

Beck had been a strong supporter of his fellow Mormon Mitt Romney during the primaries. Now he was quoting Ezra Taft Benson. Was it possible that he really believed in the old hanging-thread prophecy that was popular with a small minority in his adopted faith?

The answer arrived five days after the Benson speech, on November 4. That morning, on *The Glenn Beck Program*, Beck and Utah senator Orrin Hatch discussed the election of Barack Obama. The two Mormons agreed that the Democratic victory was weighted with meaning—the kind of meaning that only the select few can truly understand.

"When I heard Barack Obama talk about the Constitution," Beck told Hatch, "I thought, we are at the point, or we are very near the point, where our Constitution is *hanging by a thread.*" Hatch responded, "You got that right." When Beck reiterated that we are "so close to losing our Constitution," Hatch repeated Beck's words. "Well, let me tell you something," said the senator. "I believe the Constitution is *hanging by a thread.*"

The weirdest man in media was about to get even weirder.

7

Beck Unbound

Glenn Beck is a collector. With his wealth he has assembled congeries of vintage radio equipment, old American flags, historical gold coins, and very expensive watches. His most cherished item in this last group is a timepiece given to him by German luxury watchmaker Michael Kobold. It is the same watch worn by Kiefer Sutherland during a few episodes of the Fox television series *24*, one of Beck's favorite shows. The model retails for slightly more than $5,000 and is known as the Phantom. Kobold designed the stainless black steel "tactical chronograph" to blend in with the outfits that are worn by Special Forces while they operate in the thin oxygen shadows of U.S. foreign policy. Kiefer Sutherland wore the watch while pretending to be a special agent; Beck wears the watch while pretending to be Kiefer Sutherland pretending to be a special agent. But Beck doesn't wear it much. "It's probably the watch I wear the least," he once said. "It's irreplaceable. I don't want to beat that one up."[1]

Because Beck is so protective of his black *24* watch, he did not wear it for his debut appearance on *Fox & Friends*. It was January 13, 2009, six days before Beck's 5 p.m. launch on Fox News, and the network promos for the new show were in heavy rotation. Echoing his old Headline News promos, the spots touted Beck as his own man, beholden to no party or ideology. Glenn Beck, they declared, went beyond "left and right" to focus on "right and wrong."

This deeply ethical-sounding approach made Beck a perfect guest for *Fox & Friends* that January morning. Indeed, the discussion centered on one of the greatest questions of right and wrong the country had ever known: torture.

The fictional hero who wore Beck's favorite watch is known for his own moral clarity on the issue. In an episode of 24 that has since become a post-9/11 cultural landmark, Kiefer Sutherland's character, Jack Bauer, famously waterboards a terrorist to stop a nuclear attack on Los Angeles. But he does not torture himself over the decision. When a weak-kneed congressman in Washington objects to his methods, Bauer smacks him down.

Although the television dramatization of the issue has little to do with the real world—the "ticking nuke" scenario has never occurred; all evidence shows that torture yields false confessions; and most members of Congress have been generally sanguine about the Bush administration's experiment with "enhanced interrogation techniques"—influential conservatives publicly embraced the episode as if it were a documentary.

"Jack Bauer saved Los Angeles," Supreme Court Justice Antonin Scalia told an audience in 2008. "He saved the lives of hundreds of thousands of people."[2] Fox News anchor Chris Wallace answered a question about torture by declaring, "I'm with Jack Bauer on this one."[3]

Beck is among those who draw inspiration from the prime-time conservative fantasy. Like Scalia, Wallace, and others on the right, he believes that Bauer's specific use of torture proves the general righteousness and value of the tactic. "It's going to take somebody who sits in front of Congress and does what Jack Bauer did," said Beck on *Fox & Friends*. "And that is say, 'Yes, I did torture, and I'm proud of it.'"

The absurdity of this was lost on Beck's new colleagues, each of whom nodded along sagely. A week before the new *Glenn Beck* entered the annals of television history, it was clear that the host, after two years in the Headline News wilderness, was home.

Glenn Beck and Fox News were always destined for each other. The man and the network share more than politics; they share professional biographies. Both Beck and Fox began in popular entertainment. Like *The Glenn Beck Program*, Fox News struggled in minor markets before penetrating New York. (On Fox News' first day of broadcasting in 1996, Roger Ailes had to invite the New York press corps to the studios so they could write their reviews.) Just as the 2000 Florida recount gave Beck his first ratings breakthrough, the story gave Fox its first pole position in the three-way cable news race. The 9/11 attacks then put Fox over the top, just as they sent Beck national.

In January 2009, these two Bush-era brands shared a common challenge. Having come of age and thrived during an era of Republican dominance, Beck and Fox faced a Democratic White House for the first time in their relative maturity. How would they wield their clout from the outside of power looking in?

Ostensibly, Beck handled the transition calmly. For weeks, Fox News in-house ads for the new *Glenn Beck* promised a postpartisan bridge builder. "I'm tired of the politics of left and right," Beck said in the ads. "It's about right and wrong. We argue back and forth: 'If you haven't voted for the donkey, you're just a hatemonger.' The other side: 'Oh, those donkeys are trying to turn us into communist Russia.' Stop!"

The Beck being advertised—a sensible man in the middle—bore no resemblance to the polarizing hate jock heard daily on *The Glenn Beck Program.* Nor did the Beck being advertised resemble the television host last seen on Headline News in October. After the 2008 election, Beck continued describing President-Elect Obama as a "socialist" with "Marxist tendencies."[4] During his final days on Headline News, Beck went beyond even the most slanderous Republican National Committee talking points and turned up the volume on the "two Americas" idea, which excited the party base but drove independents and moderates from the McCain-Palin ticket.

Only the furniture was new. The Fox News set of *Glenn Beck* (the show's name stayed the same) was larger, airier, and decked out in a sleek modern design of red, white, and blue. Nothing remained of Beck's homey, brick-walled Headline News loft. If anyone doubted which Beck would show up at 5 p.m. on January 19—the heavily promoted postpartisan or the same old talk-radio hard-right flame thrower—those doubts were erased minutes into the first episode.

Beck fixed the course of the new show with his inaugural guest, Sarah Palin. By now, the two had formed a mutually beneficial alliance, if not a friendship. Beck had interviewed the Alaska governor numerous times since first mentioning her on Headline News the previous April. It is obvious in that first meeting that Beck had been recruited to drum up conservative support for the then unknown Palin in her vice-presidential candidacy. Despite a transparent attempt to hide his intentions—he claimed that he didn't "want to make this about politics"—Beck delivered a message tailored to the GOP base: she is one of us; let's get her on the ticket. Beck talked about Palin's special-needs child—and, of course, his own special-needs daughter—and described the little-known governor as an "incredibly accomplished, smart, powerful woman" who has been given a special-needs child "by God" because she is "truly amazing."

Nine months later, Palin was there for Beck on his big night. The two had come to know each other well throughout the previous summer and fall as Palin emerged as a champion of Beck's Real America conservatism. In the final weeks of the campaign, Palin rallied conservatives by stoking racial fears and rumors about Obama's foreign roots and extremist ties. She remained silent as cries of "nigger!", "terrorist!", and "kill him!" became staples of her campaign rallies.[5] With her guilt-by-association smears, attacks on Obama's urban community-organizing background, and tendency to talk in incoherent circles, Palin imported Beckian tactics and rhetoric into presidential politics.

"[Obama] is not a man who sees America the way you and I see America," Palin famously said in a late-campaign stump speech. Her campaign events that autumn represented a scorched-earth approach to cultural politics, in which appeals to the base rested less on policy differences than on different social styles, life experiences, and past associations. It was, according to one of many condemnatory mainstream-press editorials, an "appalling campaign" based on a strategy of "division, anger and hatred."[6]

In other words, Beck's kind of campaign. The host beamed as he welcomed Palin on January 19, declaring her "my kind of leader." This declaration of allegiance was followed by one of the creepiest on-air flirtations of the host's career when, with a twinkle in his eye, Beck called Palin "one hot grandma." He then took the predictable romp through his own biography, choking up over his palsy-afflicted daughter, Mary, who one can only hope was watching the show in her college dorm room, wondering in disbelief if her father would ever stop using her disability as a cheap emotional prop.

The nine-minute interview that followed set the tone for Beck's approach to the Obama era. When Palin expressed obligatory pride in Obama's historic victory, Beck waved her off the subject. The day before the inauguration is traditionally a brief holiday from politics, but Beck wanted to talk about what he perceived as gathering threats. "Are you concerned," he asked, "about the seeming global effort to discredit capitalism?"

Yes, Sarah Palin was worried—"scared to death," in fact. Together with having children with disabilities in common, Glenn Beck and Sarah Palin already shared a gut feeling that something "just wasn't right." Soon the media star and the hockey mom would ride that feeling to joint leadership of grassroots conservatism in opposition. This movement, whose symbol is a bag of tea, was conceived in October 2008, gestated throughout the following winter, and finally plopped out of America's womb, screaming and kicking, on tax day in 2009. When this movement announced itself to the nation on April 15, it did so with banners that said PALIN-BECK 2012.

The new *Glenn Beck* shocked even the host's most jaded critics. Its defining feature was a sustained campaign to equate President Obama's earliest signature initiatives and policies—expanding AmeriCorps, the economic stimulus package, health-care reform—with two of history's most monstrous regimes: Joseph Stalin's Soviet Union and Adolf Hitler's Third Reich. If the new show had a sound track, it was not the musical theme that began each show, but the implicit thunder of approaching jackboots.

In seeing so many genocidal and tyrannical foreign ghosts in the Democratic administration, Beck helped to write a new chapter in the tome of conservative-opposition hyperbole, which is as old as party politics. When Thomas Jefferson assumed the presidency in 1801, signaling the first transition between established parties, many Federalists warned of a Jacobin reign of terror in the New World. Writing shortly before Jefferson's victory over Alexander Hamilton, the Federalist president of Yale University asked, "Can serious and reflecting men look about them and doubt that, if Jefferson is elected and the Jacobins get into authority, those morals which protect our lives from the knife of the assassin, which guard the chastity of our wives and daughters from seduction and violence, defend our property from plunder and devastation and shield our religion from contempt and profanation, will not be trampled upon?"[7]

Whig writers and politicians expressed similar fears after the election of Andrew Jackson, whom they compared to the perceived tyrants of history: Julius Caesar, Oliver Cromwell, and Napoleon Bonaparte. Similar opposition rhetoric greeted the rise of Abraham Lincoln, Woodrow Wilson, and FDR.

During his first term, Franklin Roosevelt became the first U.S. president to be compared with Stalin and Hitler. "No candid observer, friend or enemy of the New Deal," wrote midcentury conservative James Burnham, "can deny that in terms of economic, social, political, and ideological changes from traditional capitalism, the New Deal moves in the same direction as Stalinism and Nazism."[8] As Roosevelt established the framework for the modern welfare state in the United States, market purists warned of a totalitarian result. Albert Jay Nock's *Our Enemy, the State* and Friedrich Hayek's *The Road to Serfdom* were just sophisticated versions of the blunt dread that was being expressed daily on the editorial pages of the anti–New Deal press.

The tradition was still warm when Beck came to it late in George W. Bush's second term. In 1995, House Majority Leader Tom DeLay described the Environmental Protection Agency as "the Gestapo of government." Republican power broker Grover Norquist turned heads in 2003 for comparing the estate tax with the Holocaust. Congressman Ron Paul, a 2008 Republican presidential candidate and a philosophical descendant of Nock and Hayek, helped to bring the old anti–New Deal language into the new century.

"We now have moved a major step in the direction of socialism," Paul told the Conservative Political Action Conference in March 2009. "We are close to a fascist system where the government has control of our lives and our economy."

But no one had ever leaned on the horn like Beck. Weeks into his new show, Beck made a hard turn that sent him flying off his banana seat into a brightly colored Oz of overstatement.

It began with a new segment called "Comrade Updates." Using retro-Soviet design elements, the bits were devoted to painting Hitler and Stalin mustaches on every White House policy initiative. Salary caps for bailed-out executives today, gulags tomorrow. "I'm going to show you how these things . . . happening today line up with some of the goings-on in history's worst socialist, fascist countries," Beck announced on February 4.

Two days later, on February 6, he repeated himself. "We are really, truly stepping beyond socialism, and we're starting to look at fascism. We're putting business and government together." Demonstrating that he had no idea what he was talking about, Beck held up Goldman Sachs—which owed its continued existence to taxpayer money and its deep ties to senior officials in the Treasury Department—as an example of a company that chose to opt out of the deepening state-government nexus. "It didn't take too long before . . . Goldman Sachs, they started to see the writing on the wall and went, 'Whoa, whoa, whoa, whoa, whoa. You guys are getting out of control here. What are you guys doing?' And they couldn't get out of it fast enough."

In March, Beck hit full stride. With each show, he climbed ever more commanding and dizzying heights of hyperbole. In a typical "Comrade Update," Beck spoke over strains of the Soviet national anthem and blamed "the destruction of the West" on "Comrade Obama" and "the good work [of] the agents that we've planted inside our great worker organization, the AFL-CIO."

If this could be written off as half-serious camp, the same could not be said for the next stage in Beck's rhetorical attack: the use of the language of good versus evil and accusations of slavery. On March 2, he described a White House plan to slightly restrict tax deductions on families earning more than $250,000 per year as "evil" and tantamount to "enslaving people."

Beck had growing company. The March 23 issue of the *National Review* featured Obama in a Soviet-style propaganda poster against the words OUR SOCIALIST FUTURE. In previous years, that cover might have been considered at least somewhat ironic. In 2009, suddenly one couldn't be sure.

What policies did Beck tout as the thin wedge of totalitarianism? By any sane standard, they amounted to very thin dictatorial gruel: health-care reform; commonsense gun control legislation; the expansion of AmeriCorps; limits on the use of public funds for executive bonuses; a market-friendly approach to capping carbon dioxide emissions. It was a revealing list of priorities. Beck huffed about a three-point increase in the income tax but remained untroubled by Guantanamo or warrantless wiretapping. He saw Stalin's ghost not in secret midnight renditions and torture cells—the most significant features of totalitarian regimes—but in closing the gun-show loophole and letting the Bush tax cuts expire.

Much of Beck's scorn was reserved for the American Recovery and Reinvestment Act, better known as the stimulus bill. Unlike the Toxic Asset Relief Program, Obama's stimulus bore no Bush fingerprints and could be attacked without implicating the previous administration or the titans of Wall Street, whom Beck would soon be defending against ACORN "rent-a-mobs" and "radical" unions.

Economists of all ideological persuasions were debating the merits of the stimulus, but Beck's criticisms were of a decidedly lowbrow, look-what-the-eggheads-cooked-up nature. Even if he didn't understand the bill, he was sure it was bad. On January 28, Beck mocked the recovery package for including billions of dollars for carbon-capture demonstration projects. Looking confused, he added, "I don't even know what the hell that is." At the bottom of the screen, a graphic read "Economic Apocalypse."

Beck's rhetoric was part of a devolutionary process into ahistorical nonsense that began during the presidential campaign. As with Beck's steroidal postelection version of this campaign, the right's anachronistic name-calling focused on Obama's tepid campaign promises to redress the growing imbalances that defined the Bush economy. Between 2000 and 2008, nearly 90 percent of the new income generated accrued to the top 10 percent of the population while the average family income dropped $2,000.

After eight years of extending the U.S. lead as the most unequal of all industrialized countries, popular discontent was real. Republicans attempted to deflect it not by arguing the merits of their own failed economic policies but by dusting off and hurling at Obama every insult in the conservative arsenal, including a battery of old favorites such as *extremist, radical, Marxist, socialist,* and even, by way of his prior association with former Weatherman activist William Ayers, *terrorist.*

Little of it stuck. Among independents and moderate Republicans, the attempt to paint the Democratic candidate red failed. Obama not only maintained a stable lead throughout the desperate Republican barrage, he also increased his positives in the traditionally Republican territory of taxes. The final national polls before the election showed that most Americans liked the idea of "spreading the wealth." Poll after poll found that likely voters preferred Obama's moderately progressive tax plan to John McCain's overblown antitax rhetoric by as much as 20 points.

The Republican attack line was always dependent on extreme historical amnesia. Since Obama pledged that any expansion of social programs would be deficit-neutral, the Republicans claimed that allowing the Bush tax cuts for the rich to lapse would represent a radical break with tradition. But this was false. Obama's proposed top income-tax rate of 39 percent was not only a far cry from Soviet Russia, it was also low by U.S. standards. For much of the twentieth century, the top income tax rate in the United States slid between 50 percent and 90 percent, peaking at 94 percent during the final two years of World War II. The top marginal rate held steady at 50 percent for no less than five years under that great conservative hero, Ronald Reagan, at which point he lowered it to 39 percent. (In 1988, he brought it down to 28 percent.) "Throughout the modern era, the public has supported moderately progressive taxation," says Dean Baker, codirector of the Center for Economic and Policy Research.

The election did show that the *socialist* label, once so effective, didn't work very well twenty years after the end of the Cold War. This was not a pleasant realization for conservatives. Right-wing fright over growing immunity to cries of "socialism!" was expressed clearly right before the election by *Investor's Business Daily.* Published at the height of the McCain campaign's frenzied rhetoric, the piece applauds Senator McCain for "finally call[ing] Barack Obama's agenda by its proper name." But the paper's conservative editors worried that the word had lost its power. "If he assumes voters understand what he means when he uses the word 'socialism,' he assumes too much. Sadly, most people under 60 in this country went to schools and universities where socialism isn't considered a bad thing."[9]

But the editorial conflates two distinct groups: those who don't understand the word and its wide spectrum of gradations and those who do but don't mind living under most of them. What these two groups have in common is that together they constitute a permanent majority in a country in which the word *socialist* carries an ever weakening stigma. The election proved that when Americans are hurting, they don't mind a little socialism, as long as it's pointed their way. And even when they aren't hurting, what is the U.S. highway system but socialism? Everyone pays, everyone uses. Europe, with its toll roads, often wonders why the United States is so socialist when it comes to transportation but not health care.

Of course, Beck and his fellow conservatives have never been very interested in what the Europeans think of the United States. In the weeks after Obama's inauguration, Beck carried the flag for dead-enders who refused to let go. Since *socialism* wasn't scary enough to stop Obama's election, perhaps *communism* and *fascism* could kill his reform agenda.

Viewers flocked around Beck's Fox News act in startling numbers. In February, its first full month on the air, *Glenn Beck* netted 2.2 million viewers for the network's 5 p.m. slot, more than twice as many as the previous year's show at that time. The numbers dwarfed those Beck had drawn at Headline News by a factor of five. *Glenn Beck* quickly established itself as the third most watched program in all of cable news, after *The O'Reilly Factor* and *Sean Hannity*. Beck's success mirrored that of Fox News as a whole, which enjoyed a 29 percent spike in viewership in the weeks after Obama's inauguration.

The *Los Angeles Times* was the first outlet to send a reporter to investigate Beck's new persona and ratings success. When the *Times* reporter asked Beck about the increased pitch of his screechingly apocalyptic tone, the host played dumb. "You've never met anybody who wants to be wrong more than I do," he said. "I have nothing to gain and everything to lose. If I'm right, what do I have? I don't grow my business. I have no reason to say these things."

Moments after uttering these words, Beck asked his producer about the previous night's ratings. When the answer came back—another two-million-plus night, more than the combined total of CNN, MSNBC, and HNL, as Headline News was now known—Beck broke into a smile.

"We're closing in on O'Reilly," he said, suddenly without a trace of angst. "I'm coming for him."[10]

The extreme rhetoric that defined the new *Glenn Beck* both reflected and fueled a growing extremism among grassroots conservatives. Inside the closed media universe in which Beck's stock was rising to new heights, every Obama initiative heralded the end of the republic. Citing the growth of such rhetoric on Beck's broadcasts and ultraright

Web sites like NewsMax, WorldNetDaily, and NewsBusters, some observers began to draw parallels between the new Obama-era paranoid conservatism and previous bursts of right-wing overreaction, the most recent example of which was the militia movement that found new energy in the election of Bill Clinton and peaked with the 1995 bombing of the Oklahoma City federal building.

Signs of this new hard-right movement were evident during the election, when much of the Republican base rallied around a conspiracy theory about Barack Obama's citizenship. The theory continued to thrive after the election, leading some on the right to wonder nervously where it was all headed. In a much-discussed article in the *National Review*, David Horowitz became the first to warn of an "Obama Derangement Syndrome."[11]

Coming from a man who sees socialist and Islamist conspiracies in every university to the left of Liberty University, this was a sobering judgment. The fringe was growing.

Obama Derangement Syndrome (ODS) reared its head high in late March 2009. That was when the Senate overwhelmingly passed the Serve America Act, a major plank in Obama's domestic agenda, by a vote of seventy-eight to twenty. The bipartisan bill, championed by Orrin Hatch and Ted Kennedy, seemed harmless enough. It expanded national-service opportunities by investing $5 billion in a volunteer corps focused on education, clean energy, health care, and veterans' issues.

In a symbolic gesture, the bill also designated September 11 as a National Day of Service, expanding the post-9/11 concept of patriotism. The 9/11 survivor organizations, literacy advocates, veterans' groups, and the American Association of Retired Persons (AARP) all hailed the bill upon its passage. Along with providing work for the young and unskilled, the act promised to help millions of people learn to read, go to college, stay warm, and connect with their fellow citizens.

On *Glenn Beck* and other hotbeds of ODS, the biggest question raised by the legislation was whether Obama had shape-shifted from Stalin into Hitler or had morphed into some grotesque dictatorial hybrid unique to history. The outrage and fear with which grassroots conservatives greeted the bill threw into sharp relief their unmooring from reality and the distance opening up between themselves and the Republican establishment in Washington.

On March 26, Beck opened his Fox News show by sounding the alarm about the Serve America Act. "Yesterday, the Senate passed a watered-down version of the AmeriCorps bill, aka the GIVE Act, which apparently we have problems with now," he explained. "It basically indoctrinates your child into community service through the federal government."

The next morning, March 27, Beck welcomed one of his favorite members of Congress, Minnesota Republican Michele Bachmann, onto his radio show, *The Glenn Beck Program.* The two discussed the bill's dangers as well as Bachmann's concern that the Treasury Department was planning to replace the dollar with a new "global currency." Later, on her own, Bachmann expanded on the indoctrination theme, telling a Minnesota radio station that the act would establish "reeducation camps for young people" where they would "get trained in a philosophy that the government puts forward and then go to work in some of these politically correct forums."[12] Hours after his Bachmann interview, Beck returned to the service bill on Fox during an interview with Michelle Malkin. Both agreed that the bill was proof of Obama's plan to make Americans "slaves" to the federal government.

The "slavery" rhetoric was not new. It had been gaining volume on the Right since the primaries, when Obama laid out his public service agenda. Specifically, the meme took root after a July 2, 2008, speech Obama delivered in Colorado Springs in which he first discussed his intention to expand the ranks of AmeriCorps volunteers to two hundred and fifty thousand. One line in particular set the conservative imagination aflame in a way that hinted of things to come. "We cannot continue to rely on our military in order to achieve the national security objectives we've set," said Obama. "We've got to have a civilian national security force that's just as powerful, just as strong, just as well funded."

Some conservatives took this literally, even though the basics of the service agenda had bipartisan support and would require funds in the low-single-digit billions, nothing near the more than $700 billion annually allotted to the Pentagon. But on conservative Web sites where Beck was lionized, Obama's words were taken as a blueprint for hundreds of thousands of liberal brownshirts. Hard-right commentators compared Obama's service army to everything from the Imperial storm troopers of *Star Wars* to Hitler's thugs.

Resistnet.com, the self-described "Home of the Patriotic Resistance" and an online purveyor of Beck's books, warned that "brown shirts" lurked under every red AmeriCorps windbreaker. Judi McLoud of *Newsmax,* another Beck-connected site, wrote of "forced labor" and evoked the sign WORK MAKES YOU FREE that greeted the arrivals at Auschwitz.

The Right's response to the Serve America Act combined poor reading comprehension skills and willful distortion. Although it's true that the AmeriCorps Web site has a red, black, and white color scheme reminiscent of the Nazi flag, the Serve America Act's fascist overtones stopped there.

Much of the conservative outrage focused on a detail of early drafts of the House version of the bill that instructed Congress to investigate the feasibility of a mandatory national-service requirement. But that clause died in the Senate. The final bill that was signed by the president merely expanded existing programs (some founded under presidents Richard Nixon and George H. W. Bush) such as AmeriCorps, SeniorCorps, and Learn and Serve America. The increased funding went toward service-earned scholarships and programs for disabled youth and foster children, among other Hitlerian initiatives.

As a condition for receiving Serve America Act funds, the bill required public secondary schools to integrate "service learning" into their curricula. This is the clause that Bachmann and Beck had in mind when they agreed on the danger of leftist "indoctrination camps." In their view, the lessons amounted to brainwashing, after which the government's "slaves" would be sent to do the devil's work of retrofitting energy-inefficient homes, providing emotional support to homeless veterans, and tutoring poor children in math and English.

Of what would these brainwashing lessons consist? According to the bill, the service-oriented educational programs are designed to "promote a better understanding of (A) the principles of the Constitution, the heroes of American history (including military heroes), and the meaning of the oath of allegiance; (B) how the nation's government functions; (C) the importance of service in the nation's character."

Ironically, the service-learning curriculum actually bears a closer resemblance to the conservative courses championed by Lynne Cheney than the "PC liberal indoctrination" feared by Bachmann and Beck. But nothing in the actual bill could have distracted those afflicted with ODS from their deepest, darkest fears, born of antigovernment paranoia and racial resentments being stoked nightly on the new *Glenn Beck*.

Two generations of conservatives had fought since the early 1960s to keep their movement distinct from the world of far-right conspiracies, a political dead zone inhabited by the John Birch Society that William F. Buckley Jr. called "the fever swamps." That battle, whose victory once seemed so secure, now appeared lost. In the months between Obama's July 2008 Colorado speech and the March 2009 passage of the Serve America Act, a Swamp Thing movement had emerged from the steaming bottoms of conservative Internet sites, talk radio, and Fox News. Crowning its angry, confused face was a familiar blond crew cut gone white at the temples.

The passage of the Serve America Act inspired Beck to ramp up his act in the spring. He promoted the new administration from comparisons with the most reviled regimes in history to comparisons with the scariest creations of literature. On his Fox News program, Beck aired a graphic showing Obama and other Democratic leaders as fanged vampires.

"The government is full of vampires," he said, "and they are trying to suck the lifeblood out of the economy." Beck then suggested "driv[ing] a stake through the heart of the bloodsuckers."[13]

He would soon begin describing the government as Satan itself. "You don't get into bed with the devil," he declared on his June 24 radio show. "The government is the devil."

The religious language supplanted, but did not replace, the historical analogies. On April 1, Beck launched a new Fox News segment called "Flirting with Fascism." "They're marching us to a nonviolent fascism," he said as the screen filled with images of goose-stepping Nazis. "Or to put it another way, they're marching us to 1984. Big Brother. Like it or not, fascism is on the rise."

If anyone thought that this might have been Beck's idea of an April Fools' Day joke, he quickly destroyed that theory. "Those who don't know history are destined to repeat it," he said, while onscreen images of Obama and Prime Minister Gordon Brown of Britain were juxtaposed with those of—who else?—Hitler and Stalin.

When Beck ran out of actual policies to distort and caricature, he relied on pure fantasy. On April 6, he told his radio audience that Obama "will slowly but surely take away your gun or take away your ability to shoot a gun, carry a gun. He will make them [guns] more expensive; he'll tax them out of existence. He will because he has said he would. He will tax your gun or take your gun away one way or another." He also promised to "find out what's true and what's not with the FEMA concentration camps."

In a rare bow to reality, Beck was forced to drop the FEMA concentration camps story when his research team was unable to come up with any evidence for their existence.

But if the FEMA concentration camps didn't exist, Guantanamo did. By early April, many Democrats and libertarians were beginning to speak out about the Obama administration's failure to roll back the worst excesses of the previous administration in the area of civil liberties and state secrecy, as he had promised to do during the campaign. While Beck, the self-professed libertarian, was crowing about make-believe gun taxes, Obama administration lawyers were borrowing legal arguments from the Bush administration to defend unlawful policies and practices, from torture to warrantless wiretapping. It is these policies, not progressive taxation or even universal health care, that most meaningfully define the totalitarian societies Beck routinely evoked.

This contrast illustrates the hollowness of Beck's self-professed libertarianism. Even as he became enthralled with Ron Paul's controversial monetary theories, he completely ignored the other half of the antistate coin. He simply could not reconcile his bloodlust and inner thug with the other half of the libertarian philosophy. He touted only the libertarian positions that would reduce his taxes and leave the poor to fend for themselves and ignored those he didn't like or couldn't understand.

Beck gave no indication that he was aware of this incoherence as spring turned to summer. It's unlikely he would have had much time to reflect on core principles, anyway. He had a stage show to prepare and a new book to plug. With fascism on the rise, the United States needed a good dose of "common sense." Beck was just the person to provide it.

Common Sense is the name of both Beck's 2009 comedy tour and his first "serious" book. Unlike *The Real America* and *An Inconvenient*

Book, the new slim volume—"inspired by Thomas Paine"—contains no knock-knock jokes about Michael Moore's body fat and no observational humor boxes labeled "A.D.D. Moment." Co-authored with Joseph Kerry, the book has a tone throughout of puffed-up gravitas, expressed in prose that could have been transcribed from a colonial-themed animatronic display.

"Many an erstwhile patriot has sold his birthright," declare the authors, "by failing to remember the delicate balance between master and minion."[14] With such language, *Common Sense* invites readers to suspend their disbelief and imagine Beck in a candle's midnight glow, gently dabbing his quill into an inkpot surrounded by piles of leather-bound volumes. The 107-page "case against an out-of-control government" thus announces the unlikely pupation of Beck's persona from rodeo clown into revolutionary movement leader.

As proof of Beck's total dedication to the cause, his face isn't even on the cover.

It's unlikely that Thomas Paine would have appreciated this sacrifice on Beck's part. Everything we know about the revolutionary suggests that he would have been horrified to find Beck speaking in his name. Paine was a devout deist to his last breath and considered churches "human inventions set up to terrify and enslave mankind, and monopolize power and profit."[15] The secular rationalist also possessed what was known at the time as a "leveling tendency." A firm believer in the idea of a commonweal, Paine was a prototheorist of the modern welfare state and a supporter of the graduated-income and estate taxes. The Jacobins in Paris may have considered him a conservative, but he was well to the left of most of the landed elite of colonial America, including the founding fathers.[16]

Then there is the little question of selflessness. Unlike Beck's book of the same name, Paine refused to accept royalties for his own *Common Sense*. Instead, he donated every penny to the Revolutionary Army of George Washington. The one possession Paine allowed himself during the crisis was a New York farmhouse left behind by an absconding member of the Tory cause.

The content of *Common Sense*, which debuted at number one in June 2009, is standard Beckian corporate-populist quack-quack. Underneath the colonial theme-park prose are the usual bromides held together by spit and venom. It is spiced with idiotic historical assessments

("Our collective experience since the Founding has taught us that all governments are fascist in nature")[17] and sprinkled with Mormon dispensationalism ("Great and powerful miracles are about to unfold before us").[18]

What's most interesting about the book is the frequency with which the authors remind their readers not to kill anybody. The book literally opens with an exhortation against murder. It precedes even the title page. "You might find yourself wondering what can be done to change our nation's course," read the first words in *Common Sense*. "I lay out several options, but I want to be clear that none of them include violence."

A few pages later, the authors repeat themselves and add, "Violence is the easy way out."[19] For good measure, they later remind readers a third time, "Leave your muskets at home."[20]

Glenn Beck knows his audience. Later that summer, a Beck fan named Nancy Genovese was arrested "scouting out and taking pictures" near an Air National Guard base with a trunk full of guns, including an assault rifle, a shotgun, and five hundred rounds of ammunition. Her MySpace page documented the inspiration she drew from an episode of *Glenn Beck*. "I just saw Glenn Beck tell it like it is!" she wrote in her online diary.[21]

The episode that inspired the heavily armed Genovese to case a government facility aired on June 17, the week after *Common Sense* hit the bookstores, which followed a rollout centered on a nationally simulcast stage performance of the same name. Genovese's arrest was an appropriate coincidence of timing. Though riddled with pleas for readers to leave the muskets at home, *Common Sense* is based on a false premise that logically leads to violence. It then develops that false premise with language that reinforces this logic.

"Today we find ourselves back in 1776," Beck declares in *Common Sense*. This is clearly not true. To pick one major difference, a foreign monarch does not rule the country. But if Beck is going to argue that Barack Obama is equal to George III, then he must also accept that the Revolutionary War was a just war fought by militias armed with muskets. If Beck believes that our present political situation is analogous to 1776, then he cannot also argue that the present situation is, at the same time, completely different. Either we are in 1776, or we aren't. Either we are approaching levels of state oppression such as that practiced in Nazi Germany, or we aren't.

Since Beck is a fan of comparing Democratic rule to genocidal regimes, it is an interesting exercise to review his own language with genocide in mind. But rather than just throw the word around and flash a picture of Hitler, let's ask the question: What are the historical conditions and practices that have led to mass state or ethnic violence in the past?

It would surprise Beck to learn that many people around the world have actually dedicated themselves to this question. They have accorded it the seriousness it deserves, often inspired by real-life experience under genocidal regimes. One umbrella organization that has invested considerable thought and study to the subject is the International Commission to End Genocide (ICEG). Based on the input from scholars, survivors, and activists, the ICEG has classified a list of the eight most common social phenomena that precede and accompany genocide. Beck's career is based on three of them.

First, there's *dehumanization*, in which one group denies the very humanity of another group. Historically, this stage has involved one group equating members of an ethnic group or social class with animals, vermin, insects, and diseases. Dehumanization is important because it helps to overcome the strong human revulsion toward murder. From Nazi Germany to Hutu-ruled Rwanda, hate propaganda in print and on the radio has been used to vilify the victim group. Consider the following quotes from *Common Sense*, each of which represents countless other comments that Beck has made on radio and television over the years:

> Our political leaders have become nothing more than parasites who feed off our sweat and our blood.[22]

> The snakes responsible for this scheme know that it isn't going to work.[23]

> Politicians: More Staying Power Than Cockroaches[24]

> [Progressive] hypocrites . . . truly are cockroaches who care nothing about liberty and freedom.[25]

Then there's the stage known as *classification*. Immediately preceding the violence, if not instigating it, propagandists divide society into "Us" and "Them." Beck's radio and television programs have long been hives of "We surround them" rhetoric. Then there's this in *Common Sense*:

> Make no mistake, this is a fight of Us versus Them. "Us" comprises those who believe in liberty, as described in the opening lines of the Declaration of Independence. "Them" comprises those who believe that the definition of liberty must evolve with the times.[26]

Beck specializes in *polarization*. This covers all attempts to drive groups apart rather than find common ground. This is often accompanied by extremist terrorism that targets moderates and seeks to intimidate and silence those in the center. Again, from *Common Sense*:

> Enemies Within: Tread Carefully . . . Progressives don't think like you. . . . They just don't see the world the same way, and they are working to make sure that you and your children succumb to their views.[27]

> We need a reminder . . . of who is really in control [and] how we got to a place that bears less and less resemblance to the America we remember from our childhoods.[28]

> There are many in Washington who want to leave you defenseless. . . . [These same people] have armed guards, send their children to private schools, and can afford to live in gated communities.[29]

If a Beck fan does go rogue and take the fight to "Them" with a truck bomb, it's a safe bet that Beck will take another page from the genocide playbook: *denial*. This is the eighth and final stage that always follows the violence. Those responsible deny that crimes were committed or that they had any hand in it. Blame is often placed on the victims, and all attempts at investigation are blocked.

Common Sense isn't all chilling echoes of genocidal and eliminationist rhetoric. There are also moments of brilliant, albeit unintentional, conservative dark comedy. On page 80, Beck compares eminent domain laws to the internment of Japanese Americans during World War II. But even that takes second place to Beck's discussion of the moderately progressive U.S. tax code, a centerpiece of the book and exhibit A in Beck's case for the forward march of American fascism. Beck holds up the 2008 election-debate example of Joe the Plumber, a convicted tax evader, as a case of political persecution at the hands of a vindictive Internal Revenue Service (IRS).

"This isn't a new political tactic," explains Beck. "Do you think it's purely a coincidence that Martin Luther King, Jr., was targeted as a tax cheat or that both Jesse Owens and Joe Louis were investigated for tax-code violations after they spoke out against the government?" And who is it today that stands on the shoulders of Owens and Louis? Why, ExxonMobil. "A complex and confusing tax code," explains Beck, "can be used to intimidate enemies (windfall profits tax on oil companies) and punish the innocent but politically unpopular person (a 90 percent tax on corporate executives)."[30]

This is a prime example of Beck logic. First is the self-serving and boneheaded reference to persecuted minority groups. Second is the sheer lack of sense. The fact that the government sometimes uses the IRS to punish political enemies has nothing to do with whether the tax code is *progressive*. A politically motivated audit can just as easily be ordered based on a flat tax. Moreover, the fact that politicians abuse IRS power now and then doesn't mean that we shouldn't have an IRS, any more than instances of police brutality mean that we should no longer have police.

If progressives are the villains of *Common Sense*, persecuted corporate executives are its most commonly evoked victims. In Beck's view, they are persecuted in much the same way as other long-oppressed groups in the nation's history. "African-Americans have long understood dual justice. One set of laws for whites and one for blacks," Beck explains. Now "vengeance and vigilantism" is setting up dual systems of justice for corporate executives. Beck finishes this comparison with a plea: "Wake up America!"[31]

No serious observer of the U.S. scene could look at the events on Wall Street in recent years and conclude that Corporate America is suffering at the hands of injustice or state oppression. But Beck is not serious and never has been. If America fails to heed his warning and rush to the defense of corporate bonuses, Beck suggests that history tells us what will follow, as sure as night follows day.

"A simple reading of the stories told by those who survived under the regimes of Hitler, Mussolini, Stalin, Lenin, Castro, Chavez, or Kim Jong-Il should tell you everything you need to know."[32]

• • •

On the evening of July 14, with *Common Sense* still dominating the best-seller lists, Beck changed character. Instead of defending Wall Street from populist "vigilantes," he devoted an entire segment of *Glenn Beck* to mapping out Goldman Sachs' ties to the U.S. Treasury and its role in the debate over the decision to bail out the insurance giant AIG (and thus save Goldman Sachs) to the tune of $85 billion. The famous Wall Street giant was, in Beck's words, behind a "web of bubbles."

"We are being spun in a web of lies, and we are caught up in this web!" he said. "Wall Street owns our government."

It was a stunning turn. Aside from vague rants against "bankers and elites," Beck had never gone into the weeds of systemic Wall Street corruption or questioned enormous corporate profits. But Beck's July 14 lecture sounded mostly progressive populist notes. The logical conclusion to be drawn from his chalkboard sketch of Goldman's ties to the Treasury was stricter regulation of finance.

Yet when Beck's guest, Patrick Byrne of Overstock.com, congratulated Beck for his interest in Wall Street's "capture" of progressive banking regulations, the host wasn't so sure. Beck was already having doubts about discussing what Byrne called the "oligarchy" running the country. "I wonder if it's good," Beck mused, half to himself, "or if I'm suddenly on a very dangerous boat to hell."

Alas, Beck's "Goldman moment" was every bit the anomaly it appeared to be. For unknown reasons, Beck quickly turned his boat around and never revisited the subject.

We now know that Beck had other targets in mind besides billion-dollar corporations with a chokehold on the Treasury and the power to thwart reform of the financial sector. It had come to Beck's attention that a White House adviser working out of the Council on Environmental Equality had a past in radical politics. Within days of his Goldman moment, Beck was back on familiar corporate conservative–approved territory, waging total media war against a Yale-educated community organizer turned environmental activist, who as a younger man once sold radical pamphlets on the street corners of San Francisco.

8

False Victory

Glenn Beck is exceptionally loud and proud in his disdain for all things environmental. He has zero tolerance for climate research that links global warming and atmospheric carbon counts. He spits at government efforts to protect the American wilderness and the flora and fauna of threatened ecosystems. Often his wrath seems designed to aggravate his crunchier enemies. He once devoted a *Glenn Beck* segment to blasting the use of stimulus funds to protect sea life along the California coast. For the bit's payoff, he argued that federal funds should go only to turtles and otters with guns that patrol the U.S.-Mexican border.

Beck's caveman environmental politics go beyond jokes about Teenage Mutant Vigilante Turtles. When it comes to the linchpin issues of energy and climate, his views are neatly captured in a T-shirt he sells on his Web site. Available in sizes S through XXL, the blue cotton garment features a baby polar bear set against a red bull's-eye. The caption reads, DRILL THROUGH THEIR @$$ FOR CHEAPER GAS.[1]

The host has a long history of using animals, animal-rights activists, and environmentalists as props, targets, and wedges. While working as a deejay in Baltimore in the early 1990s, he invited parking-lot protests against his show by People for the Ethical Treatment of Animals (PETA) through a series of stunts using animals. When the protests materialized, he welcomed them. They generated free publicity, he explained to a colleague. What's more, they were sure to win sympathy from the key demographic of what Beck called "the normals."

149

This strategy became more sophisticated when Beck switched from pop music to politics, but not by much. Beck has always possessed a gut hatred for environmentalists, antiwar protesters, and black social-justice activists. If one person ever came along who embodied all three, it's likely that—to borrow one of Beck's favorite images—the blood would never stop shooting out of his eyes.

Which is exactly what happened.

Beck did not have to wait long to find things to hate about the new Democratic administration. Within moments of President Obama taking the oath of office on January 20, Beck already had a list. High on that list was Obama's inaugural promise to "restore science to its rightful place" and promote the development of green technology. The host immediately began channeling his ire into a satirical radio gag called "Spotlight on Science." Each episode, explained an ironic voiceover, is "dedicated to President Obama's passion for everything science."

Sitting at the intersection of science, environment, and government activism, green jobs would have formed a particularly fat target for Beck regardless of who occupied the White House. With a black president, he could go even further. In a July 23 edition of "Spotlight on Science," Beck for the first time floated the theory that green jobs, like health-care reform, were not just socialist but also a form of stealth "reparations."

The face for this theory was a young adviser on the Council on Environmental Quality named Van Jones, who held the grand-sounding title of "green jobs czar." Jones's presence within the administration told Beck everything he needed to know about green jobs. Stumbling over Jones's name and title, Beck sketched out this profile in progressive villainy:

> [Obama's] new science czar, what is this guy's first name, Jones? Van Jones. Van Jones is a guy that was all caught up in the Rodney King trial and he was actually arrested. He was a radical communist. He hasn't shed that. He's still a radical. He is still a black nationalist. He is also now your green job czar. . . . Your country is being hijacked. They are using things like green jobs as a front. They are using health care as a front. In the context of Obama-style

reparations, that's what they're doing. [Jones] is yet another community organizer. This is yet another black nationalist in the same way that Reverend Jeremiah Wright is a black nationalist. . . . America, you need to wake up, because this country is being transformed. It is way beyond socialism. It is into black nationalism.[2]

It was an audacious leap. Beck's listeners were not only in danger of losing "their" country, but they were on the verge of becoming white chattel. One day, a Yale-educated lawyer like Jones is employed on the Council of Environmental Quality; the next day, Old Glory is drained of red, white, and blue and is retrofitted like some energy-inefficient office park with red, black, and green. After racializing health-care reform by describing it as a backdoor form of repayment for slavery, Beck had now locked the same template over green jobs.

Van Jones was the key to the strategy. Beck had bigger plans for the green jobs czar than mere "Spotlight on Science" fodder. For the next six weeks, he used much of his four hours of daily national airtime as an anvil on which to pound away at Van Jones and the radical rot he symbolized. Beck's goal was to blend certain themes and images in the conservative mind: Van Jones, Barack Obama, Jeremiah Wright, black nationalism, revolutionary communism, climate change, "street" community organizing, and the very ideas of social and economic justice.

Much of the groundwork had been laid over the course of the previous year on AM radio and Fox News. Van Jones, with his street style and his radical past, was almost too good to be true; Beck grasped this immediately. By the time Jones offered the White House his resignation on September 5, Beck was being hailed as a right-wing power broker of the first rank. He had, after all, singlehandedly taken down one of Obama's radicals by "just asking questions."

Or had he?

Phil Kerpen is a busy man. Along with coordinating the legislative agenda for Americans for Prosperity, he produces a daily podcast called *Washington Update*, is active in the high school and college debate scenes, and writes regularly for a number of conservative outlets such as *Fox Forum* and the *National Review Online*. He's also a frequent guest on *Glenn Beck*.

During the summer of 2009, Kerpen's top priority was defeating a cap-and-trade bill ostensibly designed to reduce carbon emissions and spur a new generation of clean technologies. It was an unpopular piece of legislation from the start, almost as hated on the left as it was on the right. Environmentalists criticized the bill as toothless at best and a massive industry giveaway at worst. The bill's conservative critics immediately dubbed it "cap and tax."

Conservative commentators did their best to generate heat over the bill, but it was soon overshadowed by the debate over health-care reform. Electric bills are less personal than doctor's visits. How could one excite and maintain grassroots opposition to the bill and other pieces of the White House environmental agenda? Kerpen was mulling over this question in July when he found a newspaper profile of Obama's young green jobs czar, Van Jones.

The article, published in 2005 by the Bay Area weekly *East Bay Express*, detailed Jones's radical political activities during the early and mid-1990s, most notably his involvement with a revolutionary organization called Standing Together to Organize a Revolutionary Movement (STORM). The profile explained that Jones had renounced revolutionary communism by 1996, but for Kerpen this was good enough. If Jones's past could be connected to the present, it would put a radical (and black) face on the Obama administration's broad environmental agenda, from cap-and-trade to green jobs.

Kerpen e-mailed the article to Beck's Fox News producer on July 9. He attached the following note: "Please share with Glenn this article about green jobs czar Van Jones, a self-described communist who was radicalized in jail. Confirms 'watermelon' hypothesis."[3] Kerpen knew that Beck would understand the watermelon reference because two weeks earlier he had discussed the hypothesis with him on Fox News. During a June 26 appearance on *Glenn Beck*, Kerpen described the cap-and-trade bill as having "the thinnest green on the outside, [but] inside, it's deep communist red."

America's only prop commentator then produced a large watermelon from under his desk and cut it in half.

Kerpen's July 9 memo provided Beck with the missing piece to the complete metaphor: the seeds of "black nationalism." Beck waited two weeks before using Kerpen's initial info dump. Once Beck began his attack, he was tenacious. He went after Jones almost daily, repeating the facts of his former radicalism and describing him each time as a "self-avowed" communist. Between July 23 and Van Jones's resignation on September 5, Van Jones garnered 267 mentions on *Glenn Beck*—more than anyone else, and 227 more than Osama bin Laden.[4] Beck played and replayed audio and video recordings that, he maintained, proved Jones had not changed since his days in STORM. He frequently played a clip of Jones describing green jobs as a way to "change the system."

Beck's summer-long multimedia campaign centered on three lies. When the White House tapped Jones to advise on green jobs, he was neither a self-avowed communist nor a black nationalist. Beck also twisted and then disregarded the known facts of Jones's 1992 arrest. He said that Jones had been arrested for participation in the 1992 Los Angeles riots and was a "convicted felon." Both claims were false. The easily accessible truth was that Jones was arrested while working as a volunteer legal monitor during a protest in San Francisco. Never mentioned by Beck was the fact that the state of California later declared Jones's arrest unlawful. After an investigation and a hearing, the state dropped all charges against Jones and awarded him a settlement.

The racial undertones of Beck's campaign against Jones were present from the start. The host introduced the green jobs czar not as part of a discussion of his green jobs portfolio but in a wild blaze of innuendo over an extremely marginal political movement—black nationalism—with which Jones had no affiliation. At other times the racial innuendo was farther beneath the surface. As he ran down what became a familiar list, Beck frequently mentioned Jones's support for "cop killer" Mumia Abu-Jamal. As with Jones's own arrest, however, Beck failed to address the known controversy surrounding Abu-Jamal's death sentence. Beck also overstated the radicalism of Jones's opposition to this sentence, which is shared by a long list of others, including Nelson Mandela, Amnesty International, and the NAACP.

The consistent evocation of radicalism and race, both overt and subtle, gave Beck something to talk about besides the real issues that Jones was hired by the White House to address. In this, Beck reflects the bankruptcy of the conservative agenda as represented by Kerpen, and it is Beck's skill in distracting—the job of every rodeo clown—that makes him so valuable to conservative causes. Lacking answers to the problems addressed by green-economy advocates—energy, climate, and job creation—Beck created a compelling political sideshow out of the youthful radicalism of a low-level functionary. Beck is unique not for using someone like Van Jones as a stand-in for a real debate, but for his ability to maintain a full-throttle focus for nearly two months, all the while spinning a diversionary tapestry out of nothing but a few audio clips and thin air.

These clips included multiple statements by Jones in which he simply described the fundamental premise of the environmental justice movement. One of Beck's favorites came from an interview Jones gave as the head of the Ella Baker Center, in which Jones explained, "The white polluters and the white environmentalists are essentially steering poison into the people of colored communities."[5] The extent to which this is true is debatable—indeed, the environmental justice movement has been heavily criticized by greens and progressives, most notably by Michael Shellenberger and Ted Nordhaus—but it's hardly outside the boundaries of mainstream political discussion in the United States. It was a Republican president, George H. W. Bush, who created the Office of Environmental Justice in the Environmental Protection Agency. The Clinton administration extended Bush's interest, issuing an executive order that directed federal agencies to study how pollution from industrial projects disproportionately affects poor communities of color. Moreover, there is a vast literature created over twenty years that Beck could have referenced on the environmental justice movement, had he been interested in the subject.

Instead, the host repeatedly doubled down on his ignorance. Never was this strategy more glaring or abhorrent than during the September 1 edition of *The Glenn Beck Program*. This was when Beck dismissed Jones's comments about environmental racism by comparing them to what he considered another black urban legend: the Tuskegee Syphilis Study. He followed a Jones audio clip with one of Jeremiah Wright stating a simple, uncontested fact of American history: "The government lied about the Tuskegee experiment." For most Americans, the Tuskegee experiment—a forty-year clinical study conducted by the U.S. Public Health Service in which black subjects with syphilis were experimented on and allowed to die even after the discovery of penicillin—is an infamous chapter in black America's long and frequently nonconsensual relationship with experimental medicine, one that does much to explain the lingering anger and suspicions of a generation of African Americans, including Jeremiah Wright.[6] For most, it also more than justified the creation of the Office for Human Research Protections, a federal body formed in Tuskagee's wake that typifies the kind of government activism Beck so despises.

For Beck, who knows nothing about Tuskegee or the well-documented tradition of which it is a part, it is just another bit of radical nonsense spouted by America's black nationalist enemies within. "I only have a staff of seven," Beck said proudly after airing the Jones and Wright clips. "And all of a sudden we can come up with these things. Gee, you'd think the FBI or the president of the United States would surely be able to find these things."

Gee, indeed.

Then there was a snippet from a speech that Jones gave at the 2009 PowerShift conference, a volunteer environmental organization consisting mostly of college kids. It was a vague and boring speech, panned at the time by many greens, in which Jones discussed the need for a new energy grid. In one section, he spoke of a "new system" in the following terms:

> This movement is deeper than a solar panel. Deeper than a solar panel. Don't stop there. Don't stop there. No, we're going to change the whole system. We're going to change the whole thing. We're not going to put a new battery in a broken system. We want a new system. We want a new system.

What did Jones mean by a "new system"? The answer was always as near to Beck as the local bookstore. Had Beck possessed genuine interest in Jones's current political views, he could have simply read Jones's best-selling 2008 book, *The Green Collar Economy*, in which the author argues that the government's role in building a green economy is "strategic and limited."[7] The ultimate purpose of government involvement, Jones explains, is to spur new and lasting growth in the private sector.

"We need open markets," Robert F. Kennedy Jr. writes in the book's foreword. "The energy sector needs an initiative analogous to the 1996 Telecommunications Act [that] instantly precipitated the historic explosion in telecom activity."[8] Jones then builds on Kennedy's foreword, describing in detail the "pivotal role" to be played by entrepreneurs and venture capitalists, whose voices fill *The Green Collar Economy*.

The paperback edition of Jones's book hit the stores in June, shortly before Beck unveiled Kerpen's "watermelon hypothesis." Ironically, Jones's book joined Beck's *Common Sense* on new-release displays in bookstores across the country. With Beck's looming crusade in mind, the books make for an interesting contrast.

Beck's book features repeated pleas to readers not to engage in violence; Jones's book features repeated pleas to readers to get involved in their communities and learn about energy policy. Beck's book refers to his political opponents as cockroaches, vermin, and cancers; Jones's book argues rationally for bipartisan cooperation, broad coalition building, and public-private partnerships. Beck's book is a jumble of clichés and emotional appeals about "what feels right"; Jones's book logically lays out an argument in extensive technical and historical detail.

Perhaps the most revealing contrast between the two books is found in their appendices. *The Green Collar Economy* ends with a fifteen-page compendium of more than a hundred supplementary resources that include university research centers, think tanks, nonprofit groups, and private companies. *Common Sense* points readers to the Beck-affiliated Web site of the 9.12 Project and a mere ten suggested titles, four of which feature the byline of the radical-right conspiracy crank Willard Cleon Skousen.

The two books do have some commonalities. Jones and Beck both praise personal responsibility and condemn the culture of easy credit. In some cases, the two men sound like kindred spirits. Consider the following.

The Green Collar Economy: "The notion that we could go forward indefinitely by relying on excessive debt and credit rather than on smart savings and thrift (the way our grandparents did) [is] the first fallacy. . . . Homeowners began to hock their houses just to buy flat-screen TV's. . . . No nation can go on forever relying on overseas credit rather than domestic creativity, on borrowing rather than building."[9]

Common Sense: "Let's apply some common sense to the idea that 'debt isn't bad'. . . . Our parents and grandparents relied on debt only to buy a home or a car or put someone through college. . . . Suddenly our flat-screen televisions were all 'purchased' with debt."[10]

Had Beck ever invited Jones onto his show, the two men might have talked about their thrifty grandparents and bemoaned the disappearance of U.S. manufacturing, the revival of which is at the heart of the green jobs agenda. They could have talked at length about what Jones means by "changing the system" and why that phrase currently sits squarely within mainstream discourse on energy policy.

But Beck is not much of a debater and never invites smart and informed liberals onto his shows. Although he published a book called *Arguing with Idiots*, he is terrified of actually talking to those "idiots" on the air. It is much easier to play sound bites of Jones's speeches. Probing much deeper than that would have mucked up Beck's portrait of Jones as V. I. Lenin by way of Huey Newton. It risked complicating the watermelon hypothesis and revealing Beck's racially loaded diversionary tactic for what it was. For those who are not taken in by his act, the host was proving what might be called the "jack-o-lantern hypothesis" of conservative antienvironment rhetoric: capable of scaring a child on the outside, empty on the inside.

"The Van Jones affair reflected the conservatives' complete lack of ideas," says Joseph Romm, former assistant secretary of energy during the Clinton administration. "They hate the notion of green jobs because their entire antienvironment message is built around the false notion of a trade-off between reducing pollution and jobs. They have only one job-creation message—lower taxes for the wealthy—which failed. So their only remaining message is negative: do nothing. Attack."

Beck once attempted to prove the trade-off between reducing pollution and jobs not by smear and personal attacks but by referencing an actual study. His proof was a paper written by researchers at Spain's King Juan Carlos University, which argued that green jobs initiatives kill two old jobs for every new one created. But the case was not very convincing. As with most every other allegedly academic study cited by Beck, the report's chief researcher was on the ExxonMobil payroll.

When officials with the U.S. Department of Energy's National Renewable Energy Laboratory examined the Spanish report, they concluded, "The primary conclusion made by the authors—policy support of renewable energy results in net jobs losses—is not supported by their work." Among the report's many faults, it assumed that fossil fuels would remain cheap and abundant indefinitely and that climate change would not negatively affect economies in the twenty-first century. The Spanish study, the U.S. official review concludes, "deviates from the traditional research methodologies used to estimate jobs impacts, lacks transparency and supporting statistics, and fails to compare RE [renewable energy] technologies with comparable energy industry metrics."[11]

Of course, drawing conclusions not supported by facts or logic is Beck's specialty.

Not only was Jones no longer a self-avowed communist when he was tapped to advise the White House, he was internationally acclaimed for being on the cutting edge of capitalism. Among the radicals who held this view were *Time* magazine, which named Jones a 2008 "Hero of the Environment"; *New York Times* columnist Thomas Friedman, who had lauded Jones in one of his famously promarket columns; and 2010 GOP California gubernatorial candidate Meg Whitman, who declared she was "a huge fan" of Jones's "marvelous" work.

None of this is to say that Jones was a perfect man, or even a particularly good official representative for the green jobs movement. In the end, his own past did catch up with him. But Jones's eventual forced resignation had nothing to do with his time with STORM, black nationalism, or communist goals. It also had nothing to do with Glenn Beck.

At the end of August, Beck's campaign was still in high gear but had little to show. Despite more than a month of the same accusations being repeated day after day, Jones remained in the White House. Beck's audio archive of Jones sound bites grew in size but not in traction. Thus Beck and his allies stepped up their opposition research. On September 1, the Web site DefendGlenn.com circulated a video of Jones referring to congressional Republicans as "assholes" during a lecture at the Berkeley Energy and Resources Collaborative. Jones publicly apologized, bringing wider attention for the first time to Beck's agitation. Yet it was hardly a fatal blow.

In the end, it was neither Beck nor DefendGlenn.com that forced Jones's resignation. On Thursday, September 3, the conservative blog GatewayPundit.com reported that Jones had signed a 2004 petition calling for "immediate public attention to unanswered questions that suggest that people within the current administration may indeed have deliberately allowed 9/11 to happen, perhaps as a pretext for war." The petition's wording did not claim that the government was responsible for organizing the attacks, but it was vague enough to push Jones onto the political third rail of what has become known as the 9/11 Truth Movement. The next day, Senator Kit Bond, a Republican from Missouri, called for a hearing on Jones's "fitness" to advise the president.

The hearing never took place. Jones proffered his resignation to the president the next day, Saturday, September 5.[12]

What Beck had failed to do in nearly two months of huffing and puffing, GatewayPundit accomplished in two days with a single-page document. Still, most media reports mistakenly described Jones's resignation as a "victory" for Beck despite the fact that none of Beck's charges ever made waves outside the insular world of conservative media. Only in September did the story break, driven by discoveries that were made independently of Beck's shows. As the former Bush speech-writer David Frum told CNN's *American Morning* on September 7, "[Jones] could have survived, laughed off all of [Beck's] empty accusations. What happened was, GatewayPundit got the goods."

This didn't stop Beck from taking the credit for Jones's fall, however. He dismissed talk of victory not because he had little to do with what led to Jones's resignation, he let on, but because he had so much more work to do. Even though no policies had been derailed and no communists had been smoked out of the White House, his ratings spiked, and the taste of blood was fresh in his mouth. He wanted more. On the Monday after Jones's resignation, Beck promised to continue unmasking Obama's many communist czars. "We will continue to demand answers," he promised. "This is not over."

How could it be? For Beck, the Obama administration held an embarrassment of imaginary radical riches. As he surveyed the menu, Beck sounded as if he were high off the scent of new communist prey, charged with a newfound sense of power. Hours after Jones's resignation was made public, Beck issued an urgent directive to his followers. It came in the form of a Twitter message declaring war on three current and potential members of the Obama administration. "Find everything you can on Cass Sunstein, Mark Lloyd, and Carol Browner," it said.

One week later, on September 12, around eighty thousand Americans answered Beck's call to gather en masse on the National Mall. They came to protest the president in terms they learned from Beck. Hundreds of signs combined Soviet and Nazi iconography with historically inaccurate references to czars. Among the many racially charged signs on display that day, very few mentioned the petition that forced Van Jones's resignation. More popular were signs stating flatly what Glenn Beck could not. For example: OBAMA'S PLAN = WHITE SLAVERY.

9

"A Deep-Seated Hatred for . . . the White Culture"

It was a few minutes past 7 a.m. on Tuesday, July 28, 2009, and the sofa-sitting triumvirate of Fox News's top-rated morning show, *Fox & Friends*, was engaged in the usual breakfast-hour banter. The hosts were giggling over a segment about a champion bodybuilder when Glenn Beck appeared at the edge of the studio set, his arm curled in a mock flex.

One of the show's hosts, the weatherman Steve Doocy, seized on the gesture to move the conversation into the next topic of discussion: Barack Obama's upcoming backyard "beer summit" between a black Harvard University professor and the white Cambridge, Massachusetts, police officer who had arrested him at his home. Obama was in the news for touting the racially charged incident as a "teachable moment." Conservative commentators, Beck among them, were vociferously condemning the president for saying that the Cambridge police had "acted stupidly."

"You'd better get that [bicep] ready," Doocy told the flexing Beck. "Because on Thursday night at the White House, they're going to have a beer fest!"

"That is *un-be-lievable*," Beck shot back. When *Fox & Friends* cohost Brian Kilmeade asked him to elaborate, Beck threw an arm over the couch and settled in to present his theory:

> This president has, I think, exposed himself as a guy, over and over and over and over again, as a guy who has a deep-seated hatred for

160

white people, or the white culture, I don't know what it is. But you can't sit in a pew with Jeremiah Wright for twenty years and not hear some of that stuff and not have it wash over [you].

Among the three hosts of *Fox & Friends*, only a smiling Gretchen Carlson seemed unaware that something extraordinary had just taken place.[1] After a confused pause, Kilmeade stammered that Obama couldn't be racist, because his senior staff includes so many white people. "Seventy percent of the people we see every day are white," he said. Beck brushed the argument aside.

"This guy is, I believe, a racist," he said. "Look at the people he's surrounded himself with, his new green jobs czar, Van Jones—black liberation theology, a black nationalist, also an avowed communist."

The following morning, July 29, after drubbings from across the political spectrum, including a group beat-down by the cast of MSNBC's *Morning Joe*, Beck addressed the controversy for the first and last time on *The Glenn Beck Program*—not to apologize but to assume his favorite pose: that of aggrieved victim. Standing by his words, he dismissed the mounting criticism as "the latest rage in the Glenn Beck tear-him-apart business."

This was true. The outrage that greeted Beck's comments about the president was the latest rage in a long series of rages stretching back to his days as a Top 40 deejay. At some point in his career, Beck has been condemned, sometimes more than once, by organizations representing Asians, Hispanics, Arabs, Jews, gays, and blacks. Throughout the years of engendering this rainbow of resentment, Beck had never once suffered serious consequences. He not only survived each rage intact but emerged more famous than before. Why, he must have wondered, should this time be any different?

Nearly two months after Beck's *Fox & Friends* appearance, Katie Couric of CBS News asked him to explain what he meant by "the white culture." The host demurred, saying, "I don't know how to answer that, that's not a trap."[2] But the evasion didn't mean he hasn't answered the question. In fact, Beck *has* been answering it, not in sound bites but in full, every weekday for nearly a decade.

To understand what Beck means by "the white culture," a good starting point is the title of his first and most personal book, *The Real America: Messages from the Heart and Heartland.* The concept of an American heartland continues to animate Beck's political imagination, and it explains much about how he sees the world. For Beck and his conservative audiences, the term *white culture* is not really about race, or at least not just about race. It is a synonym for an entire moral, political, and cultural universe, which Beck (among others) has nicknamed the Real America.

It is no coincidence that this idea found its loudest champion in Beck's political superhero, Sarah Palin. Nor is it coincidental that Palin pounded this idea most forcefully during the racially charged homestretch of the 2008 presidential campaign. Beck and Palin share a fan base in part because they both trade without shame or fear in the enduring idea of an American heartland that is somehow more real than the rest of the country. This myth is at once geographic and nongeographic, racial and nonracial, real and imaginary.

In speeches and writings, Beck and Palin's Real America is defined by conservative political and cultural traditions. It also has strong, usually implicit, racial overtones. Real America looks much like the red-state stereotype made famous by the 2004 election map: small-town, antigovernment, religious, blue-collar, gun-toting. It just so happens that the states closest to this stereotype are also the country's last demographic bastions of whiteness. Anyone who challenges this ideal is, by definition, an enemy of the Real America—or, in Beck's bold usage, "the white culture."

The challengers can be white, black, or, biracial. The important thing is that they embody the threat of "fake" America to the "real." This "fake America" is another mix of reality and myth. In the conservative mind, it is urban, socialist, godless, educated with all the wrong ideas, unable to create anything of lasting value, and tracking darker every day. By threatening to overwhelm and extinguish Real America, the fake is hostile in every way: anticapitalist, antifamily, and—the part of the triad that usually dares not speak its name—antiwhite.

Beck takes the idea of a heartland fortress literally. This became clear in June 2009, when author Brad Thor appeared twice on *The Glenn Beck Program* to discuss his latest patriotic thriller, *The Apostle.* The conversation soon veered into the twin threats of liberalism and Islamist terrorism. Thor, a longtime friend of the show and a contributing editor to Beck's magazine, declared, "I think we have people here who hold office who are under the influence of foreign operatives. I don't think it's a lot, but I think there are a handful of them. I think they have been here for a while."

This got Beck thinking about a possible jihadist invasion along the lines of the late–Cold War films *Red Dawn* and *Invasion U.S.A.* Should such an event come to pass, Beck mused aloud, the "sheep in America's Northeast" would be "easy to occupy." Only in the Real American state of Texas and the nearly all-white states of the intermountain West, Idaho and Utah, would the invaders encounter meaningful resistance.[3]

These two Americas—real and fake, strong and weak, white and non-white—form the frame in which Beck sees Obama as racist. This frame explains how Beck can accuse Obama of being a racist and in the same breath maintain that he's "not saying the president hates white people." Beck was born fluent in the symbolic language of this conservative heartland. He's been telling the same easy joke about the pointlessness of abstract art for years.* *The Real America* wistfully recounts weekends on his grandparents' Iowa farm watching the iconic whipping post of greater heartland popular culture, *The Lawrence Welk Show.* He is also a longtime champion of "square" sensibilities, or what he calls "the stereotypical corny stuff."[4]

In his embrace and elevation of the "corny stuff," Beck speaks straight from the playbook of angry modern heartlanders like Spiro Agnew, who once described the "disease of our times" as a "vague uneasiness that our values are corny."[5] Like Nixon and Agnew with their "silent majority," Beck rallies his corny army to surround the fashionable leftist elitists who threaten to drown his precious culture. But Beck's army is different from Nixon's. It is neither silent nor any longer a majority. It is a shrinking army fighting a desperate rearguard battle in the form of Tea Party protests and 9.12 Project marches.

It fits that Beck has emerged as a leading voice of this new, harder-edged version of the heartland myth. As Thomas Frank and others have chronicled, the modern conservative heartland is in large part a construct of Beck's own industry, broadcasting.

As recently as eighty years ago, the heartland was defined not by images of rural tranquility and fidelity to free-market verities but

---

*The joke's punch line involves Beck visiting a museum and growing confused while staring at a modern painting titled *Blue*. "It's just . . . blue," says the host. "Just the color blue."

by the radical populists and the unions that organized U.S. factory workers. With the advent of mass radio, this feisty progressive heartland ideal began a transformation into the current conservative pastoral fantasyland populated by commonsense, self-reliant yeomen who like their assault rifles loaded and their tax burdens lifted.

Reality was not allowed to interfere with this transformation as it took place. As the cities of the Midwest industrialized and diversified, the symbolic heartland's boundaries were simply expanded south and west. When during the 1960s heartland centers like Detroit and Chicago exploded in violence, they were excised from the heartland map altogether. In the words of Kansas University cultural geographer James R. Shortridge, they became "extra-regional."[6] They were simply cut out from the symbolic heartland map.

One city above all others has always posed the greatest threat to the coherence of the conservative heartland myth. It is the city where Jane Addams pioneered community organizing, where an anarchist-labor alliance won the eight-hour workday, and where Saul Alinsky unionized the meatpackers. If one man could represent a wrench in the mental machinery behind the construct of Beck and Palin's Real America, it is an urbane black Democrat from the heartland's old capital, Chicago.

Beck's heartland politics found a natural home at Fox News. Since the network's launch in 1996, it has employed the nation's leading maestros of the cultural-racial dog whistle. Before Beck showed up, Bill O'Reilly and Sean Hannity were the star soloists in an ensemble working in philharmonic perfection, with Roger Ailes conducting.

By the time Rupert Murdoch tapped Ailes to head his new network, Ailes already had nearly two decades of experience in the subtle, and sometimes not-so-subtle, manipulation of white racial anxiety. It is a history that went back to Ailes's work with Richard Nixon's 1968 presidential campaign, the first successful use of white racial fears in post–Jim Crow national politics. As the campaign's media adviser, Ailes designed and calibrated the racial component of Nixon's "silent majority" message.

In *Nixonland*, the historian Rick Pearlstein describes how Ailes sought to blunt the overtly racist appeal of third-party candidate George Wallace by co-opting and sanitizing the racist rage fueling the Wallace insurgency. "Ailes hit upon [the] idea," writes Pearlstein, of planting

a "good, mean, Wallaceite cab-driver" in the audience at a televised
Nixon campaign event:

> "Wouldn't that be great? Some guy to sit there and say, 'Awright,
> Mac, what about these niggers?'" Nixon then could abhor the
> incivility of the words, while endorsing a "moderate" version of
> the opinion. Ailes walked up and down a nearby taxi stand until he
> found a cabbie who fit the bill.[7]

Ailes would later employ racially charged imagery and rhetoric in
campaigns for George H. W. Bush and Rudy Giuliani. Shortly before
launching Fox News, Ailes produced Rush Limbaugh's television show,
where a Wallaceite hostility to gays and ethnic minorities simmered
constantly just beneath the surface and sometimes broke through. It
was with the "good, mean . . . cab-driver" still in mind that Ailes crafted
the original lineup of Fox News. From the start, the strongest voices
on Fox prime time belonged to Bill O'Reilly, who patrolled race in
modern America like a swaggering Tammany-era Irish cop, and Sean
Hannity, whose radio program during the 1990s frequently welcomed
Hal Turner, a well-known white supremacist.[8]

Then came Fox News's coverage of the 2008 campaign. When Barack
Obama emerged as a serious contender for the Democratic nomination, the network went to work inflaming racial fears and cultural
resentments among conservatives. The network's anchors reported
false stories about Barack Obama's madrassa education, described his
wife, Michelle, as his "baby mama," and—conflating the fear of a black
president with national security—described his famous fist bump with
Michelle in Denver as a "terrorist fist-jab."[9] On no other network did
the videos of Reverend Jeremiah Wright play longer or more often.

Beck's July 28 comments were a throwback to the wild GOP attacks on
Obama that defined the homestretch of the 2008 campaign. Since Beck had
been at Headline News at the time, he might have thought he had missed
out then and now wanted to make up for the lost opportunity. Whatever the
case, Beck's bosses did not appear troubled by the outburst. Bill Shine, Fox
senior vice president of programming, issued a curt statement defending
Beck's "freedom to express his opinions." There was no official reprimand
or forced apology. The network forbade Beck to mention the controversy
on Fox, but he was free to do so on the radio. It seemed that another rage
in the "Glenn Beck tear-him-apart" business was destined to flame out.

Fox News management wasn't the only force on Beck's side. So too was history. In the annals of cable news controversies, consequences follow only when the hosts "punch down" on the young or the defenseless. Don Imus had punched down on the Rutgers University women's basketball team. David Shuster punched down on Chelsea Clinton during the 2008 primaries. Both suffered official censure. But whatever Beck said about Barack Obama didn't matter, because his target was the most powerful man in the world. People may have found his comments outrageous, dangerous, and revealing of deeper problems with the host, but it was hard to feel pity for the president of the United States.

Although it wasn't immediately clear, this case of "punching up" was destined to be different. Beck's Obama comments were part of a larger pattern of race-baiting on Fox, and patience in some quarters had been wearing thin for a long time. There was a deep hunger to strike back.

But how? Until July 28, 2009, liberals had responded to Beck's incendiary comments by blogging about them. Maybe they wrote an easily ignored letter of protest. What they hadn't done is target the companies that underwrite Beck's shows. Among those who thought it time to try such a strategy was the four-member staff of a young Oakland-based civil rights group called Color of Change.

Color of Change was conceived during a conference call.

It was the spring of 2005, and a dozen of the Bay Area's leading activists were on the phone discussing the local agenda for the summer. Among the participants was James Rucker, the thirty-six-year-old director of grassroots mobilization at MoveOn.org. Rucker had joined the liberal new media group in 2003 after an early career with a succession of Silicon Valley startups. At the time of the conference call, he'd begun toying with an idea for a new organization.

"I wanted to see the model we created and evolved at Move On put to work for black folks, brown folks, and others," says Rucker. "We saw the power of what was being created with Move On, but it wasn't reaching many of the communities that needed such a mechanism the most—whether black, brown, or low-income. These communities were the least represented and the most shut out of the political process."

Also on the conference call was the thirty-five-year-old director of the Ella Baker Center for Human Rights, who was also known for his work on police accountability and criminal justice reform in the Bay Area. His name was Van Jones. He was immediately struck by Rucker's idea of a new organization like MoveOn.org, and the two men stayed in touch throughout the summer.

By September, Rucker and Jones were in the early planning stages when Hurricane Katrina devastated New Orleans, presenting what Rucker calls the "perfect organizing moment." Within a month of announcing Color of Change in early September, they had enlisted ten thousand members. Two years later, Color of Change had grown to become the country's dominant online civil-rights organization, with a membership of more than six hundred thousand. (Van Jones left Color of Change in 2007 to focus on the green jobs agenda.)

Color of Change primarily focuses on new-media protest campaigns. It also links traditional civil rights groups with the mostly white liberal blogosphere and the mainstream media. The group is "reaching a demographic of sixteen- to forty-five-year-olds who no longer have a relationship with black newspapers," NAACP chief Ben Jealous has said. "[It is] taking over the role that the black press has traditionally held: publicizing injustices and rallying public sentiment against them."[10]

When Beck made his remarks on *Fox & Friends*, Color of Change had already organized two campaigns around Fox News. The first pressured the Congressional Black Caucus (CBC) to pull out of a 2007 primary-season debate it was planning to cosponsor with the network. After rallying its members to contact members of the CBC with their concerns, the debate was scuttled. The organization next launched a more general campaign highlighting the steady flow of inflammatory racial comments that defined Fox News' coverage of the 2008 general campaign.

Color of Change's four-member staff came to work on the morning of July 28 expecting to focus on Lou Dobbs, who had recently joined in stoking right-wing hysteria over Barack Obama's birth certificate. Those plans were interrupted when Rucker opened his e-mail account and found a clip of Beck's appearance that morning on *Fox & Friends*.

"As soon as we saw the video, we knew," says Rucker. "It was just one of those moments. Beck's comments about the president perfectly captured what has been going on at the network for a long time. It just took it to another level. We knew immediately that it would be easy to organize around and started drawing up an advertiser list."

The campaign that followed was unorthodox. Normally, the first contact with an advertiser follows a long organizational buildup, but Rucker and his colleagues decided to start moving on both tracks simultaneously. While Color of Change drew up and circulated a petition, it also began crafting a message to be delivered to Beck's advertisers that week.

"Beck's rhetoric was so clearly beyond the pale," says Rucker. "If we could get well-known companies to visualize their brands being associated with what was coming out of Beck's mouth, we knew they would be very uncomfortable, and we presumed that they'd want to excuse themselves from Beck's circle fast."

To help get the word out, the group turned to Sunshine, Sachs & Associates, a respected Manhattan PR agency that Color of Change had worked with in the past and whose client list includes liberal celebrities like Ben Affleck and Leonardo DiCaprio. (Its cofounder, Ken Sunshine, is a close friend of Matt Hiltzik, Beck's PR flack.) Color of Change announced its campaign to the world on July 30, just two days after Beck's comments.

The initial press release was headed "ColorofChange.org Members Urge Glenn Beck Advertisers to Pull Ads in Wake of Recent Race-Baiting Comments on 'Fox & Friends.'" The release touted the organization's large membership and cited market research forecasting that the buying power of African Americans would soon surpass $1.1 trillion. Armed with this press release, a petition, and a transcript of Beck's comments, staffers began calling corporate communications departments on July 30.

The first victory came within seventy-two hours. Fitting Color of Change's roots in new media, the company was Lawyers.com. Then the dominoes began to fall. By day three, GEICO, Procter & Gamble, and Progressive Insurance all announced that they would stop advertising on *Glenn Beck*. The latter two companies not only promised to drop their ads, they also apologized and called their previous ad buys during the show "errors." By August 13, Healthy Choice, Roche, Sanofi-Aventis, and Radio Shack had all pledged to pull their ads.

Four days later, a large cluster of major brands joined the list, including Best Buy, CVS, and Wal-Mart.

As the list grew, so did the ambitiousness of the campaign. "At first it was all a little shocking," says Rucker. "But when we hit twenty companies, we started to realize we could go for everybody. It suddenly made perfect sense by design that these advertisers should abandon a pariah. The campaign became self-reinforcing by creating a public story that there was something seriously wrong with this guy."

The conservative push-back started on August 12, in classic Beckian fashion. NewsBusters.com published an article attacking Color of Change as "an extremist racial grievance group that tries to stir up racial antagonism in order to promote a socialist agenda." Conservative bloggers soon joined the effort. Within hours of the News Busters story, Color of Change began receiving the first of what would become hundreds of harassing phone calls and hate letters. A trickle of abusive e-mails became a torrent on August 14, when the *New York Times* described the boycott campaign as "unusually successful."[11]

Beck never addressed the widening boycott directly, but on television and radio his war on Van Jones continued to escalate. To many observers, the timing of the two phenomena was a little too perfect. It seemed Beck and Color of Change were waging a war by proxy. To Beck's critics, the host was attacking Jones as a stand-in for Color of Change; to his supporters, Color of Change was attacking Beck on behalf of Jones (and even the White House).

But a closer look at the players and the time line suggests that the timing was just a strange coincidence. Van Jones was no longer associated or even in touch with Color of Change by the summer of 2009, and Beck had only just begun to focus on Jones when he made his July 28 comments.

"We didn't even realize that Beck had attacked Van when we started the campaign," says Rucker. "And even when we recognized that, it was so pale it wouldn't have been the kind of thing that would have motivated us, or our members, at all. If the story were about Beck attacking Van, the vast majority of our members really wouldn't have cared. And we wouldn't, either. We get attacked all the time by the Far Right. It's just part of doing business."

As the summer came to a close, business on *Glenn Beck* was worse than ever.

As news of the successful boycott spread, Beck announced that he was taking a weeklong mid-August vacation. The timing sparked widespread speculation that Fox News had forced Beck to take a leave of absence in the hope that the story would pass. If that was the intent, the effort failed miserably. During Beck's vacation, twenty-two companies joined the exodus from his show. The names included blue-chip giants AT&T, Johnson & Johnson, and, perhaps most painfully for Beck, Orson Welles's old sponsor, the Campbell Soup Company. The Color of Change staff, meanwhile, more than doubled its number of volunteers and temp workers.

"We knew something remarkable was happening when we received a phone call from a company called AirWare," says Gabriel Rey-Goodlatte, the Color of Change campaign director. "They really wanted us to know that they had dropped Beck. But we hadn't even contacted them."

Another sign that the campaign was having an impact was the growing volume of hate mail and phone calls received by Color of Change. "The hate mail picked up once Beck started talking about Van all the time," says Rey-Goodlatte. "Along with letters and calls, hundreds of racist messages have been posted on our site."

Beck often shares hate mail from liberals on his Web site. In the spirit of reciprocity, below are some of the letters that Beck's fans have sent to Color of Change since the boycott began. Each represents dozens more just like it:

> From: Joe Drager
> Date: Monday, August 24, 2009, at 3:55 a.m.
> Do you have to be a spade to join your organization?

> From: Morgan Snow
> Date: Tuesday, August 25, 2009, at 12:47 p.m.
> You people are disgusting subhuman worthless animals. I will no longer do business with any company that has canceled ads on Glenn Beck's show because of you idiots.

> From: Michael Chambers
> Date: Tuesday, August 25, 2009, at 10:37 a.m.

Aren't you special! If niggers like you spent half your energy they do screaming racist into supporting their own black family America would be better off!

From: Tory NOBAMA Donegan
Date: Monday, September 14, 2009, at 11:22 a.m.
FUCK NIGGERS. GLENN FOR LIFE!

From: Kerry
Date: Monday, September 14, 2009, at 9:53 a.m.
hey rucker, if I ever see you I'm going to beat your Black Trash face in!
    Glenn Beck is kicking your ass! You are a Black Trash Hillbilly!

From: Mark Gregory Compton
Date: Wednesday, September 16, 2009, at 7:01 p.m.
I think Obama and you-all are exactly what you are. Forget the word racists OK. . . . You just do not like white folks just like I do not really care for porch monkeys . . . so let's stop joking around and kidding each other OK. . . . Glenn Beck be right . . . deep inside you know it . . . and want it. . . .
    Love and Pass them Greens, Mark

From: Carlos A Sanchez
Date: Wednesday, September 16, 2009, at 10:08 p.m.
Bottom line for you pinkos, don't fuck with FNC or talk radio. ACORN is cut from the same cloth as all you ghetto rattlers who have no product other than to assist the nation's lowest rung in how to cheat the system. You are truly a cancer in the asshole of this great country and no amount of race baiting will fix that.

From: Robert & Leona
Date: Thursday, September 17, 2009, at 10:01 a.m.
RUN YOU BLACK THUGS, BUT YOU CAN'T HIDE, TALK RADIO IS BRINGING YOU BLACK ASS THUGS TO THE SURFACE AND THERE IS NO PLACE TO HIDE.

From: Bill Terror
Date: Monday, September 21, 2009, at 5:47 p.m.
You and you're racist black trash terrorists better stay away from me and my family.

From: Ed Ryan
Date: Monday, September 21, 2009, at 4:10 a.m.

And Van Jones is gone. And ACORN is destroyed. Beck:
2—Niggers: 0
　　Suck it, boy!

From: Bruce Fultz
Date: Wednesday, September 23, 2009, at 10:42 a.m.
i saw glenn beck's program last nite about your hero obama. you
nigger's attack him cause he tell's the truth and liberal's can't handle
truth & logic. we all know obama has an agenda to change america into his radical minded warped govt'! glenn is a true patriot
and those are becoming harder to find. but he's getting the message out there. you nigger's need a reality check. i'm so glad fox is
standing behind glenn beck. and not allowing your nigger group to
intimidate them!! you fucker's go after beck's sponsor's. but yet you
support those little nigger thug's who beat the hell out of that white
dude down there. nigger logic!

From: RedNeckCraka
Date: Thursday, September 24, 2009, at 9:38 p.m.
FUCK YOU IDIOT NIGGERS YOU ARE A WASTE TO
DECENCY AND LIFE. GO PISS ON YOUR FUCKING
MOTHERLAND THAT YOU MISS SO MUCH, GET THE
FUCK OUT BEFORE IT'S TO LATE

On and on did Glenn Beck's "Real America" let its voice be heard.

Beck returned to the air on Monday, August 24. The rodeo clown was
angry. Without addressing the boycott directly, Beck made no secret
of the fact that he believed his best defense was ratings, sweet ratings.
As he pleaded with his radio audience to watch his Fox show all that
week, it was clear that the boycott campaign had raised his persecution
complex to a screaming pitch.

"Watch the show tonight," he begged. "You may not save my life. But
you'll save the republic. They need to destroy me because I'm on to
them. You can dismiss someone who's not a threat. But I'm a threat. The
opposition is growing." Later that night, he brought the same message
to his Fox News audience. "America," he said, "I ask you to call a friend
and ask them to watch the show this week."

The Color of Change campaign met with even more success after Beck's return. In response, Beck's push-back devolved into unconcealed desperation. "I'm begging you," he said toward the end of the August 26 edition of *The Glenn Beck Program.* "Call everyone you know. Get them to watch the show." He even acknowledged his radio fans' concerns about the transparency of what he was doing. "I don't care if you—if you don't wanna watch it because of ratings, whatever," he continued. "Question me all you want, tear me apart all you want. Listen to the truth. I ask that you watch tonight, tomorrow, and Friday. Tell everyone you know! Tivo them! Fox News Channel, five p.m."

It worked. The week after his mysterious vacation, Beck's ratings broke the record for the 5 p.m. slot on any cable news network. More than three million viewers tuned in on one night, making Beck second only to O'Reilly for the day. Most shocking was that he had 888,000 viewers in the prize demographic, beating O'Reilly's 8 p.m. show by a nose.[12]

If numbers were capable of beating the boycott, these would have done it. In late August, Beck still had a few major-brand sponsors, including some blue chips.

It didn't happen, however. Despite the record audiences the show was drawing, advertisers continued to abandon *Glenn Beck.* On August 27, ten companies whose ads had recently been seen during Beck's program announced they were pulling out. They included a slew of corporate icons: Applebee's, Bank of America, General Mills, Kraft, and Travelers Insurance. By Labor Day, the number of companies to drop Beck had surpassed fifty, and the number was growing every day.

Beck still had his fans. Among those heartened by the viewer support for Beck was former Ku Klux Klan leader David Duke. "A lot of stuff is happening in the world of race relations and little of it points towards a post-racial society," Duke noted on his Web site. "Beck is steadily losing advertisers, but his viewers seem to be sticking with him. White desperation is manifesting itself in various forms."[13]

David Duke wasn't the only avowed "white nationalist" who was encouraged by Beck's words and the way they resonated with Fox News viewers. On the nation's leading discussion board for racists, Stormfront.org, Beck's July 28 claim that President Obama harbors a

"deep-seated hatred for white people, or the white culture" was met
with attention and appreciation.

Some participants saw Beck as an important ally in the white
nationalist cause. Others were skeptical, viewing him as a clueless conservative version of Lenin's "useful idiot." But some of Stormfront's
most active members generally agreed that whether or not he was fully
aware, Beck was nudging his audience toward an embrace of racial
consciousness.

"Glen Beck can be useful," wrote one Stormfront member who posts
under the name SS_Marching. "When Glen beck said 'Obama Has A
Deep-Seated Hatred For White People' he is able to reach a much
wider audience than we can. They will [be] predisposed to the idea
and the next time Obama pushes an anti-white policy they will see it
as such."[14]

Stormfront member PowerCommander agreed. Beck, he wrote:

> seems to have ignited a flame under the asses of some folks with
> similar ideas by pushing the right buttons. It appears as if the cur-
> rent regime [is] directly blaming GB and fox news for throwing a
> wrench in their machine. Is Beck's rambling getting America fired
> up and ready to fight? Has Beck told enough of the truth to start
> something bigger? Even an engine needs a starter to get fired off
> and go down the road.[15]

Thor357, a Stormfront sustaining member who has posted on the
site more than thirty-five hundred times, had this to say:

> Glenn Beck and Alex Jones [a controversial conservative media
> figure who asserts that 9/11 was an inside job and that environ-
> mentalism is the new eugenics] are the front line in the war of
> Ideals we grapple with, they are far from perfect and are some-
> what compromised. But every person in the last 2 years that
> I have introduced to the WN [white nationalist] Philosophy have
> come largely from Alex Jones, Glen Beck and the Scriptures for
> America founder Pastor Pete Peters. Baby steps are required
> for people like these, but the trio Beck, Jones, Peters are the
> baby food that feeds potential Nationalists. . . . Glenn Beck is not
> far behind as his Mormon background indicates to me as most
> Mormons I have met are not friends of Jews like the Church was

years ago. Most Mormons I know are arming themselves, with guns, bullets and food.[16]

Later in the same discussion thread, Thor357 added:

> I have talked to 6 people in two days because Glenn Beck woke them up, it's amazing how angry they are. They are pissing fire over Obama, this is a good thing. Now I educate them. If out of 100 of the Glen Beckers I keep 20 then I have won 20 more to cover my back side. I never lost the 80 as they never were.[17]

Carolina Patriot, whose member picture features a kitten aiming an assassin's rifle, was conflicted but admiring:

> Every now and again when an infomercial takes the place of hunting or fishing, I'll turn over to Glenn Beck if he's on and watch his show. Sometimes it is amusing, sometimes it is informed, and sometimes, I think he comes to SF [Stormfront] to steal show idea's.[18]

UstashaNY offered up an analogy to substance abuse, with Beck as the soft-stuff hook:

> Beck, Dobbs etc. are like gateway drugs. If it wakes up one person to learn something about whats really going on and that person does the research, looks deeper and deeper into WHO and WHAT is behind all of this, then its a win for the movement. NOBODY in the msm [mainstream media] is reporting the stuff Beck does, let him keep talking. It will wake people up, believe me. . . . He is more of a help to us then you may think. Until we have a REAL voice in the msm, guys like him and Dobbs are a stepping stone right into our laps. Its only a matter of time.[19]

Even those who don't think Beck understands what he's doing appreciate his instincts. According to WhiteManMarchesOn88:

> There is no doubt that Beck is not a WN [white nationalist], but I have to agree that he does raise a lot of really good questions that do promote White survival. I'm sure he would go a lot farther with

a lot of his questions, but ZOG [Zionist-occupied government] would more than likely kick him off television if he did.[20]

"By no means do I think [Beck] is aware of the racial issue, and for the moment that is ok," wrote Stormfront member QHelios. "He is stirring the pot, and I thank him for that."[21]

Corporate America and the average white nationalist agree: Declaring that the president hates white people is a good way to stir the pot. But it's not the only way. Beck is nothing if not a man of many spoons.

"Show me your friends," Beck likes to say, "and I'll show you your future."

In his losing battle against the Color of Change campaign, Beck has had no more generous or energetic friend than Gary Kreep. A California attorney and a veteran of extreme-right causes, Kreep is the president of the United States Justice Foundation, under whose name he registered DefendGlenn.com in August. At first, Kreep attempted to hide his involvement. An article on the Web site of the ultraconservative World Net Daily announced the group's founding by describing it as run by an unnamed "husband and wife" team representing Beck fans "with real purchasing power, unlike the instigators of this phony Astroturf boycott."[22]

Designed to rally public support for Beck and his dwindling number of advertisers, the site was part of a larger campaign, in which Beck was a leading participant, to indirectly discredit Color of Change by attacking one of the organization's cofounders, Van Jones. Visitors to DefendGlenn.com were instructed to contact companies that had dropped Beck and inform them that Jones had gone to prison for helping to incite the Rodney King riots of 1992 and had accused President Bush of giving troops orders to shoot black people in New Orleans. Both claims were false.

The use of lies and slime was consistent with Kreep's career. Since the 1980s, Kreep has associated with some of the nation's most thuggish far-right organizations and individuals. Most recently, prior to his defense of Beck, he was party to a federal lawsuit, *Captain Pamela Barnett v. Barack Hussein Obama*, which sought to prevent Obama's inauguration on the grounds that he was not a U.S. citizen. Kreep has also defended anti-immigrant vigilante groups, radical pro-life groups, and Reverend Wiley Drake, the California Baptist preacher who briefly made headlines in June 2009 for openly praying for Obama's death.

DefendGlenn.com failed to stop the bleeding. September arrived with eleven new companies announcing they would no longer advertise on *Glenn Beck*. One by one, the last holdouts among the big names fell: Capital One, Dannon, Discover, HSBC, Infiniti, Mercedes-Benz, and Simplex Healthcare. In October, the total number climbed to eighty. When two British firms joined the list, including the makers of Guinness and Tanqueray, the campaign became international.

As of this writing, in December 2009, *Glenn Beck*'s advertising roster resembles the show's guest list of right-wing freaks and geeks. The list is down to a combination of direct-marketing companies, gold dealers— most notably Beck's longtime sponsor, Goldline—and ideologically supportive outfits that live off foundation money. Not a single nation- ally recognized brand is left. Many of those that remain are closer to a *Saturday Night Live* spoof; for example, EggGenie—"Eggzactly what you've been waiting for! Order now!"

Prominent among this rump group of advertisers are groups that are fronted by conservative activist-publicist Rick Berman and philanthropist Philip Anschutz. Both men are best known for setting up nonprofit front groups for corporate interests. In the case of Berman, who is known as Dr. Evil for his work flacking for the tobacco indus- try, this means ads for the Center for Economic and Entrepreneurial Literacy and the Employment Policies Institute, which produces the Web site RottenAcorn.com. Among the Anschutz-tied groups that sup- port Beck's show are the Foundation for a Better Life and *The Weekly Standard.*

Ads from other corporate front groups include Americans Against Food Taxes, American Coalition for Clean Coal Electricity, Americans for Prosperity, Conservatives for Patients' Rights, National Republican Trust PAC, GOPTrust.com, TeaPartyExpress.org, and United Against a Nuclear Iran.

As 2010 loomed, *Glenn Beck* was reduced to Fox's only hour of ide- ologically sponsored programming. The free market had listened to Glenn Beck and his critics, considered its options, and spoken.

• • •

Fox News maintains that the mass transatlantic advertiser bolt from *Glenn Beck* has never affected its bottom line. It's possible its executives are telling the truth. Maybe EggGenie, Goldline, and *The Weekly Standard* are paying top rates for their slots. But the boycott has, for the first time, introduced Beck to the reality of consequences. Along with embarrassing the host, it has also bloodied the Beck brand. Early in the campaign, some critics expressed hope that Fox News would drop Beck. But that was never likely. Beck is the future of the network, its fresh face for the post-O'Reilly era, and the value of that cannot be measured in advertising dollars.

The same is true of his value to conservative causes in general. No matter how poisonous he may be, or yet become, to mainstream corporate advertising campaigns, his peerless skills as a rabble-rouser and a manipulator of discontent ensure his survival on Fox News, regardless of where GEICO buys its ad time. If Koch Family Foundations is one day forced to underwrite each episode of *Glenn Beck* just to keep its host on the air, it'll be smart to do it.

10

ACORN

In early May 2009, James O'Keefe, a twenty-five-year-old business student in New York, received a phone call from Hannah Giles, a twenty-year-old journalism student in Florida. Giles, like O'Keefe, was a budding conservative activist. She was calling to express her admiration for O'Keefe's recent video sting against Planned Parenthood, which he had posted on YouTube. The sting failed to fell the icon of reproductive rights, but Giles had found herself inspired by the attempt. While jogging, she told O'Keefe, she had been struck by her own idea for a sting operation. Giles later described her eureka moment to Sean Hannity:

> I had never seen an ACORN office, I really didn't even know that they existed, and I jogged into the wrong part of town, saw some homeless people and street ladies, and I put two and two together when I turned around to get back into a safe neighborhood. And it's like, what if these people went into ACORN? A prostitute and—what would come from that? No bills, no nothing—would they get a house?[1]

Giles's statement offers a revealing look into the unique architecture of the conservative mind, in which a first contact with poverty slides quickly toward thoughts of hurting one of the poor's few champions. Of all of the questions being in "the wrong part of town" might raise for a young political activist and journalist, Giles found herself most haunted by this one: *Could a poor prostitute get a house?*

O'Keefe agreed that it was a fascinating question.

Of course, theirs was no innocent curiosity. O'Keefe and Giles shared the right's long-standing animosity toward the Association of Community Organizations for Reform Now. The ACORN sting that ensued was intended to embarrass, damage, and possibly—hopefully—destroy the organization. O'Keefe has traced his own animosity to the day he viewed a video depicting ACORN workers breaking the padlocks off foreclosed homes and reclaiming them for the evicted. Giles, for her part, has a harder time putting a finger on her deepest motivations, but they are strong. "Why go after ACORN?" Giles explained to the *New York Post*. "Because I love America, I love God, and corrupt institutions don't help that."[2]

And so, during July and August 2009, O'Keefe and Giles traveled around the country, secretly recording walk-in visits to ACORN offices. The offices they visited were established to provide tax advice to the poor as well as guidance through government red tape. In an undisclosed number of cities, O'Keefe and Giles, the latter dressed in her best blaxploitation approximation of hooker attire, requested advice from ACORN in setting up a local prostitution business. (Although Giles and his conservative media allies later did their best to hide this fact, he did not dress as a pimp while visiting the ACORN offices; rather, he dressed like a preppy college student—in slacks and a buttoned-down shirt.[3]) The brothel, they sometimes explained to staffers of various degrees of credulity and interest, would employ underage girls from Central America. In several cities, ACORN staffers passively and actively obliged their requests for help. In other cities, ACORN staffers refused, rebuked, and even mocked the requests.[4]

The duo posted the first recording of these encounters on September 10 at BigGovernment.com, a new Web site founded by conservative media entrepreneur Andrew Breitbart. The edited footage captured a couple of vacant-eyed ACORN staffers in Baltimore nonchalantly offering to help O'Keefe and Giles. Throughout the next week, four videos with similar content were posted on the site and covered extensively on leading conservative Web sites, AM talk radio, and Fox News.

By the time the videos became a sensation on the right, Glenn Beck was well known for his own personal crusade against ACORN. Indeed, it had been a dominant motif of his broadcasts since the 2008 election. That winter and the following spring, he had welcomed ACORN whistle-blowers onto *Glenn Beck* and compared their concern for fiscal irregularities within the organization to the efforts of civil rights heroine Rosa Parks.

Weeks before the video scandal, Beck discussed ACORN with California Republican congressman Darrell Issa, a member of the House Oversight and Government Affairs Committee who is also the richest man in the House; his private fortune is estimated at $250 million. Issa was on *Glenn Beck* because he had just released a report that recycled the conservative talking points against ACORN. It was titled "Is ACORN Intentionally Structured as a Criminal Enterprise?"* Beck's show was an ideal setting in which to break the story of Issa's report, whose title reflected Beck's own modus operandi of smear and innuendo cloaked within a pose of "just asking questions." It was also the summation of the Republican Party's sustained five-year attack on ACORN, which had consisted largely of exaggerations and lies regarding alleged voter fraud.

Because of his proven record of dedication to the anti-ACORN cause, Beck was invited in on the video scandal. Breitbart threw Beck a crumb compared to what Hannity received, but it was better than nothing. On September 15, Giles appeared on *The Glenn Beck Program* and debuted fresh audio clips from her conversation with ACORN staffers in San Bernardino, California. Beck welcomed Giles as an "American hero" and urged his audience to contact their local newspaper editors and demand coverage of the videos.

By then, such efforts were no longer necessary. When Giles appeared on Beck's radio show, the story had already leaped from AM radio and Fox News to the wider media world. The wheels were also in motion in Washington, where Republican members of Congress were spearheading efforts to sever each of ACORN's tenuous ties to the government.

This they accomplished with astonishing speed. On September 11, the U.S. Census Bureau, which had recruited ACORN to help with outreach during the 2010 census, rescinded its invitation. On September 14 and 17, respectively, the Senate and the House passed the Defund ACORN Act, which canceled all present and future federal grants and

---

*The answer to Issa's question, according to the nonpartisan Congressional Research Service, is no. In a report released in December 2009, the CRR concluded that the various accusations against ACORN—including alleged "voter fraud"—are bogus. Its findings, ignored by Glenn Beck, were clear. In no instance did individuals who were allegedly improperly registered to vote by ACORN or its employees "attempt to vote at the polls." Nor could the CRR find instances in which ACORN "violated the terms of federal funding in the last five years."

contracts, most of which went to ACORN's Housing Corporation for home-ownership counseling.

On September 23, the IRS dropped ACORN from its tax-assistance program. (For years, ACORN had provided an antipoverty program for the working poor: free tax advice to low-income families so they could get the benefits from the Earned Income Tax Credit. ACORN's work put millions of dollars in the pockets of low-income families.) Finally, adding insult to injury, on September 24 the Treasury Department singled out ACORN by name while announcing a probe into the government's oversight of tax-exempt organizations.

ACORN's abandonment by Washington's political class was startlingly swift. But the damage to ACORN didn't stop at the banks of the Potomac. In the weeks and months after the video scandal, ACORN lost most of its funding from national foundations. It was forced to lay off much of its national staff and close chapter offices around the country. This rapid attenuation should have ended the conservative myth of an all-powerful ACORN. It is telling that it did not.

Even after achieving the goal of totally isolating and defunding their target, the critics on the right continued to ratchet up their attacks. The Republicans who had opposed the use of a special prosecutor to investigate torture and illegal detainment now called for one against ACORN. Breitbart rolled out new videos during September and October, which Fox News aired with relish. In November, Breitbart demanded that Attorney General Eric Holder launch a probe into the organization. If he didn't, Breitbart threatened to release more video timed to the 2010 midterm elections, with the aim of hurting Democratic prospects.[5]

A foreign observer might have thought that ACORN posed an existential national security threat. But those familiar with the right's long siege on the organization weren't surprised when the pile-on continued into autumn. Conservatives had been trying to destroy ACORN since long before its hourly-wage staffers were caught on tape offering to assist in illegal activity. If the conservative critics couldn't destroy ACORN, they sought to make it into an outsized monster whose shadow could play tricks on the public mind. These tricks were nowhere as effective as among the conservative grass roots, which since the 2004 election had been trained to see ACORN as the left's rampaging golem, wrecking precious liberty with every thunderous step.

By the time the first Giles-O'Keefe videos were released, anti-ACORN hysteria on the right had reached new and ever more hallucinatory heights. The phantom menace was seen as wreaking havoc even in areas of the country where ACORN was inactive, such as rural communities on the Canadian border. Two months after the passage of the Defund ACORN Act, Conservative Party congressional candidate Douglas Hoffman blamed ACORN for his off-year loss in a Republican-leaning farming district in upstate New York. A decade earlier, Hoffman's accusation would have fallen flat, but in 2009 it resonated. On the anniversary of Barack Obama's decisive victory over John McCain, a national poll found that a majority of Republicans believed that ACORN "stole" the 2008 presidential election.[6]

It wasn't just ACORN that stole the election, in this view. The conservative campaign against ACORN has always been about more than just one organization. No conservative commentator has been more up front about this than Beck. "This isn't just an ACORN scandal," Beck told his radio audience on September 15. "This is about the whole philosophy behind community organizing."

Truer words had never been spoken into the host's microphone. But Beck's honesty raised the question of what he meant by "the whole philosophy behind community organizing." What philosophy? And more to the point, given Beck's own well-known forays into conservative community organizing, whose communities?

Before the 2008 Republican National Convention, few Americans knew anything about the world of urban community organizing. They didn't know much about it after the convention, either. But if the convention had a dominant theme other than John McCain's suffering inside a North Vietnamese prison, it was the attack on community organizing. And that theme was always designed to raise suspicions, not enlighten.

During the buildup to McCain's acceptance speech on September 4, speaker after speaker invoked Barack Obama's past as a community organizer on the South Side of Chicago. They cited this experience as reason enough to distrust him with executive powers. On the night that Sarah Palin was introduced to the country, George Pataki, Rudy Giuliani, and the vice-presidential candidate each took to the podium and mocked the very idea of community organizing. When Palin sneeringly compared community organizing unfavorably with the job of small-town Alaskan mayor, the Republican audience clapped, hooted, and hollered.

The attacks had obviously been coordinated; their purpose was transparent.[7] The strategy bore the smudgy fingerprints of former Republican operative and current Fox News chief Roger Ailes, who more than anyone else pioneered the GOP strategy of using the spectre of inner-city blacks to stoke white suburban fear, anxiety, and resentment. In St. Paul, the Republicans erected an enormous framework, to be used in the campaign to follow, in which urban community organizing stood opposed to "real work" done by "real Americans" in places like suburban Ohio and rural Alaska.

The GOP first used ACORN as a proxy—for cities, for blacks, for "socialism"—in 2004. During John Kerry's attempt to unseat George W. Bush, the Republicans grew increasingly alarmed by ACORN's voter registration efforts in key battleground states such as Ohio, New Mexico, and Florida. By registering tens of thousands of poor and working-poor first-time voters, most of whom were likely to vote Democratic, ACORN threatened to tip the electoral scales. The Republicans answered this threat with smears and frivolous legal efforts to stop ACORN's work.

Throughout September and October, the chairman of the Bush-Cheney campaign called for an investigation into allegations of voter fraud against the organization. According to the Bush campaign, ACORN threatened to "ultimately paralyze the effective ability of Americans to be able to vote in the next election."[8]

It was a curious attack line coming from the party that had recently been caught illegally scrubbing the names of blacks from voter lists in Florida. As detailed in a 2007 report by Project Vote, the Republican Party has long engaged in systematic attempts to limit and challenge the voting rights of some Americans: almost always those who are poor and black. This is often done through the passage of so-called ballot-security measures implemented for the purposes of compiling challenge lists, a technique known as *voter caging*. Sometimes it is done through more direct means, such as robo-calls, direct mail, and bogus lawsuits designed to frighten and intimidate.[9] In 2004, just as the GOP released its ACORN voting-fraud meme, a report for the Center for Voting Rights and Protection chronicled in damning detail the GOP's long history of using ballot-security programs that "almost exclusively target heavily black, Latino, or Indian voting precincts."[10]

The GOP's campaign against ACORN, often repeated uncritically by the major media, used the term *voter fraud*—an extremely rare crime for which ACORN could be held responsible if caught engaging in it—to describe the very different phenomenon of *attempted voter registration fraud*. The latter is not a crime and did not implicate ACORN as long as ACORN officials alerted election authorities, which they consistently did. According to Lorraine C. Minnite, a scholar of voter fraud at Columbia University, records show that only twenty-four people were convicted of or pleaded guilty to illegal voting between 2002 and 2005, an average of eight people a year. More Americans were struck by lightning.

The absence of substantiated reports of voter fraud did not stop the GOP from describing ACORN in apocalyptic terms. The organization, according to the Republican mantra in 2004, was in the midst of waging a war on the pillars of American democracy that threatened to turn the country into a banana republic. Fox News led the charge, reporting allegations of voter fraud while flashing images of black ACORN employees. The purpose, it seemed, was to set up a "blacks stole the election" narrative in the event that Bush lost.

"The reports of voter fraud in Ohio are some of the most alarming in the nation," Republican National Committee Chairman Ed Gillespie said two weeks before Election Day. In the key swing state of Florida, Governor Jeb Bush launched a statewide probe into voter registration fraud that singled out ACORN's Florida office, which had registered more than two hundred thousand new voters, many of whom had been illegally denied the right to vote in 2000. Republican officials raised similar concerns across the country. In some cases, Republican officials took action. One month before the election, New Mexico's attorney general raided ACORN's offices and confiscated its computers and files.

Conservative outlets kept the ACORN story warm and ready for use in the run-up to the midterm elections of 2006, during which Republican politicians again challenged and attempted to obstruct ACORN's voter registration efforts. Behind the scenes, Bush adviser Karl Rove guided the Justice Department as it pressured Republican attorneys general to investigate and indict ACORN, regardless of the evidence. Those who refused to play along were fired.

Best known among those who were fired is David Iglesias, the Bush-appointed U.S. attorney in New Mexico. After forming a task force and investigating dozens of allegations of voter fraud, he found them baseless. When he failed to issue a politically motivated indictment against ACORN, he was replaced. The firing of Iglesias and others eventually led to Alberto Gonzales's forced resignation as U.S. attorney general.

ACORN reemerged as a story during the 2008 presidential election. The more the McCain campaign floundered, the more desperately it attempted to connect Obama to ACORN and an image of inner-city lawlessness based almost entirely on imaginary charges of voter fraud. In mid-October, the McCain campaign pushed a heavy flurry of horror stories about ACORN. The allegations served a twofold purpose: to distract voters from bad economic news, and to shift the blame for the financial crisis away from unregulated Wall Street firms and toward ACORN and the urban poor.

The plan met with some success: more than 60 percent of all stories about ACORN since 2007 appeared in the month of October 2008.[11] The centerpiece of the GOP's all-out offensive was a McCain campaign Web ad titled simply "ACORN." In the ad, a voiceover rehashes Obama's history of working with ACORN's Chicago branch, then asks, "What did ACORN in Chicago engage in? Bullying banks. Intimidation tactics. Disruption of business. ACORN forced banks to issue risky home loans. The same types of loans that caused the financial crisis we're in today."

The effort may have hurt ACORN's public image, but it failed to win McCain an advantage in the polls. On the day of the final presidential debate, October 15, McCain trailed, despite Obama's well-known past as a community organizer. Still, the McCain campaign refused to give up faith that ACORN was the campaign's silver bullet. ACORN, McCain declared during the debate, "is now on the verge of maybe perpetrating one of the greatest frauds in voter history in this country, maybe destroying the fabric of democracy."

McCain's nationally televised last-ditch attempt again failed to move the polls. It succeeded, however, in pouring fuel on conservative anger toward ACORN. The next day, eighty-seven ACORN offices around the country reported receiving hundreds of hostile e-mails, many of them containing racial slurs. After the ACORN offices in Seattle and Boston were vandalized, the FBI stepped in. "We believe that these are specifically McCain supporters," an FBI official told McClatchy Newspapers.[12]

As ACORN hysteria on the Right reached a boiling point, conservative commentators kept up the heat. Among them was Beck, then airing his final episodes on Headline News. Two weeks before the November 4 election, Beck spoke as if ACORN had already stolen both the election and "his" country.

"When did we lose our country?" he asked on October 14 during a segment focused on ACORN. "It has been taken over by thieves and criminals and socialists and Marxists and God only knows what."

Not even its staunchest defenders would argue that ACORN is a well-managed organization. This is partly by design and partly by necessity. A shoestring national operation, ACORN has put almost all its funds into organizers, researchers, and people who provide counseling on tax and housing problems. Little of its budget has gone into management. Indeed, its success has been due to a conscious decision to favor growth and local control over hierarchy and oversight. It has sometimes failed to live up to its own ideals, such as when the National Labor Relations Board ruled in 2003 that ACORN had underpaid its workers and subjected them to unsafe working conditions. There have also been fiscal irregularities. Temporary part-time canvassers have in many instances attempted to scam ACORN by turning in scores of false registration forms across the country.

Yet even the fullest accounting of ACORN's shortcomings and misdemeanors cannot account for the disproportionate energy that the Republican Party and conservative media have spent attacking the organization. Despite its rapid growth in forty years, ACORN remains a comparatively powerless organization compared to major business and labor groups. Its successes against powerful opponents such as banks and corporations have won incremental improvements in the lives of poor people. As proven by the rapid bipartisan passage of the Defund ACORN Act, it carries zero clout in Washington. As a gobbler of state largesse, it barely registers: it has received a little more than $50 million in federal funding in fifteen years.

For more than three decades, the national media ignored ACORN. Between its birth in 1970 and its profile in the 2004 election, ACORN was never considered an interesting national story. Although the community-organizing group traces its lineage to the civil rights movement of the 1950s and 1960s, its work is generally devoid of high-impact media spectacle. It does not organize massive gatherings or promote national leaders, and it focuses on local fights instead of sweeping, era-defining federal legislation. In its style and its program, ACORN shares more in common with the welfare-rights movement. Most of ACORN's work consists of backroom dealing, red-tape clearing, and pavement pounding in low-income communities of color. Moreover, its activities are too diffuse for any one convenient handle. So the national media for a long time treated ACORN like everything else happening in America's inner cities: they ignored it.[13]

Not everyone enjoyed the luxury of being able to ignore ACORN, however. As it grew in size and effectiveness, it became well known to politicians, civic leaders, and business leaders who worked in the same communities. Although Rudy Giuliani and John McCain later claimed ignorance about and contempt for the organization, both men have in the past spoken at ACORN events or praised the organization for its work in their backyards. Local businesspeople grew to understand ACORN as a force to be partnered or reckoned with on a range of issues affecting the lives of the urban poor, including predatory banking, the redlining of poor communities, minimum wages, and tenant rights.

As long as ACORN agitated locally, they made enemies locally. Although it has been making a national impact since the mid-1970s, when it played an instrumental role in the passage of legislation regulating banks in poor neighborhoods,[14] the stories about ACORN remained limited to regional media. This pattern continued to hold even into the late 1990s, when ACORN, by then operating offices in more than a hundred cities, emerged at the forefront of the living-wage movement.

This attempt to bypass federal and state inaction on the minimum wage drew the negative attention of industries that employ low-wage workers, especially food, retail, and hospitality. The conservative think tanks that represent these groups, most notably the D.C.-based Employment Policies Institute (EPI), were the first to mobilize against ACORN on a national scale. In 1996, EPI launched a Web site called RottenACORN.com.

Aside from its specific agenda, the threat that ACORN posed to conservative interests was more diffuse. For decades it has served as an incubator for and an influence on a new generation of progressives, including a young Barack Obama, who worked with ACORN on the South Side of Chicago in the 1980s.

"Like the United Farm Workers in the past, ACORN has become a school for organizers for the wider progressive movement," says Peter Dreier, the director of the urban and environmental policy program at Occidental College. "In its forty years it has trained hundreds of organizers who have gone on to start other organizations or do other effective progressive political work, including with unions but with many other kinds of groups. Its overall influence on progressive politics is enormous because of the many people it trained and inspired over the years."

Combined with its voter registration efforts, this made ACORN—powerless by most conventional measures—a formidable enemy to those who take a narrower view of American democracy.

Beck's first major attack on ACORN came in the context of the financial crisis of 2008. Joining his fellow conservative commentators, he blamed the banking collapse on a piece of legislation for which ACORN successfully agitated during the Carter administration. Passed in 1977, the Community Reinvestment Act (CRA) cracked down on racism in lending, required banks to lend in low-income neighborhoods where they took deposits, and forced government mortgage insurers to reduce minimum loan requirements. In 1986, ACORN created the ACORN Housing Corporation to work with banks and assist first-time home buyers.

During the 2004 GOP convention, numerous speakers bragged about the Bush administration's role in expanding poor and minority home ownership to "all-time highs," despite the administration's weakening of the CRA. In 2008, minority and low-income home buyers were the GOP's favored villains. The McCain campaign led the way with an ad that juxtaposed Freddie Raines, the black former head of Fannie Mae—who had nothing to do with the Obama campaign—with an elderly white woman meant to symbolize the crisis's victims. The ad asked: "Obama and his liberal allies? Mum on the market crisis."

Beck was less interested in the intricacies of the crisis on Wall Street than the poor, mostly minority people who bought homes for the first time after the Bush administration's weakening of the CRA. "You're going to understand who is responsible for this credit crunch and this credit crisis, and you ain't gonna like the answer," he told his radio audience on September 18, 2008. "The Community Reinvestment Act. It was started, it was a 'feel-good' measure, back in the 1970s, and Jimmy Carter started it."

The problems with Beck's echo of the latest GOP talking point were by then well known. It was less the CRA that caused the crisis than the lack of regulation of Wall Street (and of the CRA, which led to better-performing loans than those untouched by the "feel-good" legislation). Not even the lenders tried to blame the long-hated CRA for the crisis. In the business press, which was never a fan of the CRA, the speciousness of the argument was freely admitted.

"The idea that a lending crisis created from 2004 to 2007 was caused by a 1977 law is silly," noted a *BusinessWeek* writer. "But it's even more ridiculous when you consider that most subprime loans were made by firms that aren't subject to the CRA."[15]

Writing in *Barron's*, Barry L. Ritholtz, who heads the Wall Street research firm Fusion IQ, listed the widely accepted causes of the crash without mention of the CRA. "We used excessive leverage, failed to maintain adequate capital, engaged in reckless speculation, created new complex derivatives," he wrote. "We focused on short-term profits at the expense of sustainability. We not only undermined our own firms, we destabilized the financial sector and roiled the global economy, to boot."[16]

None of this concerned Beck. On his shows, poor black people caused the crash, period. They were enabled by bipartisan "feel-good" legislation enforced by ACORN's protest-happy "thugs."

When Beck began to discuss ACORN on a regular basis in 2009, he switched tracks along with the rest of the conservative train and began to focus on ACORN "corruption." The numbers, however, have never been kind to conservative claims of epic ACORN corruption, any more than they have been to the claims that ACORN caused the financial crisis. In the wake of the video scandal, the organization's few political defenders easily exposed the sham furor about ACORN corruption with a few statistical comparisons. Florida congressman Alan Grayson, for example, noted that Halliburton's criminal misconduct while contracting with the Pentagon is measured in billions of tax dollars, compared to ACORN's $53 million in total federal funding. Every dime ACORN received from the government, noted Grayson, "is roughly equal to what the taxpayer paid to Halliburton each day during the war in Iraq."[17]

It wasn't necessary to go back even that far. The very month that Congress pulled ACORN's funding, pharmaceutical giant Pfizer was fined $2.3 billion to settle criminal and civil cases with the government, including Medicaid fraud. Yet no groundswell of support emerged behind a Defund Pfizer movement in Congress. Beck was likewise untroubled by Pfizer's actions and saved his wrath for ACORN's "thieves and criminals and socialists and Marxists and God only knows what."

Just as Van Jones topped the list of most mentioned individual targets during Beck's first six months on Fox, ACORN was the most frequently mentioned organization, garnering 1,224 mentions (Al Qaeda, in comparison, netted 50 mentions).[18] The media watchdog group Media Matters for America has calculated that even in the absence of charges against ACORN, Beck was approximately thirty-five times more likely to discuss the organization than he was any of the military contractors convicted of billion-dollar fraud, extortion, and murder. He was also twenty-four times more likely to discuss ACORN than to talk about convicted Republican felons such as Jack Abramoff and Bob Ney.

What distinguishes Beck's ACORN attacks from those of his Fox News colleagues is his honesty. He readily admits that his real problem is not with corruption, or even ACORN. Rather, it is the whole philosophy of social justice.

For its conservative enemies, social justice is a villain best kept in the abstract and in caricature. The real-world results of social justice struggles, once achieved, quickly become popular and politically incontestable. In the last century, the battles that have been fought under the banner of social justice include the universal franchise, the minimum wage, Social Security, the progressive income tax, and desegregation.

Faced with the prospect of further popular policies that increase social and economic justice, the modern Right has sought to defeat them by playing on racial fears and resentments. In 1964, Barry Goldwater spoke in favor of "states rights" and against "social activism." Four years later, Richard Nixon used code words for inner-city violence in his campaign against Lyndon Johnson's Great Society (and third-party candidate George Wallace's more overt racist appeals). In the 1980s, Ronald Reagan spoke of "Cadillac-driving welfare queens," a car associated with inner-city pimps and hustlers, even though no such specimen existed and most recipients of social welfare benefits for the poor are white.

This is the tradition Beck represents when he attacks ACORN and groups associated with social justice, as well as when he describes health-care reform and green jobs as "stealth reparations." He understands intuitively what polling data prove: many whites are more likely to oppose social welfare policies if they think they will disproportionately benefit poor blacks, whom conservatives subtly but systematically depict as lazy and undeserving of funds provided by "hardworking" taxpayers. Scholars have given this various names, including "symbolic racism," "laissez-faire racism," and "racism in drag."[19]

Beck is a bold "symbolic racist." Before and after the 2008 election, his attacks on Barack Obama and his moderately progressive policies were frequently matched with images of urban blacks. Sometimes he doesn't even pretend to be doing otherwise. On October 8, 2009, he warned the listeners of *The Glenn Beck Program* to beware of not just ACORN but any group that shares its mission of social justice. In the process, Beck leapt a little too quickly from ACORN to the previous year's conservative racial panic button, the Reverend Jeremiah Wright. Follow the bouncing ball of Beckian logic:

> Whenever you see something that says something about a "strong democratic movement" or "strengthening democracy," you're in trouble. If you see anything that talks about social or economic justice, you're in trouble. When you see those words, run. Because social justice is what Jeremiah Wright preaches. Run. And don't listen to anyone who is telling you differently.

In conflating the forces of "social and economic justice" with Jeremiah Wright, Beck was merely recycling his battle-tested Van Jones strategy.

For Beck and for certain far-right members of his audience, there is more at work than just garden-variety white suburban anxiety and resentment. Within the apocalyptic conservative tradition embodied by Beck, there has long existed paranoia that urban gangs would one day be sent inland from the coasts to form the shock troops of the "One World Government," the ultimate right-wing conspiratorial bogeyman. In the mid-1960s, members of the Utah branch of the John Birch Society created panic in Salt Lake City with rumors of an impending invasion of "black militants." Three decades later, at the height of the Clinton-era militia movement, the Senate Judiciary Committee held hearings in which militia members shared their belief that "urban street gangs" would be part of the "New World Order" invasion force sent to disarm the "Patriots."[20]

The right wing's New World Order paranoia is a snug fit with its conspiratorial view of ACORN. When Congress passed the Serve America Act in March 2009, the hard Right honed in on ACORN's "eligibility" for the act's funds. "Both the House and Senate bills are designed to funnel money to a semi-militarized wing of the Democrat Party," wrote the conservative blogger Doug Ross. "ACORN appears to be at the center of this wing."[21]

Beck went one step further, asking whether Obama's "civilian service army" might involve not just ACORN but all sorts of shadowy collections of urban youth. In a memorable television segment on August 27, 2009, Beck segued from the Serve America Act to a series of visual non sequiturs showing organized black American youth: Black Panthers standing in front of a polling station, Louis Farrakhan addressing his congregation, and, most bizarre of all, a room full of unidentified young black men engaged in pseudo-military calisthenics. "Because of Barack Obama," one of the boys declares with menace, "I'm going to be a lawyer."

What did this last clip of young aspiring lawyers mean? What was its provenance? Beck didn't know. But like Richard Dreyfuss playing with a pile of mashed potatoes in *Close Encounters of the Third Kind*, he knew it must hold some sort of key. "We've been looking for two weeks for connections on this [group of exercising black kids], but we can't find anything," explained Beck. "I'm not suggesting the president of the United States has anything to do with these groups."

Then why show the images? Why point out that there are militant-looking black Americans who support the president?

He wasn't sure, but something in Beck's gut told him that these images held enormous explanatory power. According to Beck, the images proved that militant black groups had "infected the system" and threatened "our" freedom. Black Panthers. Communists. Community organizers. "This is the new Democratic Party," he explained. "It is not the Democratic Party of your father and [your] grandfather."

That Democratic Party was, of course, the Democratic Party of the New Deal and the Great Society. But Beck's grasp of history has always fallen far short of his reach. In his mind, a plague is ravaging the land as never before—the plague of "social justice." As Beck routinely explains it to his audience, ACORN is a carrier of this plague, but it is just one of many carriers. Like the people ACORN serves, social justice will still be a threat even after ACORN is vanquished once and for all.

The financial crisis of 2008 and ACORN's response to it threw a spotlight on the central paradox of Beck's faux-populist demagoguery. Beck's politics required that he simultaneously indulge in contradictory impulses: bash the greedy investors and bankers, and bash the social justice groups that were seeking to hold accountable those who were responsible for the crisis.

After initially criticizing the Bush bailouts for not being big enough, Beck quickly corrected course. By the time he arrived at Fox News in January 2009, he was arguing that troubled Wall Street firms should be allowed to fail and that the creative destruction of capitalism be allowed to follow its natural progression. Yet his antiregulation ideology and gut-level disgust with true economic populism stopped him from joining those "street social justice organizers" who were actually doing the hard and thankless work of trying to hold the guilty (and powerful) responsible.

Beck's populist response to the crisis always had a forced feeling to it. His true loyalties were apparent in the disproportionate anger he directed at ACORN, Freddie Mac, and Fannie Mae, rather than at AIG, Goldman Sachs, and Lehman Brothers. He released much more fire at the Democrats' stimulus bill (which saved the jobs of teachers and firemen) than at the Bush bailouts (which kept investment bankers employed and rolling in bonus cash), despite their roughly equal price tags. Nor was Beck very concerned with new regulations proposed by the liberal members of Congress. After briefly examining how Goldman Sachs had used its clout to game the system and bilk taxpayers, Beck fled the subject, never to return. He preferred to attack financial institutions in the abstract, with passing references to "Wall Street." He reserved vicious personalized attacks, not to mention serious research, for Van Jones, ACORN, and union leaders.

Beck's faux populism evaporated the instant the White House and community organizers became the face of accountability. When the White House proposed restricting the use of taxpayer money to fund AIG bonuses, Beck screamed "mob rule." Even in a crisis, he argued, contracts are sacrosanct. Under no circumstances could the government step in to "void legally binding contracts."[22]

But that was true of only some contracts. Beck did not extend the same sanctity to the contract held by the United Auto Workers (UAW). He fully supported the voiding of the UAW contract after GM's bailout. A month before rising to the defense of million-dollar corporate bonuses, Beck had devoted a segment to attacking the union with disinformation, claiming that the average UAW member earned $154 an hour, including benefits, when the real number was just a little over $50.[23]

When ACORN emerged in the debate over executive bonuses, Beck's elitist sympathies barreled even more powerfully to the fore.

One Saturday afternoon in late March, the ACORN-affiliated Connecticut Working Families Party organized a protest of taxpayer-funded AIG bonuses. The protest took the form of a bus tour of the tony suburbs of Fairfield, Connecticut, in which some AIG executives lived. Involving about forty protesters, the event was dubbed "Lifestyles of the Rich and Infamous." The idea was to highlight the lavish lifestyles of those who had brought the economy to ruin by trading wildly in mortgage-backed derivatives, then requested federal assistance to bail themselves out, and were now receiving lavish bonuses on the taxpayers' dime. The organizers delivered letters of protest to the manicured, guarded homes of two leading AIG executives, then joined an ACORN-organized rally outside the Wilton, Connecticut, offices of AIG's Financial Products Division, the closest thing the financial crisis had to a crime scene.

Beck, who himself lives in a lavish suburban Connecticut mansion, was horrified. His narrative of Wall Street greed suddenly became one of Wall Street persecution. ACORN's direct-action protest, he asserted, was another sign of encroaching fascism. He condemned the bus tour as an example of "fake populist anger" being directed at "faceless bonus recipients"—as if the whole point of the tour was not to put faces on the recipients.

On the Monday after the tour, Beck invited former Bush media representative Mark McKinnon onto Fox to join him in venting against the protest. The two men discussed what they called a "dirty little secret": that ACORN and the Service Employees International Union (SEIU) had organized the "rent-a-mobs." In fact, it was no secret at all who the organizers were, but Beck described the event conspiratorially, flashing images of protesting ACORN members, most of whom were black.[24]

The well-known relationship between ACORN and the SEIU—two of the largest and most influential mass-based groups working to improve the lives of poor and working Americans—was a revelation for Beck. In the following months, he would place the ACORN-SEIU nexus at the root of what he called the "tree of radicalism and revolution."

Unveiled in September, Beck's revolution tree was presented as a sort of grand unifying theory of progressive politics. The time line covered by the tree was familiar territory for Beck's audience. The seed was planted under Woodrow Wilson, it was watered by Saul Alinsky, and it achieved maturity with the ACORN-SEIU alliance, which Beck believed now threatened the republic.

One important stage in this tree's development, Beck believes, is the so-called Cloward-Piven Strategy. The name comes from a 1966 *Nation* magazine article written by a husband-and-wife team of Columbia professors, Richard Cloward and Frances Fox Piven. In the article, the authors lay out a plan to "overload" the welfare system as a way to encourage the establishment of a guaranteed national income. The National Welfare Rights Organization (NWRO), which Piven and Cloward helped to found, adopted the strategy. And while there was an ACORN connection—ACORN's founder, Wade Rathke, had been an NWRO organizer—the Cloward-Piven Strategy was more of a Great Society relic than a living idea when one of Beck's most reliable conservative defenders, David Horowitz, resuscitated the strategy in the contemporary context of the conservative march against ACORN.

Like Beck, Horowitz is a fan of imagined master plans and progressive plots. Through his Web site, DiscovertheNetworks.org, Horowitz—a onetime radical leftist who now makes his home on the radical Right—has done much to give shape to Beck's postelection theories, including the idea that ACORN and the SEIU are stealthily trying to implement

Cloward and Piven's plan to overload the electoral system and pave the way for socialism. As described on Horowitz's site:

> The new "voting rights" coalition combines mass voter registration drives—typically featuring high levels of fraud—with systematic intimidation of election officials in the form of frivolous lawsuits, unfounded charges of "racism" and "disenfranchisement," and "direct action" (street protests, violent or otherwise). Just as they swamped America's welfare offices in the 1960s, Cloward-Piven devotees now seek to overwhelm the nation's understaffed and poorly policed electoral system. Their tactics set the stage for the Florida recount crisis of 2000, and have introduced a level of fear, tension and foreboding to U.S. elections heretofore encountered mainly in Third World countries.

Listening to Horowitz and his hand puppet Beck, you'd think that Cloward and Piven are the Lenin and Trotsky of the modern Left. Cloward died in relative obscurity in 2001. Piven still teaches sociology at the City University of New York, but she would have a hard time getting a cover story in the *Nation* these days. Her name barely comes up in the archives of the country's leading progressive online and print publications. Her biggest practical legacy is probably the "motor-voter bill" of 1993, which allows Americans to register to vote while renewing a driver's license. Even in the 1960s, the goal of her most radical writing was the eradication of urban poverty according to the stated goals of the Johnson administration, done in a way that shifted state spending more than it created it—using federal assistance to remove the burden from the cities and the states.

For Beck, ACORN carries the flame of his confused understanding and overblown fear of the Cloward-Piven strategy. And through their ties to ACORN, so does every other group in the progressive constellation. This is especially true of the SEIU. ACORN and the SEIU form the most dangerous branches in Beck's giant radical tree, which threatens the Constitution like the giant demonic oak that grabs Toto in Frank L. Baum's *The Wizard of Oz*.

In Beck's fevered mind, the connections among ACORN, the SEIU, progressive funding networks, and joint projects like the Apollo Alliance are secret maps to a communist takeover. In reality, they are no more secret than are the ties among some corporations, right-wing foundations, Republican donors, and conservative think tanks—or between the Employment Policy Institute and RottenACORN.com, and Americans for Prosperity and Glenn Beck.

But Beck is dealing with a Democratic administration for the first time since his political awakening in 2001. For him, everything is a revelation. Here's Beck in a typical rush of connect-the-dots discovery:

> The Apollo Alliance, OK—oh, look, it's ACORN. ACORN founder Wade Rathke is former chairman of Tides Center. That's weird. Rathke was on the Tides board! ACORN, Tides, Apollo, Van Jones, Jeff Jones, Weather Underground—uh-oh. But the good news is there's no funny business going on here. [George] Soros gives money to Health Care for America Now, which is weird because the two organizations that are doing that are ACORN and SEIU. We already know about ACORN . . . Wow! It's almost like these three are all connected. Isn't that weird?[25]

Actually, no, it's not weird at all. At least, it's not for anyone who possesses more than a child's understanding of Democratic coalition politics. Much "weirder" than George Soros's funding of a health-care reform initiative is the fact that a national media figure thinks that Jeremiah Wright and the Weather Underground have anything to do with the Apollo Alliance, which began as a joint attempt by the United Steelworkers and the Sierra Club to reduce U.S. reliance on foreign oil and revive the country's manufacturing base.

Weirder still is the fact that Beck has successfully grown a mass following while stumbling through a remedial self-education in U.S. democracy, which reflects the carnival mirrors inside his mind as much as it does the reality he struggles, in ever-so profitable futility and desperation, to comprehend.

11

Brother Beck Presents: Mormon Masterpiece Theater

Every July 4, Glenn Beck emcees the Stadium of Fire celebration in Provo, Utah. The patriotic extravaganza is the most elaborate Independence Day celebration in the country, drawing more than fifty thousand people to Brigham Young University's LaVell Edwards Stadium for a program of family music, star-spangled speeches, military displays, and a magnificent array of fireworks. Sponsored by the conservative Mormon group Freedom Festival, the Stadium of Fire is the closest thing in the country to an institutionalized Rally for America. It is not surprising, then, that this is among the high points of Beck's calendar year. "There's nothing like Utah on the Fourth of July," he likes to say.

The Jonas Brothers were the biggest commercial act on the 2009 Stadium of Fire program, but the chaste Disney boy band didn't headline. That honor went to an enormous American flag, 155 feet by 90 feet, which was ritually burned during the show's climax. It was Beck's job as emcee to narrate the rite as it was carried out according to an elaborate official protocol. When a cauldronlike container at the center of the field was set afire, an emotional Beck declared, "If our American flag could speak, oh, the stories she would tell." With those words, the Stadium of Fire became a Coliseum of Crying. "Many people teared up," reported the *Deseret News*, "including event emcee Glenn Beck, who emphasized to the audience what a special ceremony they were witnessing."[1]

Except that they weren't. A few days later, Provo's fire chief admitted that the nylon flag had not, in fact, been burned, as the crowd was led to believe. Because of safety concerns, a less volatile material had been quietly substituted for the flag in the giant cauldron. Like the emcee's famous tears, Provo's patriotic inferno was not what it seemed.

If people know one thing about Glenn Beck, it is that he cries. He is the Crying Conservative. Alone among cable news and talk-radio personalities, he frequently chokes up, quivers his lips, wipes his eye, and holds tortured misty pauses until he can hold them no more. For more than a decade, Beck has been crying on the radio, on television, on stage, in interviews, and even in scripted commercials. Sometimes the tears are implied; at other times, such as during a 2009 stage performance, he gets into a fetal position on the floor and bawls. But whatever the gradation, he owns the scale. It defines him like nothing else.

This is not an accident. As they were always intended to do, Beck's tears have become a distinctive corporate-brand handle. They mark him clearly from everyone else in the broadcasting industry. When Beck began his career in conservative commentary, the field was thick with tough-guy know-it-alls—from the lace-curtain boor O'Reilly to the cigar-chomping blowhard Limbaugh.

But the cast of the late 1990s was incomplete. It contained no emotional Nancy, no repentant prodigal son, and no needy Twelve Stepper. Beck, a careful student of positional marketing theory since his days in Baltimore, identified and exploited the open niche. He began practicing the act during his transition from Top 40 to talk radio in the late 1990s. According to his Connecticut colleagues, he was known for being both genuinely emotional and able and willing to fake-cry on cue.

"There were definitely times the crying was a tactic," remembers Vinnie Penn, Beck's former cohost in New Haven. "He'd be crying on-air. Then we'd go on commercial break and he'd phone in an order for a bacon-and-egg with cheese. Then we'd come back on-air and the tears would be back." In Tampa, too, he was known for turning on the waterworks for dramatic effect.

The role of Crying Conservative is well suited to Beck's dramatic ambitions and emotional needs. But that alignment doesn't make his execution of the character any less cynical. Sometimes Beck's use of tears is so patently faked that it's funny; at other times, it's just nauseating. The best example of the latter is the time that Beck Freudian-slipped while choking up over the tragedy of someone else's missing child. "Two years ago," Beck said somberly one night early in his Fox News tenure, "I made the father a promise that I would not let this story dry—er, *die* . . . ."[2]

Beck's tears are low-hanging fruit for parody, which no Beck hater can resist. It didn't take long, however, to figure out that Beck was laughing the hardest of all, in the back seat of his limo. The trailers for Beck's stage shows tout the star as "America's favorite hysterical, fear-mongering, TV and radio crybaby." The back cover of his best-selling book, *Arguing with Idiots*, shows the author pointing to a juicy tear on his right cheek, as if to say, "Make fun of me all you want, you fools. Please, don't stop."

Then there is the July 2009 *GQ* photo shoot in which Beck applied Tiger Balm to activate his famous tear ducts. It was from this shoot that the image for his September 2009 *Time* cover was drawn. Beck now uses the image as the screen saver on his office computers.

"It is not whether you really cry," Ingrid Bergman once said. "It's whether the audience thinks you are crying." In Beck's case, it's not whether you really cry. It's whether people are talking about whether you are really crying.

Making a joke of his tears, as he does, is not the same as copping to emotional dishonesty. Beck bristles whenever his crying is used not as joke material but as evidence of a larger, deeper fraudulence. Admitting that he is a charlatan is one bridge that Beck cannot afford to cross, even if his denials often serve to confirm the obvious. "I'm a crybaby. I'm such an easy target. I'm surprised *SNL* [*Saturday Night Live*] hasn't come after me," Beck once told a reporter.[3]

"If you're going to make that case [that he's faking it], I deserve a frickin' Emmy," he said in the same interview. "That's unbelievable act-ing. Do you think that a *grown man* crying on the air is something I wouldn't get hammered *relentlessly* for?"[4]

As Beck knows very well, being hammered relentlessly has its uses. When *SNL* finally did come after Beck, he was thrilled. Heavy attacks by liberals only publicize and reinforce Beck's faux vulnerability among the only people who matter to his business: conservatives who hate liberals.

Beck likes to say that his tears are biologically determined, that he's "90 percent 'chick' in that category."[5] It's a revealing statement, not just for himself but for his more macho peers as well. With his constant crying and effeminate hand gestures, "Glenda" Beck apotheosizes the gender blending that has always been at the heart of right-wing talk radio.

"On talk radio in the 1980s and 1990s," writes Susan Douglas, a media historian at the University of Michigan, "masculinity was constructed as a fusion of traditionally 'male' and 'female' traits. Boys were supposed to be boys, meaning white, heterosexual boys, [but] they were also gender poachers, recuperating masculinity at the end of the century by infusing it with the need to chat, the need to confess insecurities, the need to be hysterical and overwrought about politics, the need to make the personal political."[6]

When it comes to public crying as vaudeville, Beck owes less to universal womanhood than to a very specific brotherhood. He's not stereotypically premenstrual as much as classically Mormon. Like so much else that baffles people about Beck, his approach to public tears has been shaped in the crucible of his adopted faith. It was the lachrymose Latter-Day Saints who turned an amateur crybaby pro.

During the first weekend of October 2009, the Church of Jesus Christ of Latter-Day Saints held its semiannual general conference in Salt Lake City. For two days, church leaders sermonized on the power of the Holy Spirit and railed against pornography, a "potent tool of Lucifer." In turn, the speakers described powerful spiritual experiences in highly personal terms. Throughout the telling, often at similar dramatic moments, many speakers appeared on the verge of being overwhelmed by emotion. Sometimes the emotion broke through. Voices cracked, throats caught, eyes misted over. To the uninitiated, it seemed as if the speakers were all imitating Glenn Beck.

Among the practices that distinguish Mormonism from other forms of Christianity is a highly stylized social ritual known as *bearing testimony.* On the first Sunday of each month, Mormons gather at their local ward house to speak about "what they know to be true." The format is something like a cross between an open-mic poetry slam and an Alcoholics Anonymous meeting. One by one, the congregants give semistructured speeches—testimonies—that deal with a central theme; each one usually lasts no longer than a few minutes. These testimonies, structured like radio monologues, describe the feeling of being overwhelmed by the love of Jesus, of struggling against temptation, and of maintaining full dedication to the restoration of the gospel. As the speakers relive these feelings, it is common for them to emote within circumscribed boundaries.

Because they are such emotional events in which pure feeling trumps argument or rhetoric, some consider the ritual to be the Mormon equivalent of speaking in tongues. The *Encyclopedia of Mormonism* describes it as follows:

> Bearing testimony is based on [the belief] that the power that motivates individuals to live as Christ taught is the power of the Holy Ghost, rather than the power of logic or the eloquence of gospel teachers. . . . This is illustrated by Brigham Young's account of his own conversion when an LDS missionary bore his testimony: "If all the talent, tact, wisdom and refinement of the world had been sent to me with the Book of Mormon, and had declared, in the most exalted of earthly eloquence, the truth of it, undertaking to prove it by learning, and worldly wisdom, they would have been to me like the smoke which arises only to vanish away. But when I saw a man without eloquence, or talents for public speaking, who could only say, 'I know, by the power of the Holy Ghost, that the Book of Mormon is true, that Joseph Smith is a prophet of the Lord,' the Holy Ghost proceeding from that individual illuminated my understanding, and light, glory, and immortality were before me. I was encircled by them, filled with them, and I knew for myself that the testimony of the man was true."[7]

Those who study Mormon rituals and rhetoric say that the fingerprints of bearing testimony can be found all over Beck's public tearfulness. "Beck's ability to 'cry on cue' appears to be a combination of Mormon culture and the practiced delivery of a media professional," says

Daymon M. Smith, a Mormon doctoral candidate in anthropology at the University of Pennsylvania. "He is using Mormon tactics to spread Mormon ideas, such as the gospel of Cleon Skousen, under the cover of secular political revelations."

"Beck's emotional performances are very like Mormon testimonies," agrees David Knowlton, a Mormon cultural anthropologist at Utah Valley University. "Beck has married two rhetorical styles: the quiet, Mormon sense of emotion present during key moments in testimony, and the bombast of more mainstream evangelical performances. Mormons and evangelicals simply do not trust reason to the same degree they trust feeling. George W. Bush also tapped into this with his elevation of gut over mind."

When viewed in the context of Mormon practice, Beck's public crying begins to make more sense. Like his millennialist politics, they cause liberals to laugh but command respect from Mormon and evangelical religious conservatives. This helps to explain the yawning comprehension gap between his religious fans and his secular critics. Secular liberals watch Beck's cheap theatrics and see unmanly, dishonest, and possibly insane behavior. Mormons and like-minded evangelicals, especially Pentecostals, see familiar signposts associated with masculinity, sincerity, and even authority.

"The tears of Mormon men are emblems of sincerity," says Knowlton. "This is the role of light crying from the stand, when one chokes up and may even tear up. Public crying gets more common as one climbs the ladder of church authority. Mormonism praises the man who is able to shed tears as a manifestation of spirituality. Testimony is both a formal genre and a performance of personhood that marks a transition from a mundane to a mystical way of knowing. The emotion involved is a symbol of righteousness."

It is also the ultimate rhetorical punch. "Nothing can silence a Mormon congregation like a voice crack from a speaker," says Brad Kramer, a Mormon anthropologist who writes on Mormon politics and culture. "The testimonial style unites an unquestioning audience, and they too may report feeling, as a sort of divine contagion, the truth of another's testimony."

It is hard to imagine a religion better suited to Beck's emotional needs and personal style than the Church of Latter-Day Saints. Mormonism has institutionalized Beck's favorite mode of speech, the sentimental monologue. It also encourages a certainty of spirit based on self-revelation that lies outside argument, fact, or logic. What Beck does on radio and television is an amped-up version of the testimony ritual: he fervently talks about what he believes—*knows*—is happening, describes the dark secrets he has uncovered, conveys the transcendent importance of these discoveries, and frames it all in a Manichean narrative—America as a battlefield on which God-fearing defenders of liberty face off against evil big-government conspirators.

The way Beck has built his movement and his audience is a microcosm of the method by which the Mormon Church grew into a worldwide religion. Like an earnest young missionary spreading the good word through emotional speeches to confused Latin American villagers, Beck has brought his gut self-revelations to national television and radio, employing emotional intensity overflowing into tears to conquer doubts of his sincerity and prove his access to powerful truths. By asking his viewers to "join him"—in the 9.12 Project, as a "constitutional watchdog," for his 100-year plan—or to "follow him" (as he says at the beginning of each Fox broadcast), he is offering viewers a chance to share in his revelation.

Bear testimony; recruit. Bear testimony; recruit.

On Thursday evening, October 15, 2009, Brother Beck's Mormon Masterpiece Theater treated Fox viewers to an especially memorable production. The one-act performance had no official title, but it quickly became known on liberal blogs as "Glenda Watches a Coke Commercial, Cries, and Goes to a Suburban Keg Party."

Beck began the performance with two well-known television advertisements from the early 1980s: one for Coca-Cola and one for Kodak. The spots represented the first time in weeks that major-brand advertising had been seen on Fox News between 5 and 6 p.m. When Beck's eyes misted over after playing the spots, it seemed that the memory of such advertising was too much for him to take.

Beck was crying for more than just the memory of blue-chip sponsorship. He was crying for the innocent America of 1980 and the great U.S. advertising agencies of that long-lost era, which conceived ads of such power and wholesomeness. Where were the advertising creatives of today who were worthy of standing on the shoulders of these giants?

Not traitorous GEICO with its limey lizard or the proud radicals at Progressive Insurance. (These two companies were among the first to join the advertiser boycott against Beck in August 2009.)

Beck explained that 1980 was "a simpler time" when Americans "were united on some basic things." He asked his audience to join him in remembering what life was like during this simpler time, when *Three's Company* was the biggest show on television, and the top marginal income tax rate was 50 percent. Beck acknowledged that America "has never been a perfect place." Then came a long, choked-up pause, during which Beck appeared to resist the urge to bite his knuckles. He launched into a rambling allegorical tale about how his viewers are a lot like teenagers at a party on a Saturday night, out way past curfew. They smell of weed and booze, but they didn't really do anything wrong. Still, they are going to be in trouble when they get home. They will be grounded and forced to stay in on the following Saturday night.

If Beck were capable of driving his most flummoxed viewers to suicide, this would have done the trick. In the Internet debates the segment sparked, many participants found themselves at a complete loss. "While watching this," wrote one person in a liberal discussion group, "I could almost hear the shotguns being cocked and loaded across the country."

Indeed, there was something about this segment that was fundamentally unanswerable. The sentimentalism of the bit was so cheaply canned, so reflexively narcissistic, and so historically obtuse that it was less a piece of theater than an act of violence. With this bit, Beck's love of vulgar sentimentalism hit terminal freak velocity. Anyone who looked directly into its light was sucked through a vortex and deposited into a strange land where *Free Willy* is *Citizen Kane*, and a sepia-toned Kodak commercial is capable of capturing all that is good and true about an America that never was.

Along with being the teariest form of Christianity, Mormonism has developed maudlin sentimentalism into an art and an industry. Mainstream Mormonism is the closest thing the United States has to a Disney religion, with an orthodox culture that has replaced the tragic sensibility with a masochistic addiction to uplift. The church produces and promotes a steady stream of LDS-approved books, music, and films that form a G-rated Wellbutrin-fueled world unto itself. In this world, the grand Wurlitzer of human experience is reduced to a single-note caricature of the redemption theme.

Like Beck's work in radio, television, stage, and publishing, official Mormon culture is more than aggressively anti-intellectual; it is infantilizing.[8] Those who stray too far outside the sandbox of accepted narratives do not fare well. In 1993, after a brief glasnost period at Brigham Young University, the school purged its faculty of feminists and liberals. Church officials gave speeches naming feminists, intellectuals, and gays and lesbians as the three greatest enemies of the church. Ever since, the BYU faculty has been required, as a condition of employment, to annually renew their endorsements by local ecclesiastical leaders. Beck, so ready to decry imaginary neo-Soviet policies in the U.S. government, is silent about the real neo-Soviet policies within his church.

Before Beck embraced this world, it confused him. In *The Real America*, he describes the curious case of the Amazing Mr. Plastic Man, an especially happy member of his future ward house. Beck describes how he and his fellow congregants were in Sunday school class discussing the Mormon concept of Zion—a place where, in Beck's words, "we can all make as much money as we want, where we can all still be capitalists, but we only take the amount we need and give the rest to help the poor, widowed or fatherless."

Mr. Plastic Man raised his hand. "There's only one way this will happen," he said. "If I truly love you and you truly love me. If deep down inside of ourselves we see people for who they really are, our literal and spiritual brothers." Beck then comments:

> He was crying and I was crying. Simple truth. . . . It was then that I decided, "I don't care if you have Kool-Aid in the basement, give me a cup. I'm so tired, I can't live with the baggage of my life any more. I can't live with the mistakes I have made. I'm laying down my sword, because I want to be like the Amazing Mr. Plastic Man."[9]

There may be no better example of Beck at his saccharine sentimental worst than his first novel, *The Christmas Sweater*. Although he doesn't advertise it as such, it is an archetypically Mormon creation. Beck claims that the plot is based on a true story, centered on the death of his mother. But the standards of Mormon sentimentalism demand more than one parental death, so the young protagonist's father also dies. Beck cowrote the number one *New York Times* best seller with another Mormon author, Jason Wright.

The result—an unwieldy collection of clichés and congealed preteen literary sugar—could easily be confused with any number of other Mormon-authored novels. One of these, Richard Paul Evans's *The Christmas List*, shares not only a cover design with Beck's book but also enough by-the-numbers pathos to melt the human brain. The biggest difference between the two Christmas books is that Beck manages to work in a swipe at the federal food-stamp program in the first five pages. The Web site of the church-owned Deseret Book Company describes *The Christmas Sweater* as a "warm and poignant tale of family, faith and forgiveness." This faint praise is the same cookie-cutter judgment Deseret's in-house critics pass on every work of Mormon popular fiction to meet the genre's rote requirements. There are simply no subjects in this blank-eyed literary canon beyond the church-approved troika of family, faith, and forgiveness.

LDS Church–produced films offer more of the same. All follow the same trajectory of cartoon tragedy to bright-light redemption with pummeling predictability. Consider the plots of Mormonism's most famous "film classics," as described in the *BYU Creative Works Catalogue*:

> *The Gift*: A twelve-year-old boy struggles to understand why his father is so hard on him. When he realizes that his father is simply trying to teach him a strong work ethic, the boy searches for the perfect Christmas gift to give in return. Since it is the depression of the mid 1930s, money is scarce, but when he decides to get up early on Christmas morning to do the farm chores, he gives him a gift that will last a lifetime.

> *Cipher in the Snow*: When a teenage boy dies unexpectedly, his math teacher is asked to notify the parents and write the obituary. Although he was the boy's favorite teacher, he hardly knew him. Shy and ostracized, the boy was considered a "cipher"—an unknown number in a class roll book. As the teacher unravels the mystery of what led to the boy's death, he commits himself to not letting others suffer the same fate.

> *The Emmett Smith Story*: When Emmett Smith has a brain tumor removed, he loses his equilibrium and is told he will never run again. With determination, the high school track coach is able to run 20 miles once again within a year. When Cindy Duncan

becomes a student at his high school, Emmett challenges her to do the same—set a goal for leaving her wheelchair to walk to the podium to get her graduation diploma.

John Baker's Last Race: When John Baker learns he is dying of cancer, he faces a choice: to end his life, or to use his remaining time to make a difference in others' lives. He chooses to dedicate himself to his young students and his citywide girls' track team, leaving them with a legacy of love and accomplishment, and an understanding of the value of determination and a positive attitude.

The roots of Mormonism's tolerance of and thirst for such stories run deep, say scholars of Mormon culture.

"Sentimentality peaked in the middle nineteenth century, around the moment of Mormonism's cultural inception," writes Joanna Brooks, a Mormon scholar of religion and literature at San Diego State University. "The kind of sentimental storytelling found in Beck's fiction is not a minor tradition in Mormonism. We hear it in Sunday school and we read it in church magazines. Where Jews have the talmudic tradition of scholarly commentary, Mormons cite this vast sentimental archive of stories about widows and dying children. Critical thinking is not strongly valued in orthodox Mormon culture."[10]

Mormon sentimentalism results in more than just bad film and fiction. It obliterates any possibility of fuller reckoning with the complexities of history. In his essay "Everybody's Protest Novel," James Baldwin argued that by cheapening tragedy, sentimental novels help to reinforce the reality that made the tragedy possible in the first place. Sentimentalism, Baldwin wrote, is rooted in a "medieval morality [of] black, white, the devil, the next world—posing its alternatives between heaven and the flames." This medieval morality is fertile ground for medieval politics. For Baldwin, the politics of sentimentalism always shares an "indecent glibness" with those "moral, neatly framed and incontestable . . . improving mottoes sometimes found hanging on the walls of furnished rooms."

In other words, Beck World politics. A world in which *The Christmas Sweater* is considered literature is also a world in which Cleon Skousen can be considered a political philosopher. It is to this story that we now turn.

12

The Ghost of Cleon Skousen

On the evening of September 2, 2009, Beck presented one of his famous Fox News lecture seminars. As with his previous chalkboard sessions, his purpose was to connect the dots of progressive influence and reveal the contours and loci of leftist political power, its secret strategies and unspoken agendas. But this lesson differed in two key respects from Beck's earlier exercises in adult political education. Rather than focus on the players in the Obama administration, Beck employed a wide-angle historical lens. And instead of marking up a green chalkboard with interlocking flowcharts of liberal nonprofit organizations, Beck narrated a digital slide show.

Glenn Beck as art history professor: it was a first.

Beck's slide show consisted of several public artifacts from midtown Manhattan, all seemingly benign. The sampling included two carved friezes, named *Industry* and *Agriculture*, that frame the entrances of 636 Fifth Avenue; a 1933 Diego Rivera mural named *Man at the Crossroads*, which hung briefly in a lobby at Rockefeller Center; a 1957 bronze by Soviet sculptor Yevgeny Vuchetich named *Let Us Beat Swords into Plowshares* that adorns the north garden of the United Nations; and a neoclassical glass wall sculpture by Attilio Piccirilli, another Rockefeller Center piece, which depicts a chariot, its driver, and a young man walking toward the sun.

Those watching the show from across a noisy bar might have sur-
mised that Beck was putting politics aside for the night to share photos
from a neighborhood walking tour. They would have been wrong.
During the nine-minute segment, Beck explained that there were two
themes in the pieces in his slide show. New Yorkers are blind to these
commonalities, but Beck saw them clearly, and he grasped the fullness
of their menace.

Beck went on to explain that the ties that bind these four works constitute a sort of left-wing Da Vinci code, which holds the secrets to
the radical-left forces arrayed against the Republic. "Those with eyes
will not see, and those with ears will not hear," said Beck, quoting a
line found in both the Bible and the *Book of Mormon*. When Beck
approached this art with open ears and open eyes, he heard the ballads
of communist revolution and saw the symbols of fascist mythology. He
asked his viewers to join him and open up their own senses. The public
art of the past held important lessons for today.

Beck pointed out the art's dastardly motifs, each in turn. There
was a hammer, a wheel, a sun, and a naked strongman pointing to a
child and a distant horizon. The strongman was Mussolini, said Beck,
and that reminded him of Barack Obama. "Gee, who's having indoctrination next week?" he asked, referring to the president's planned
address to U.S. schoolchildren, which was causing a flap in the Tea
Party movement. It was all there.

Beck even deciphered that terrifying Bronze Age symbol of agriculture and lawn care, the sickle. "Where have we seen that before?" the
host wanted to know. After cataloguing each of these images as if they
were the Christian apocalyptic "mark of the beast," Beck turned to the
camera in triumph. "This is propaganda," he declared, "hidden in plain
sight. *In plain sight!*"

This led to a troubling question: How did this leftist imagery come
to lurk in America's hypercapitalist heart, midtown Manhattan? Beck
noted that the *Industry* and *Agriculture* friezes even flanked the
plaza where NBC's *Today* show—a heartland icon and Beck's former
employer—holds summer concerts for tourists and children.

"Progressives, fascists, communists," said the host. "What do they all
have in common?"

All the pieces in his slide show, Beck explained, were found on property owned or formerly owned by the Rockefellers. The friezes on Fifth

Avenue; the Rivera lobby mural that hung, briefly, at 30 Rockefeller Center; and Vuchetich's bent sword at the United Nations, an institution built on land donated by Nelson Rockefeller—each led directly back to the Standard Oil fortune, accumulated in the nineteenth century by John D. Rockefeller Sr. and managed for the last century by his scions.

"I want you to understand who these progressives are," said Beck. "What's happening to our country has been a long time in the coming. It makes sense that we are headed down this road today. It makes sense that you feel uneasy and everything seems to be hidden. It's not, if you look."

Beck asked his audience to draw their own conclusions, but there was only one conclusion for anyone following Beck Logic: the Rockefellers may be synonymous with U.S. capitalism, but they have a history of indulging in un-American sympathies, if not activities. The immense fortune amassed by John D. Rockefeller Sr., an honest robber baron, was soon put to work by his progressive spawn to fund the devil's work. In 1933, John D. Rockefeller Jr. paid the communist Diego Rivera to paint a mural. And in 2009? Beck ended his lecture on an ominous contemporary note: "The Rockefeller Fund gave a big award and an awful lot of credibility to Van Jones, our new green jobs czar."[1]

The progressive-communist-fascist past, frozen in time throughout Manhattan, was prologue. It was as easy to see as opening your eyes.

Beck's September 2 slide show triggered the inevitable, by then almost ritualized, Beck mock-fest. "Glenn Beck: Crack(ed) Symbolist," declared *Time*'s art critic.[2] "Glenn Beck: Art Hysterian," quipped a *New York Times* columnist on his blog.[3] But hysterical about what? And why? No one seemed to know. *Los Angeles Times* art critic Christopher Knight placed Beck's lecture within the context of America's history of right-wing reaction against modern art. This phenomenon peaked during the late 1950s, when civic groups, led by the Society for Sanity in Art, crusaded against abstract paintings and sculptures they suspected of carrying subliminal communist propaganda. Beck, Knight assumed, had merely revived this tradition.

But he hadn't. Beck never advocated destroying or draping the pieces in his slide show. The Fox News foray into art criticism was no

Cold War flashback to hokey McCarthyite watchdog activism. The art was quite beside the point. The real focus of the segment was the Rockefeller dynasty as a symbol of powerful enemies within. By connecting the Rockefellers to a century of perceived left-wing propaganda and subversion—from V. I. Lenin to Van Jones—Beck was reciting the dogma of a conspiracy culture with deep and tangled roots in the history of the far right. Often diagnosable by Rockefeller fixations, recurring nightmares about the United Nations, and a burning hatred of the income tax, this conspiracy culture is generally known by the name of the phenomenon it fears, the New World Order.

Beck's art-lecture nod to New World Order conspiracism baffled his critics and casual viewers, but it was no lightning bolt out of the blue. As the ingredients of Beck's hard-right politics have changed throughout the years, the belief in a slowly unfolding secret plot involving enemies at home and abroad has remained the singular constant. Indeed, Beck has been quietly mainstreaming right-wing conspiracy culture for the better part of a decade. His Rockefeller lecture was unique only for its brazenness.

The biggest factor in the development of Beck's conspiratorial worldview was his midlife Mormon conversion. Within Mormon culture, there runs a strong current of New World Order paranoia. After joining the church in 1999, Beck aligned himself with the religion's ultraconservative strain, in which this paranoia thrives. It is through mixing in these circles that Beck encountered the legacy of Mormonism's most influential hard-right figures of the last century. These men brought anticommunist extremism to Utah during the 1950s. They interpreted the Cold War as the fulfillment of Mormon prophecy and saw radical-right organizations like the John Birch Society as embodying "proper" Mormon politics. The fruit of their efforts was a philosophy within Mormonism in which ultraconservatism, end-times prophecy, and the paranoid style freely mix. It is Glenn Beck's current spiritual home. The doormat says GOD, GOLD, AND GUNS.

Anyone who has followed Beck in recent years will recognize the deceased godfather of this Mormon current. His name was Willard Cleon Skousen. In broadcasts and in print, Beck has routinely promoted Skousen and his works since his early years in talk radio.

He has often called Skousen's books "must-reads," including the 1970 New World Order treatise *The Naked Capitalist* and the 1981 theocratic tract *The 5,000 Year Leap: A Miracle That Changed the World*. The latter is Beck's favorite book and tops the 9.12 Project reading list, which contains several other Skousen titles.

Beck's enthrallment with Mormonism's most notorious crank explains much that would otherwise remain inscrutable. It was Skousen, more than any mainstream figure on the right, who created the frame through which Beck sees the world. In this frame, powerful elites and their leftist allies seek a one-world socialist government by scheming to subvert the godly Constitution that is the sacred foundation for the Real America.

It was in *The Real America* that Beck first showed signs of familiarity with Mormonism's chief conspiracist. The moment comes midway through the book, in a chapter titled "The Enemy Within."[4] It is a short and strange chapter, unrelated to the chapters preceding and following. It consists solely of a list titled "Communist Goals of 1963." Beck identified the list as something he found "buried" in the Congressional Record, entered by Albert Herlong, a Democratic congressman from Florida from 1949 to 1969. Beck asks his readers to study Herlong's list, then check off the goals they think America's current "enemies within" have successfully achieved forty years later.

Although Beck does not identify the author (Herlong was not the author), the "Communist Goals of 1963" was written by Cleon Skousen, who featured a version of the list in his McCarthyite stump speeches during the early 1960s. Following the publication of *The Real America*, Beck continued to endorse Skousen and his obscure works more directly. This included repeated plugs for Skousen's 1958 best-selling anticommunist tract, *The Naked Communist*, as well as for its sequel, the 1970 anti-Rockefeller New World Order manifesto, *The Naked Capitalist*. Both books are elaborately imagined, feverishly argued, and poorly researched.

In *The Naked Capitalist*, Skousen describes a global megaplot in which the dynastic superrich control leftist forces around the world in pursuit of a one-world socialist government. In his own time, the book received scant attention other than ridicule outside of fringe-political circles. But apparently Skousen was just ahead of his time. In his 2007 best seller, *An Inconvenient Book*, Beck lauds *The Naked Capitalist* as a "must-read" for anyone "interested in learning more about the organizations behind [the efforts to destroy U.S. sovereignty]," including New World Order bogeymen like the Council on Foreign Relations.[5]

In recent years, Beck has also emerged as a leading advocate for Skousen's distinctly Mormon fundamentalist interpretation of U.S. history. In Beck's favorite book, *The 5,000 Year Leap*, Skousen argues that the U.S. Constitution is a revelatory document of divine provenance, written by religious men who were inspired by the political order of ancient Israel as described in the Bible. Since 2008, Beck has concentrated his considerable talent as pitchman to promote this view. In his 2009 foreword to *The 5,000 Year Leap*, Beck calls Skousen's book "divinely inspired." In Beck's best seller of the same year, *Common Sense*, Skousen's book tops the "required reading" list.[6] Skousen's tract is now the central history text for hundreds of thousands of Tea Party activists.

Like Skousen's books on the New World Order conspiracy and end-times prophecy, *The 5,000 Year Leap* was virtually unknown before Beck plucked it off the remainder pile of history. Never during his ninety-three years did Skousen enjoy a national media champion like Beck. Quite the opposite. He was widely regarded for much of his life as an embarrassing and even dangerous presence on conservatism's crank fringe. His work with the John Birch Society and other radical-right groups earned him calumny and boot prints from some of the most conservative figures and organizations of the Cold War.

Willard Cleon Skousen was born in 1913 to American parents in a small Mormon frontier town in Alberta, Canada. When he was ten, his family moved to California, where he remained until he shipped off to England and Ireland for two years of Mormon missionary work. In 1935, after graduating from a California junior college, the twenty-three-year-old Skousen moved to Washington, D.C., where he worked briefly for a New Deal farm agency. He then began a fifteen-year career with the FBI and earned a law degree from George Washington University in 1940. His posts at the FBI were administrative and clerical in nature, first in Washington and later in Kansas City.

After retiring from the FBI in 1951, Skousen joined the faculty of Brigham Young University in Utah. His life as a religion professor was suspended in 1956, when he began a tumultuous four years as chief of police in Salt Lake City. During his tenure, he gained a reputation for cutting crime and ruthlessly enforcing Mormon morals. Among Skousen's achievements were bans on public smoking and pinball machines, which the chief considered a corrupter of youth almost as wicked as rock 'n' roll.

But Skousen was too earnest, even for Salt Lake City. The city's ultra-conservative mayor, J. Bracken Lee, fired him in 1960 for excessive zeal in raiding home bingo games and private clubs where the Salt Lake City elite (including Mayor Lee) enjoyed its card games.

"Skousen conducted his office as Chief of Police in exactly the same manner in which the Communists operate their government," Lee wrote to a friend after his firing of Skousen. "The man is a master of half-truths. In at least three instances I have proven him to be a liar. He is a very dangerous man [and] one of the greatest spenders of public funds of anyone who ever served in any capacity in Salt Lake City government."[7]

While serving as police chief, Skousen had begun laying the ground-work for a career as an anticommunist speaker. In 1958, Skousen published an exposé-cum-history of the global communist movement, *The Naked Communist*. A work of laughably shoddy scholarship, the book went unnoticed by professional historians except those in Skousen's Utah backyard. His résumé to that point—failed chief of police, part-time BYU religion professor, FBI paper pusher—was not that of a scholar.

"Skousen had never read a word of Marx and didn't know what he was talking about," says Louis Midgley, a historian and a former colleague of Skousen's at BYU. "The faculty was embarrassed that he was even allowed on the staff as an instructor of theology."

Then as now, ignorance was no bar to success on the far right. *The Naked Communist* would, according to Skousen, sell more than a million copies in the five years after its publication. Many of these were sold by hand, on the road. By the time Skousen was fired from the police force in 1960, he had developed connections with groups that were beginning to bubble up on America's far-right scene. Freed from his police duties, Skousen toured the country, speaking to audiences organized by groups such as the Church League of America, the Christian Anti-Communist Crusade, and the John Birch Society. Carrying the torch of Joe McCarthy, these organizations made it their work to channel, feed, and satisfy Cold War paranoia.

Within a year, Skousen had emerged as one of the best-known figures on the far right. In 1960, he founded his own like-minded organization in Salt Lake City, the All-American Society. Here's how *Time* magazine described the outfit the following year:

> The All-American Society, founded in Salt Lake City, has as its guiding light one of the busiest speakers in the rightist movement: W. Cleon Skousen, a balding, bespectacled onetime FBI man who hit the anti-Communist circuit in earnest in 1960 after being fired from his job as Salt Lake City's police chief ("He operated the police department like a Gestapo," says Salt Lake City's conservative Mayor J. Bracken Lee). Skousen freely quotes the Bible, constantly plugs his book, *The Naked Communist*, [and] presses for a full congressional investigation of the State Department.[8]

Skousen was more than just another anticommunist opportunist; he was a fraud. Although Skousen claimed that his years with the FBI had exposed him to inside information, his employment records show that his work at the bureau was largely secretarial in nature.

"Skousen never worked in the domestic intelligence division, and he never had significant exposure to data concerning communist matters," says Ernie Lazar, an independent researcher who has studied the internal documentation of Skousen's FBI employment history.

Along with touting his imagined exposure to highly classified FBI business, Skousen trumpeted the expertise he claimed to have gained while researching *The Naked Communist*. But this research was even shakier than his résumé. Among the stories in Skousen's fantastical arsenal was the alleged treason of FDR adviser Harry Hopkins. According to Skousen, Hopkins gave the Soviets "50 suitcases" worth of information on the Manhattan Project and nearly half of the nation's supply of enriched uranium.

By 1963, Skousen's extremism was costing him. Members of the ultraconservative American Security Council kicked him out because they thought he had "gone off the deep end." One council member who shared this opinion was William C. Mott, the judge advocate general of the U.S. Navy. Mott found Skousen "money mad . . . totally unqualified and interested solely in furthering his own personal ends."[9]

When Skousen defended Birch president Robert Welch's charge that Dwight Eisenhower was a "dedicated, conscious agent of the Communist conspiracy,"[10] the last of Skousen's dwindling corporate clients dumped him. The ultraconservative National Association of Manufacturers released a statement condemning the Birchers and distancing itself from "any individual or party" that subscribed to their views. Skousen, author of a pamphlet titled *The Communist Attack on the John Birch Society*, ranked high among the nation's most prominent Birch defenders.[11]

Skousen's activities were causing apprehension within the FBI as well. Even inside the Mormon Church, a debate began in the early 1960s about Skousen's increasing double profile as a Mormon and a controversial anticommunist activist. For many church leaders, Skousen was bringing unwanted attention to the church, which until then had generally eschewed involvement in politics. But Skousen had allies in high places. The strongest and most loyal of these was a future church president and posthumous friend of *The Glenn Beck Program* named Ezra Taft Benson.

As described in chapter 6, Beck employed the voice of Ezra Taft Benson from beyond the grave just days before the 2008 election. The audio consisted of Benson recalling Nikita Khrushchev's promise to him that his grandchildren would live under communism. Beck believed that the imminent election of Barack Obama represented the fulfillment of that threat. "Listen carefully," said the host before the playing the clip. By then, Beck had more than resigned himself to a Democratic victory—he was banking on it. Beck was already planning some sort of anti-Obama movement based on the work of Cleon Skousen. So who better to assist Beck in framing Obama as the culmination of a communist master plan than Nikita Khrushchev and Skousen's longtime friend and ally, Ezra Taft Benson?

Beck is part of a minority of Mormons who believe it is important to "listen carefully" to the scratchy recordings of Benson's lectures. Like Skousen, Benson is an icon among ultraconservative Mormons, who appreciate the official cover he provided that allowed Skousen to bring McCarthyism to Utah in the form of the John Birch Society (JBS). The author of a Skousenite anticommunist manifesto called *The Red Carpet: A Forthright Evaluation of the Rising Tide of Socialism*,

Benson believed allegiance to the John Birch Society was the measure of every good Mormon. His sons, Mark and Reed, founded and led Salt Lake City's JBS chapter. Together with junior members of the Skousen clan, they organized student spy rings to monitor faculty and students at the University of Utah and at BYU.

In the mid-1960s, Skousen and Benson were allies in the JBS's efforts to demonize the civil rights movement, which the organization viewed as a stalking horse for communism. The cover of the September 1965 issue of the *John Birch Society Bulletin* declared: "Fully Expose the 'Civil Rights' Fraud, and You Will Break the Back of the Communist Conspiracy!"

Toward this end, the Skousen and Benson clans took matters into their own hands, in the process creating hysteria in Salt Lake City. Led by Reed Benson (son of Ezra) and Mark Skousen (nephew of Cleon), the Salt Lake City Birchers in 1965 began spreading rumors that the NAACP was sending two thousand Black Muslims to attack the Church of Latter-Day Saints. General panic ensued. The Utah National Guard was placed on alert and began practicing riot maneuvers in anticipation of the invasion. After calm was restored, the Anti-Defamation League and the NAACP both expressed concern over the Bircher-fomented race-war hysteria in Utah. But the campaign continued. The next month the *Bulletin* published articles describing blacks as "savages" and civil rights leaders as "animals."[12]

For most of the 1960s, the majority of radical rightists believed that the global communist conspiracy was headquartered in Moscow. The conspiracy's many U.S. agents and fronts, they believed, received their orders from the Soviet capital. But this view would not survive the decade. By the time of Richard Nixon's election in 1968, Birchers had begun developing a new and improved conspiracy, headquartered in the twin capitals of global finance, New York and London.

The key event in this transformation occurred in 1966. That was the year Macmillan published *Tragedy and Hope* by the noted Georgetown historian Carroll Quigley. Totaling some thirteen hundred pages, the book was an ambitious economic and political survey of the period between 1895 and 1965. It was well received by Quigley's fellow historians, but it sold poorly, and the publisher killed it after nine thousand copies sold.[13]

What the publisher and author didn't know was that the book was gaining cult status in far-right circles. Among groups like the JBS, *Tragedy and Hope* was embraced as the Rosetta Stone of the capitalist superconspiracy, which soon superseded the old communist plot. In Quigley's study of dynastic wealth, influential private societies, and their occasional ties to left-wing groups, the far right saw a new galaxy of hidden power that explained everything from détente in Washington, D.C., to radical chic in Manhattan.

The first sign of the book's effect on the far-right scene appeared in Gary Allen's 1968 book, *Nixon: The Man behind the Mask*. Allen, a leading Bircher, cited Quigley in support of his argument that Nixon employed anticommunist rhetoric to cloak his progressive goals, including the transformation of the Republican Party into a vehicle for socialism. Nixon, Allen believed, was able to fool so many conservatives only with the help of powerful leftist allies in the "East Coast establishment," notably Nelson Rockefeller.

Skousen shared Allen's belief that *Tragedy and Hope* was a revelatory text. Throughout the late 1960s, Skousen not only carefully annotated his copy, he sent samizdat versions of Quigley's tome to fellow BYU faculty. Attached were handwritten notes that read "This book holds the key." For Skousen, Quigley's book was the "insider account we've been waiting for" that drew back the red curtain to expose the *real* conspiracy. With Quigley's analysis, everything made sense: the Bolshevik Revolution; the socialist art of Rockefeller Center; the Council on Foreign Relations.

Eager to proselytize (and sell some books), in 1970 Skousen self-published his take on the capitalist superconspiracy revealed by Quigley. Throughout his 144-page essay, Skousen breathlessly appropriates Allen's language of "insiders" and the "establishment" to identify the forces dragging the United States toward the New World Order. He called it *The Naked Capitalist*.

Skousen began selling copies of *The Naked Capitalist* for two dollars apiece in early 1970. He hoped that in being the first to outline the new megaconspiracy, he might replicate the runaway success of *The Naked Communist*. But it didn't happen. He was beaten by his John Birch Society associate, Gary Allen, who struck publishing gold the following year with the similarly themed *None Dare Call It Conspiracy*, which sold more than five million copies. Like *The Naked Capitalist*, Allen's title paid homage to a Bircher best seller from a simpler time, John Stormer's 1964 *None Dare Call It Treason*.

The first fifty pages of *The Naked Capitalist* consist of nothing but extended quotations from *Tragedy and Hope*.[14] All of them deal with the institutions and individuals that Quigley believes are significant in the West's recent political and economic development. Skousen focuses on the origins of the Federal Reserve, the founding of the Council on Foreign Relations, and the rise of the billion-dollar corporation. He also zeroes in on the key figures behind what he calls "the world's secret power structure." These include the scions of the Morgan, Rockefeller, and Ford fortunes. "It was no coincidence that the entire site for the United Nations was donated by the Rockefellers," he writes. In a similar vein, Skousen notes that the Ford Foundation funded the "vulgar anti-white" art of LeRoi Jones and the "anti-white" politics of the National Urban League and the Congress of Racial Equality.[15] Echoes of Skousen's outrage can be heard in Beck's pointed comments about the Rockefeller Fund's past support for the "black nationalist radicalism" of Van Jones and his green jobs agenda.

The purpose of liberal internationalist groups such as the Council on Foreign Relations, argues Skousen in *The Naked Capitalist*, is to push "U.S. foreign policy toward the establishment of a worldwide collectivist society." He claims that the Anglo-American banking establishment has been agitating for this goal since the Bolshevik Revolution. Skousen substantiates this claim by citing the work of a former czarist army officer named Arsene de Goulevitch. Among Goulevitch's own sources is Boris Brasol, a White Russian émigré who provided Henry Ford with the first English translation of the *Protocols of the Elders of Zion* and later became a supporter of Nazi Germany.

The fingerprints of *The Naked Capitalist* can be found all over Glenn Beck's historical interests. Each of Beck's favorite twentieth-century whipping posts is profiled in Skousen's book. On television and radio, Beck has spent hours superficially discussing the perfidies of Walter Lippman, Woodrow Wilson, and Wilson's foreign policy adviser, Edward M. "Colonel" House. In *The Naked Capitalist*, Skousen also discusses House's long-out-of-print novel, *Philip Dru: Administrator.* Beck has mentioned the novel at least a dozen times on the air, and he frequently suggests that his listeners and guests track down a copy of the 1912 political thriller. Beck repeats Skousen's description of the novel as evidence of the totalitarian fantasies harbored by reform-minded progressives like House, a wealthy banker who championed the graduated income tax.

The superrich not only sought to control every lever of global power, Skousen argued, they were also in lockstep with one another in the march toward a socialist One World Government. Any challengers to the New World Order, such as Barry Goldwater or the John Birch Society, must be crushed. In a line that would win sympathy from Beck's 9.12 Project conservatives, Skousen describes how the superconspiracy uses its media arm to drown out patriotic messages by "pounding out a subtle (and sometimes blatant) message of 'extremist' [and] 'racist.'"

"What we are witnessing," concludes Skousen in *The Naked Capitalist*, "is a very carefully and methodically executed program designed to destroy constitutional government as we have known it and make a shambles of the society which has wanted to keep the Constitution alive. Only then can a highly centralized, socialist state be established."

Aside from their relative eloquence, these words could have been uttered by Beck or written by one of his ghostwriters.

The deranged and incoherent fantasy described in *The Naked Capitalist* resonated with many on the radical right as the 1970s opened. Ultraconservatives witnessed in horror the drift of Richard Nixon's White House. For them, nothing illustrated the socialist establishment's grip on U.S. politics more than the rise of Henry Kissinger and Nelson Rockefeller, the very faces of liberal, East Coast, foundation-connected internationalism. As Skousen notes in *The Naked Capitalist*, Kissinger's affiliations included the triple whammy of New World Order para-noia: the Council on Foreign Relations, the Rockefeller Fund, and the Bilderberg Group.

And if Henry Kissinger can't be trusted to run a vast left-wing con-spiracy, then who can be?

The publication of *The Naked Capitalist* ripped open the old debate within the Mormon Church about the political activities of Skousen and Benson. Liberal members of the BYU faculty were especially aghast that some of their colleagues were assigning Skousen's latest treatise.

Among those driven to action was longtime Skousen critic and BYU history professor Louis C. Midgley. When Midgley caught wind that Mormonism's leading scholarly quarterly was set to publish an uncritical review of *The Naked Capitalist*, he requested space to publish a rejoinder. The editors agreed. Midgley also invited Carroll Quigley to participate in a roundtable on the controversy. The result appeared in the Mormon journal *Dialogue*.[16]

Midgley and Quigley passed harsh judgment on Skousen's book. In an opinion seconded by Quigley, Midgley accused Skousen of "inventing fantastic ideas and making inferences that go far beyond the bounds of honest commentary." Skousen had not only read things into Quigley's book that were not there, he completely missed what *was* there. Midgley ridiculed Skousen for fulfilling Quigley's caricature of a radical-right conspiracist who can't discern influence from omnipotence or liberal capitalism from totalitarian communism.

"Skousen's personal position," wrote a dismayed Quigley, "seems to me perilously close to the 'exclusive uniformity' which I see in Nazism and in the Radical Right in this country. In fact, his position has echoes of the original Nazi 25-point plan."

When the *Dialogue* roundtable went to press, Skousen was at work laying the groundwork for his plan to save the republic as outlined in *The Naked Capitalist*. On July 4, 1971, Skousen opened the doors of the Freemen Institute in a converted storefront judo studio located just off the BYU campus in Provo, Utah. The purpose of the Freemen Institute, said its literature, was to "inspire Americans to return to the Founders' original success formula." It would accomplish this through a touring lecture seminar titled "The Miracle of America," to be given by its founder in locations across Utah and the United States. By the end of the summer, Skousen had raised enough money to move the base of his new organization into a larger space in a nearby warehouse. The upgrade was celebrated in a ceremony attended by like-minded ultraconservative Mormons, including LDS apostle and future church president Ezra Taft Benson.

As with his previous anticommunist message, Skousen's constitutional lessons eventually drew critical attention in Utah and beyond. Edwin Brown Firmage, a professor of law at the University of Utah, complained to the Mormon magazine *Sunstone* in 1981, "Skousen is teaching right-wing fundamentalism with a constitutional veneer. How anyone can prove that civil rights and welfare are unconstitutional is beyond me. For his people, 'Constitutional' is just a right-wing buzzword."[17] A reporter from the *Philadelphia Inquirer* named Larry Eichel reached the same conclusion after attending one of Skousen's lectures in the birthplace of the Constitution. "He preached a political return to the eighteenth century," wrote Eichel.[18]

The reporter was off by a century. What the Mormon constitutionalism pioneered by Skousen really pines after is the federal government of the nineteenth century. If Skousen could have stopped the clock anywhere, it would have been 1867, the year before the passage of the Fourteenth Amendment. Like today's Tenther movement, whose adherents cite the Tenth Amendment to advocate the sovereignty of the states over federal government power, Skousen argued that constitutional decline began when the federal government overrode the states to grant and enforce equality under the law.

Skousen's "Miracle of America" seminars not surprisingly made villains of federal agencies. He especially wanted to abolish the Occupational Safety and Health Administration and the Environmental Protection Agency. Also on his wish list: repeal the minimum wage, smash the unions, nullify antidiscrimination laws, sell off public lands and national parks, and end the direct election of senators. He wanted to kill the income tax and the estate tax, destroy the wall separating church and state, and, of course, raze the Federal Reserve system.

When the negative press around Skousen's seminars started popping up in the national media, the church hierarchy moved swiftly to avoid a repeat of the 1960s. In 1979, LDS Church president Spencer W. Kimball issued an order to every Mormon priest in the country. It stated, "No announcements should be made in Church meetings of Freemen Institute lectures or events that are not under the sponsorship of the Church. [This] is to make certain that neither Church facilities nor Church meetings are used to advertise such events and to avoid any implication that the Church endorses what is said during such lectures." According to retired BYU professor Louis C. Midgley, who was familiar with the church's deliberations, Skousen was on track to being excommunicated.

Skousen didn't advertise it in his Freemen Institute literature, but his backward-looking "Miracle of America" seminars were heavily flavored with Mormon theology. The very name of Skousen's institute was a play on a passage in the *Book of Mormon*. Skousen's call for a constitutional "restoration," meanwhile, closely paralleled Mormonism's central theological claim to "restore" the gospel of Jesus. In this view, the United States is not just an experiment in self-rule; it is the fulfillment of prophecy in the last days. A Freemen official interviewed in 1983 explained as follows:

> When we go to foreign countries, we teach a model constitution which has been drawn up by the Freemen Institute here. *It is patterned similarly after the U.S. Constitution.* We've taken certain concepts of the Restored LDS Gospel and incorporated them into our working model of what an ideal constitution should be.[19] (Emphasis added.)

Considering the historical antagonism between the LDS Church and the other branches of Christianity, one might guess that Skousen's Mormon crusade was a lonely one. It wasn't. Skousen ended the 1970s on friendly terms with many leading figures from evangelical Christianity. During Ronald Reagan's march toward the White House, Skousen found himself courted by a new political movement that was taking shape in Washington. In July 1980, more than two hundred thousand conservative evangelicals gathered to celebrate this movement under the banner WASHINGTON FOR JESUS.

Amid the summer throng that presided over the Christian Right's creation was Cleon Skousen. It was a happy time for the sixty-seven-year-old Mormon. There was a Goldwater Republican in the White House, and he was making lots of interesting new friends. Among them was a very rich and generous Korean fellow named Sun Myung Moon.

"Over the next couple of years," said an uncharacteristically optimistic Skousen in 1981, "we have a real opportunity to turn this country around."[20]

The stirrings of political collaboration between the Latter-Day Saints and other Christian denominations occurred in the context of the national campaign against the Equal Rights Amendment during the 1970s. For the first time, Latter-Day Saints formed state-level alliances with Southern Baptists and northern Catholics to help defeat the legislation.

The collaboration proved successful. Religious activists from other faiths discovered that the Mormons could be well-funded and disciplined allies. Powerful figures within the emerging movement were especially impressed by the military efficiency with which the Mormon Church hierarchy translated leadership decisions into grassroots execution.[21]

The Christian Right formalized its acceptance of the Mormon Church in 1982 by appointing Skousen to the board of the Council for National Policy. Sometimes described as the religious right's answer to the Council on Foreign Relations, the council was founded in 1981 to hash out policy ideas for the new administration. To be closer to the action, Skousen relocated the Freemen Institute to Washington, where he had lived and studied as a young man.

At the council, Skousen was known as one of the earliest and fiercest proponents of privatizing Social Security. He also used the proximity to other religious activists to develop important personal and organizational ties, most notably with the Moral Majority, the lobbying outfit founded by Virginia's Reverend Jerry Falwell in 1979.[22] By the end of Reagan's first term, the Moral Majority and the Freemen Institute were cosponsoring each other's events, and Falwell was sending his employees to study at Skousen's seminars.[23]

Skousen still found time to write. As he managed the transition from Salt Lake City to Washington, he arose every day at 4 a.m. to expand and organize the dog-eared notes he used for his "Miracle of America" lectures. The result was a three-hundred-page manuscript that he self-published at the end of 1981. Heavily peppered with photos, biblical portraits, and cartoons, its chapters were broken into bite-size chunks of a few hundred words. As a result, the book had a childlike quality. Skousen named it *The 5,000 Year Leap: A Miracle That Changed the World.*

If Skousen had predicted great success for his new book, few people would have taken him seriously. Even a self-declared prophet like Skousen's friend Moon would have had trouble believing that nine years into the next century, *The 5,000 Year Leap* would become a publishing megaphenomenon, briefly outselling on Amazon.com just about every other book ever written since the beginning of time.

The 5,000 Year Leap reads exactly like what it was until Glenn Beck dragged it out of twenty-first-century obscurity: an introductory textbook suited to tiny centers of ultraconservative Mormon pedagogy like Utah's George Wythe University, where it heads the syllabus of Government 101, alongside Ezra Taft Benson's own contribution to the literature of Christian constitutionalist studies, *The Proper Role of Government*.[24] It was the book's centrality in the George Wythe curriculum that drew Beck to the school and compelled him to become a benefactor.

"Quite honestly, the first thing that attracted me was that to graduate you have to know all of the principles behind *The 5,000 Year Leap*," Beck explained in a 2009 appearance at George Wythe. "It is *the* book to read for this period in our country's history."

Like the Freemen seminars upon which it is based, *The 5,000 Year Leap* is Skousen's contribution to the Christian Right crusade to write Jesus Christ into American history. In terms of reach, it has been more successful than most. But as a work of scholarship, *Leap* resembles the rest of Skousen's crackpot oeuvre. In the rare instances in which mainstream scholars have come into contact with the book, their judgment has echoed Louis Midgley's response to *The Naked Capitalist*.

The thesis of *Leap* is that the U.S. Constitution is a miracle. The original version, penned and ratified in 1787, is a divinely inspired, and thus perfect, document. All of the country's problems result from turning away from a Christian-oriented society of extremely limited government. Although Skousen concedes that the founders did not want the republic to have a national church, he argues that the separation of church and state at the state level has no basis in the Constitution.

In a representative instance of Skousen's use of anecdote in place of argument, he seeks to prove this claim by citing Thomas Jefferson's support while serving in the Virginia legislature for a day of fasting and prayer. As president, Jefferson retracted that support, defending a "wall of separation between church and state." But Skousen believed this phrase has been misunderstood by a succession of godless and uninformed Supreme Court justices. In Skousen's telling, the founding fathers of American democracy drew much of their civic inspiration from the Bible, both directly and secondhand. He writes as follows:

> Jefferson's "wall" was obviously intended only for the federal government. And the Supreme Court's application of this metaphor to

the states has come under severe criticism. . . . Religious precepts turned out to be the heart and soul of the entire American political philosophy. They were taken from the books of John Locke, Sir William Blackstone, and other great thinkers of the day, who took them directly from the Bible. Thus, religion and the American institutions were combined.[25]

Skousen's authorial style mirrors the method by which Mormons prepare for religious meetings. First, select quotations from recognized authorities; second, arrange by theme, making sure to exclude opposing views; third, present. Some of the authorities quoted in *Leap*, like John Adams and Benjamin Franklin, are familiar enough. Others, like Mormon leaders Ezra Taft Benson and J. Reuben Clark, are not. But more important than Skousen's sly mixing of secular and ecclesiastical authority is his abject failure to get even the basic elements of his story correct.

Skousen's biblical exegesis is as faulty as his reading of Jefferson's private letters and Carroll Quigley's *Tragedy and Hope*. Skousen cites Jeremiah 34:16 to support his claim that slavery was outlawed in ancient Israel, despite reams of scripture illustrating the contrary. He further describes "people's law in ancient Israel" as among the prime models for the founders' republican vision.[26] Although it is true that the Hebrew Bible described a system of law to which the leaders were subject, Skousen skips over the minor fact that the leaders of ancient Israel were chosen by, and thus represented, God, not their fellow Israelites. This type of leader embodied the very system of rule by divine justification that America's founders threw with force into the dustbin of history.

Despite the wispy veneer of scholarly rigor, *Leap* is an extended cut-and-paste job of argument by assertion and anecdote. It is also a recipe for turning the United States into fifty little theocracies, each dictating morality according to its own religious ethics. These ethics, argued Skousen, should be transmitted through "extensive Bible reading" in public schools.

The project of the book is clear, even if its author never comes right out and says it. Others would prove bolder in explaining the importance of *Leap*. In Ronald Mann's introduction to *Leap*'s tenth-anniversary edition, he praises Skousen for grasping America's choice of "Christ or chaos" and for acknowledging that its future depends on "accepting and demonstrating God's government."[27]

It was a sign of Skousen's rising Washington profile that he renamed his organization the National Center for Constitutional Studies after Reagan's reelection. The new moniker—more mainstream, less Mormon—reflected a new stature at the center of power. (It also reflected the increasingly public fact that the Freeman Institute's name and ideas were being taken up by Idaho-based militias and white supremacist groups.) Among those who appreciated Skousen's work and growing influence was President Reagan, who praised the renamed Freemen Institute as "doing fine public service in educating Americans."[28]

Skousen showed no signs of slowing down. Shortly after completing *Leap*, he began writing another, more ambitious work of history, *The Making of America*. He scripted a lecture seminar based on his new book and took the show where he felt it belonged: on the road. Here's how *Time* magazine described Skousen's "Making of America" seminars in 1987:

> Billed as a seminar on the Constitution, "The Making of America" is more a churchy patriotic meeting than a scholarly dissertation. Sessions open with a presentation of military colors, followed by soloists belting out the Battle Hymn of the Republic and audiences singing God Bless America. When W. Cleon Skousen, 74, steps onto the podium, he preaches that the authors of the Constitution intended the U.S. to be governed as a Christian republic "under the law of God." As he explained to a rapt gathering of 800 in Anchorage two weeks ago, "The Founding Fathers wanted to separate church and state but not religion and state, and not God and state."[29]

It wasn't long before Skousen's theocratic lecture tour ran into problems. *The Making of America*, it turned out, not only suffered from the same glaring weaknesses as *Leap*, it also presented a history of slavery that could have been written by a propagandist for the Ku Klux Klan. Skousen's book characterized African American children as "pickaninnies" and described U.S. slave owners as the "worst victims" of the slavery system.

He quoted the historian Fred Albert Shannon in explaining that "[slave] gangs in transit were usually a cheerful lot, though the presence of a number of the more vicious type sometimes made it necessary for them all to go in chains." Skousen's history of slavery also reviewed the need to monitor alleged troublemakers. "Negro preachers," explained the book, "often bred discontent by their unnecessary restraint upon pleasure, and, if itinerants, had to be watched closely for abolitionist or seditious doctrines."[30]

The controversy the book provoked provided a rare opportunity for professional historians to become aware of and evaluate Skousen's work. One such encounter involved Stanford University historian Jack Rakove. Rakove attended Skousen's lectures and examined his books after California's Bicentennial Commission came under public criticism for selling *The Making of America* as part of a fundraising drive.

"I recall being intrigued by the maps explaining how the ten lost tribes of Israel made their way to America," remembers Rakove, whose constitutional history, *Original Meanings*, won the Pulitzer Prize in 1997. "Skousen's work is a joke that no self-respecting scholar would think is worth a warm pitcher of spit."

The burst of national publicity that accompanied the bicentennial controversy was Skousen's last. When he died in 2006 at the age of ninety-two, his death went unnoticed outside Mormon circles.

Among the public figures to sing Skousen's praises at the funeral was his most successful pet political project, Senator Orrin Hatch.* Standing over Skousen's flag-draped casket, the Republican senator read an elegiac poem that he would later enter in the Congressional Record. It served as the bookend to Skousen's first appearance in the record more than forty years earlier: the "Communist Goals of 1963."

The year after Skousen was buried in Salt Lake City, Glenn Beck hosted John Birch Society spokesman Sam Antonio on his Headline News

---

*Hatch isn't the only national politician to express an affinity for Skousen. In an August 2007 interview with Iowa talk-radio host Jan Mickelson, Republican presidential aspirant Mitt Romney murmured his assent when Mickelson spoke of their "common affection for the late Cleon Skousen." Later in the interview, Romney described Skousen's *The Making of America* as "worth reading" and name-dropped Skousen's book of Mormon eschatology, *A Thousand Years*, in defense of the idea that Christ will return to earth and "split the Mount of Olives [and] stop the war that is coming to kill all the Jews."

show. After a brief discussion of illegal immigration, Beck expressed admiration for his guest's organization. "Sam, I have to tell you, when I was growing up, the John Birch Society, I thought they were a bunch of nuts," said Beck. "[But] you guys are starting to make more and more sense to me."[31]

It wasn't just the contemporary version of the John Birch Society that Beck had developed an affinity for, however.

Two months later, Beck interviewed conservative pundit David Horowitz on his radio program. He asked him, "Have you ever read any Skousen? Have you read—do you remember *The Naked Communist*? I went back and reread that; it was printed in the 1950s. I reread that recently. You look at all the things the Communists wanted to accomplish. It's all been done."[32]

Beck couldn't get Skousen's 1958 title out of his mind. The following week, Bill Bennett—Reagan's secretary of education and now himself a radio talk-show host who once asserted that crime could be eliminated by aborting every black baby—appeared on Beck's radio program and received the same treatment from Beck, who sounded like a liberal college student fresh off a first encounter with Noam Chomsky. "Are you familiar with Skousen?" asked Beck. When Bennett replied that he was, Beck gushed:

> He's fantastic. I went back and I read *The Naked Communist*, and at the end of that Skousen predicted [that] someday soon you won't be able to find the truth in schools or in libraries or anywhere else because it won't be in print anymore. So you must collect those books. It's an idea I read from Cleon Skousen from his book in the 1950s, *The Naked Communist*, and where he talked about someday the history of this country's going to be lost because it's going to be hijacked by intellectuals and communists and everything else. And I think we're there.[33]

Beck would continue to drop Skousen's name in 2008, but his attempt to revive him really kicked in as he developed the concept behind the 9.12 Project. A month before President Obama's inauguration, Beck began dropping teasers for a movement in which he would be spokesman and Skousen the intellectual godfather. On his December 18, 2008, radio show, Beck introduced his audience to the idea of a "September twelfth person":

> The first thing you could do is get *The 5,000 Year Leap*. Over my book or anything else, get *The 5,000 Year Leap*. You can probably find it in the book section of GlennBeck.com, but read that. It is the principle. Please, number one thing: Inform yourself about who we are and what the other systems are all about. *The 5,000 Year Leap* is the first part of that. Because it will help you understand American free enterprise. . . . Make that dedication of becoming a September twelfth person, and I will help you do it next year.

Indeed he did. During Beck's first weeks on Fox News, he furiously promoted *Leap*. It was a push that peaked on March 13, 2009, with Beck's teary announcement introducing the 9.12 Project. The hourlong show featured Beck personally giving each member of his live audience a copy of Skousen's book. His praise that night echoed his words in the foreword he had written for the book's thirtieth-anniversary edition. "I beg you to read this book filled with words of wisdom which I can only describe as divinely inspired," writes Beck.

The result was a publishing earthquake. More than 250,000 copies were sold in the first half of 2009. The January 2009 edition of *The 5,000 Year Leap*, complete with Beck's laudatory new foreword, came out of nowhere to hit number one on Amazon.com. It remained in the top fifteen all summer, holding number one in the government category for months.

When Beck's *Common Sense* was released that summer, *Leap* received another boost by topping the 9.12 Project's required-reading list. As of winter 2009–2010, it remains a presence at 9.12 Project meetings around the country, where guest speakers often use it as their primary source material. James Pratt, the book's Utah-based publisher, states the obvious when he says that Beck "has done more to bring the work of Dr. Skousen [*sic*] to light than any other individual in America today."[34]

The 5,000 Year Leap is not the only Skousen title to find new life on the 9.12 Project circuit. The president of the National Center for Constitutional Studies, Dr. Earl Taylor Jr., has toured the country offering daylong seminars to 9.12 Project chapters based on Skousen's *Making of America*. For $25, participants receive a bag lunch and stories about America's religious founders and the happy slaves of the antebellum South. The ads for Taylor's seminar, as featured on 9.12 Project Web sites, claim that Skousen's book is "considered a great masterpiece to Constitutional students [and is] the 'granddaddy' of all books on the United States Constitution."

Prior to his Mormon baptism, Beck had only the vaguest conservative instincts and very little knowledge of history or politics. In Skousen, he found a ready-made worldview perfectly suited to his paranoid, combative, and apocalyptic nature. After 9/11 inflamed Beck's apocalyptic side, the Skousenite strain in his adopted faith provided heavy ballast for his conviction that the United States was fighting World War III.

Beck would deny that he shares Skousen's conspiracy approach to history. In his books he has gone out of his way to distance himself from "the tin foil hat crowd" and to stress that there is no conscious conspiracy. Both *Common Sense* and *An Inconvenient Book* contain self-effacing rejections of conspiracy theories. These hedges could be Beck's words, or they could reflect nervous editing by more cautious members of Beck's large editorial team. Whatever the case, Beck's politics remain Skousenite in tone, style, and content, regardless of the disclaimers that accompany Beck's exhortations to read Skousen's books.

From Skousen, Beck has learned his truncated and narrow view of American history. Both men adhere to a decline narrative that zooms straight from the divinely inspired genius of the founders to the perfidy of the progressives (with a brief stop in 1868 to bemoan the Fourteenth Amendment). For Skousen and Beck, America's fall from grace is completed precisely in 1913. That year witnessed four of the most momentous events in the Skousenite handbook: the birth of the Federal Reserve, the beginning of Woodrow Wilson's presidency, the establishment of the Rockefeller Foundation, and the passage of the Seventeenth Amendment (which began the election of senators by popular vote).

The Skousen legacy is seen more generally in Beck's eschatalogical take on politics as an urgent crusade to surround America's godless enemies within. Skousen's Cold War writings and Beck's modern updates both burn with the language of righteous resentment against "insiders." In *The Naked Capitalist*, Skousen blames America's ills on the "Ivy League, Anglophile, eastern seaboard . . . establishment."[35] Beck's *Common Sense* is likewise full of populist-sounding rage against elites and their "Ivy League educations, family connections, and misplaced egos."[36] For both men, the enemies of America are "without honor."

Beck's apocalyptic urgency is based on a sense of time always running out, just as Skousen's was. In *The Naked Capitalist*, Skousen describes the 1970s as "the crucial period during which free men in general, and Americans in particular, will decide whether we have the stamina and intelligence to turn the tide." In *Common Sense*, Beck writes that if the Constitution is not rescued right here, right now, the next generation will be "forced to carry the yoke of servitude imposed by their domestic and foreign masters."[37]

It does not trouble Beck any more than it did Skousen that this Constitution, so in need of urgent rescue, is a thoroughly secular document that its authors found imperfect enough to begin amending as soon as they finished writing it. Bereft of references to Mosaic law, Jesus Christ, or God, its own language constitutes an unanswerable rebuke to religious hucksters, past and present, who seek to deny our shared Enlightenment heritage in the name of the voices inside their heads.

13

The 9.12 Project

Tea Party conservatism is the first protest movement in history to be launched from the floor of a stock exchange.

It was Thursday morning, February 19, 2009, not yet a month into Barack Obama's presidency. A veteran Chicago-based CNBC correspondent named Rick Santelli was reporting on his usual beat from the trading room at the Chicago Board of Trade, where as a younger man he traded cow and gold futures. During a lull before the Chicago floor opened for business, Becky Quick, an anchor on the network's early show, asked Santelli his thoughts on the administration's newly announced $75 billion plan to help distressed home owners stave off foreclosure. Upon receiving the question, Santelli shifted his left foot back slightly, as if assuming a stance, and held forth with an emotional response that has since become the stuff of Tea Party lore:

> The government is promoting bad behavior. You know, the new administration's big on computers and technology—how about this, President and new administration? Why don't you put up a Web site to have people vote on the Internet as a referendum to see if we really want to subsidize the losers' mortgages; or would we like to at least buy cars and buy houses in foreclosure and give them to people that might have a chance to actually prosper down the road, and reward people that could carry the water instead of drink the water? President Obama, are you listening?[1]

As the correspondent's anger mounted, nearby traders took notice and began to cheer him on. The hurrahs emboldened Santelli, who then floated an idea. "We're thinking of having a Chicago tea party in July," he said. "All you capitalists that want to show up to Lake Michigan, I'm going to start organizing it." Then he pointed to the raucous traders behind him. "This is America!" he yelled. "This is the silent majority! If you read our Founding Fathers, people like Benjamin Franklin and Jefferson, what we are doing in this country now is making them roll over in their graves!"[2]

Jason Roney, the analyst who was sharing a split screen with Santelli, joked that Mayor Richard Daley was most likely calling up the National Guard in response to the trading-floor call for insurrection. Another copanelist teasingly congratulated Santelli on "his new incarnation as a revolutionary leader." But it was no joke. Within minutes of the broadcast, what will be forever known as "Santelli's Rant" was being praised, posted, and echoed in conservative media as if a shot had been fired and heard 'round the world. By the end of the day, Santelli's Rant—a "10,000 volt charge of energy and anger," according to one conservative blog[3]—had earned its presenter comparisons to Revolutionary War hero Samuel Adams and fictional *Network* hero Howard Beale. For his strong words against the home owners' bailout, the CNBC reporter was hailed as a leader and a symbol of disenfranchised Americans suffering under big-government oppression and fiscal mismanagement. On sister network MSNBC, Chris Matthews told Santelli that his outburst had catapulted him "up there with Rush Limbaugh and Sean Hannity."[4]

As Santelli basked in his newfound fame, a nationwide protest known as the Tea Party movement mysteriously materialized on the Internet. A ring of Web sites came online within hours of Santelli's rant, like sleeper-cell blogs awaiting instructions from a faraway central leadership, all claiming to have been inspired by Santelli's allegedly impromptu outburst. At first glance, the sites appeared unplanned. But many were suspiciously well designed and strangely on point with their "nonpartisan" and "grassroots" statements. An investigation by Mark Ames and Yasha Levine found that the sites were heavily linked to one another and that many were connected to corporate-funded think tanks like FreedomWorks and Americans for Prosperity, which specialize in imitation-grassroots PR campaigns.[5]

Something big was clearly afoot: a new "taxpayer revolt" whose symbol was tea and whose face belonged to Rick Santelli. If Glenn Beck had anything to say about it, and he did, that would not be the case for long.

On the morning of February 20, Beck addressed Santelli's instant celebrity on the radio. He was obviously rankled by the comparisons between Santelli and Howard Beale. There could only be one modern-day Beale, and that was Beck. While playing the audio of the rant, the host at first tartly dismissed Santelli as "a showman." Only as the tape played on did Beck begin to focus on the message, not the man. And he was on board. If Santelli's rant was, as it appeared, the planned trigger for a coordinated rollout involving right-wing think tanks and high-level conservative media, Beck sounded as if he had received a full debriefing:

> When [Santelli] said, "President Obama, are you hearing this," he couldn't have spoken truer words. This is the beginning. . . . It is what I've been talking about that was coming for a very long time and that is disenfranchisement, which will turn into anger, and then turn into God knows what. So this is where it gets real. Listen carefully. You hear the [stock-trading] floor? This is what's coming. There is going to be peaceful civil disobedience. I think that is the first step. And this was the first launch across the bow of peaceful civil disobedience.

Santelli may have been "the first step," but Beck is a distance runner who understands the importance of pace. Months before Santelli's rant, Beck had begun to tinker publicly with the blueprint for his own citizens' protest movement. Its central idea was amorphous but catchy: the September 12 American.

The earliest prototype of the 9.12 Project bore little resemblance to the final product. Beck's beta version of the nine-twelver was a sort of good samaritan of the apocalypse, a rugged individualist who stocked soup and ammunition in preparation for runaway inflation and social collapse. Beck's first mention of the concept came on September 22, 2008, during a radio monologue on the financial crisis. When the economy finally crumbled and unleashed social chaos, Beck told his audience,

"You must be the person that you were on September 12, [2001,] because people are going to freak out. People are going to be very afraid and people aren't going to know what's happening. These experts don't know what's going on. You will. You need to be the leader."

A week after Obama's election, in the two-month period between his Headline News and his Fox News tenures, Beck elaborated on his gestating idea of the 9.12 Christian road warrior:

> You don't have to buy gold. You buy food. If you had three months of food, if you had six months of food. . . . With tough times ahead you are going to be prepared. [It] will be a great blessing because you are going to feel like the September twelfth person. A metaphor for what is coming is September eleventh. It's not going to be an event but it's going to be something that scares a lot of people. And you need to be the person that is either standing in [sic] the street corner with the boot, or the one that rolls down your window and puts the money in the boot at every single block. Because you're a September twelfth American.[6]

Then something changed. In the weeks leading up to the inauguration, Beck's idea of the nine-twelver evolved from a selfless soup stocker to a selfless soup stocker who crusades for free-market principles. Beck began telling his radio audience of the big plans he had for the September 12 person. This individual must not only organize and lead his neighborhood after civilization's collapse, he must also work toward national revival, with Beck leading the way. Beck did not elaborate on the substance of this movement, but he explained that it would have a bible: *The 5,000 Year Leap* by Cleon Skousen.

A month before the inauguration, Beck's vision for the 9.12 movement was slowly coming into focus. Skousen would be "the first part" of something requiring "dedication." Beyond that, Beck asked for patience. More details would be forthcoming next year. To hear them, he suggested, listeners should tune in to the Fox News Channel on weekdays at 5 p.m. Eastern Time.

Beck launched big on Fox News on January 19, 2009. By early February, *Glenn Beck* viewing parties were popping up across the country.

Sensing the new conservative mood, Beck put aside the communist-tinged survivalist lectures and pounded away on a theme of "we surround them." His 9.12 concept soon crystallized into something more than a vague, gooey promise. On February 16, Beck floated nine values and twelve principles that separated the "we" from "them."[7]

On the screen was a plug for Glennbeck.com. Beck asked viewers who agreed with these principles to e-mail him their pictures; he promised to include them on his program so viewers would know they "are not alone." The response was overwhelming and crashed the network's servers. Glenn Beck's Real America had been quickening in utero; on that night Beck broke water.

For an antitax, anti–big government movement, the politics that animated the "we surround them" concept were skewed strongly against temporary social welfare policies, which constitute a tiny fraction of government spending. On February 17, the day after outlining his 9.12 concept, Beck delivered a typical "we surround them" rant on his TV show that focused on the possible expansion of national unemployment benefits:

> I read stories, two stories this weekend in the *New York Times* where they were talking about how great this is because the unions are going to be very, very strong and the government welfare is coming. Unemployment for people who quit their job. Unemployment for people who quit their job or have been fired from a part-time job. This is good news? This to me doesn't make any sense. But you're not alone. I'm not alone.

Many of those in Beck's audience stood to benefit from the policies Beck attacked. But the viewing parties continued to multiply and grow. During the last week of February, Beck teased an upcoming special "We Surround Them" episode of *Glenn Beck*, during which he promised a major announcement for those willing to "make sacrifices." Then came Santelli's explosion of rage against mortgage support for the working poor and the middle class. This unleashed a flood of energy on the Right, partially organized and channeled by FreedomWorks. As the infrastructure for the Tea Party movement was unfurled like a fold-up combat bridge, preparations were already under way for the March 13 airing of the "We Surround Them" special. Large viewing parties were organized in Utah, Ohio, and Iraq and on the Chuck Norris Ranch. Each would be connected to Beck's Fox News set by a live satellite feed.

The show was destined to be Beck's most famous hour of television. When it was over, he became the public face of the growing Tea Party movement. Never again would anyone mistake Rick Santelli as the proper heir to Howard Beale's throne of tears ever again.

On March 13, 2009, *Glenn Beck* opened with the host behind the set. Looking like a nervous comedian poised to take the stage for his first HBO special, Beck launched into a speech that was tailored to what he imagined his typical viewer to be. With his left hand more frantic than usual, he began with a swipe at low-income home owners:

> You didn't take out a loan that didn't require proof of income. And now you're forced to bail these people out. You're concerned. It's not about politics. You actually believe in something.

A video montage replaced the image of Beck: George W. Bush at ground zero, Mexican gang members, soldiers fighting in a desert. Over the footage, Beck continued his monologue:

> The world is spinning out of control. Islamic extremism. Europe on the brink. Even pirates now. Mexico isn't safe for vacations anymore. Our companies face new union mandates, and global cap-and-trade, and the second highest corporate tax rate in the world. Major banks have stocks worth less than a frappuccino. . . . What happened to the country that stood up for the underdog? What happened to the forgotten man?

Chants of "U-S-A!" could be heard from members of the studio audience, sitting unseen just feet away from their eulogizing hero, who continued:

> Something is happening in America. The paradigm is about to change. Tonight, I will ask you to choose. To become the watch-men at the gate, to become America's next greatest generation.

The video montage abruptly ended. The screen filled once again with Beck looking at the camera. The next thirty seconds would become the most repeated clip of his career. Choking up, Beck asked the following: "Are you ready to be that person you were, that day, after nine-eleven, on nine-twelve? I told you for weeks, you're not alone!"

He looked around and above him, almost panicked, tears welling. Then he exclaimed: "I'm turning into a frickin' televangelist. Come on, America. Follow me!"

Beck ran out onto the set wearing his usual combo of suit and black Converse sneakers.* He was greeted with rapturous applause by the studio audience. Hundreds more fans cheered on the street outside the Fox News building. "You're the secret," he said, "you're the answer." He started crying again. "Sorry. I just love my country. And I fear for it."

What followed was a blur of classic incoherent Beckian treacle. Chuck Norris told Beck "he's lighting a spark." Norris's wife, Gina, smiled and nodded vigorously. An army sergeant told the story of a private in Iraq who unloaded five hundred rounds in the direction of the enemy minutes after taking a chunk of shrapnel in the throat. Beck choked up. A survivalist explained why faith in God is "the most important thing." The former CEO of Madison Square Garden said that private charity is better than government handouts. Beck again explained the nine principles and the twelve values. More tears.

In the show's final minutes, Beck again addressed the camera. His voice was soft and intimate, like a *700 Club* host fishing for first-time callers. "If you choose to be a nine-twelver," he said, "you will not only change yourself, but you will change, literally, our country." To start on this path, he asked his live audience to look under their seats. Anyone who was hoping to find the keys to a 2009 Saturn was disappointed. They found instead two paperback books: Cleon Skousen's *The 5,000 Year Leap* and Jay Perry's *The Real George Washington*. Both titles are published by the Mormon-run National Center for Constitutional Studies, founded by Cleon Skousen and currently based in a remote farmhouse in Malta, Idaho.

---

*Off-air, Beck is known to favor Louis Vuitton shoes.

Beck then launched one of his famous buildups, the kind once used to tease about fake underground theme parks in Baltimore:

> Yesterday was six months to September twelfth. . . . I'm working on a couple of projects that are gonna take me at least six months to do. I'd like to ask you [chokes up] to join me. Again, on Saturday, September twelfth. I'll share with you what I've been working on to put the values and principles to work in my own life, and you show me what you've done. We'll meet back here in six months. All right?

"All right!" Real America responded. Days later, Meetup.com announced the 9.12 Project to be the biggest social networking phenomenon since Howard Dean.

Beck's attempt to control the grassroots' protest agenda was short-lived. Much to his chagrin, the road to September 12 passed through another key date in the U.S. calendar that the master showman had not considered: April 15. In the days after *Glenn Beck*'s "We Surround Them" episode, FreedomWorks and Americans for Prosperity announced plans for tax day protests across the country.

Beck panicked. The giveaway was the curious disappearance of his famous urgency. All of a sudden, the host—who had been warning of impending fascism for weeks, complete with images of marching jackboots—now felt that everyone should relax. It was too soon for April protests, he explained, because higher taxes hadn't kicked in yet.

Despite Beck's misgivings, Fox News gave him a starring role in its all-day coverage of the protests. Between 5 and 6 p.m. on April 15, Beck had the field all to himself, broadcasting live from the Alamo in San Antonio, Texas. During the special episode, "Taking a Stand at the Alamo," Beck sheepishly explained away his original opposition to the April protests. "I said five or six weeks ago that I felt it was too early for these tax tea parties," he said. "The reason was, at that time, I said, 'We're not paying higher taxes yet.' But they're coming."

Throughout the show, Beck was repeatedly interrupted by chants of "U-S-A!" giving the feel of a Sarah Palin campaign rally reunion. Among Beck's featured guests were Ted Nugent and Texas governor

Rick Perry, who joined Beck at the Alamo after a statehouse visit to back a resolution in support of "states rights under the Tenth Amendment to the U.S. Constitution."

At the time, neo–states' rights activism—known as the Tenther movement—was becoming an increasingly loud theme on the young Tea Party scene, but it was nothing new on Beck's programs. As far back as 2007, Beck had welcomed onto his Headline News show guests associated with the League of the South (a neo-Confederate group) and other secessionist outfits. Tenther activism would soon become part of the 9.12 Project catechism. In Florida, for example, the Tampa chapter was gathering support for a series of bills compelling the state to ignore federal legislation on health care and gun control. One proposed bill, the Florida Tenth Amendment Resolution, put the state on track toward secession by reasserting "Florida's sovereignty under the 10th Amendment to the Constitution of the United States." Nine-twelvers soon began drafting copycat bills around the country.

On the Alamo stage, Beck faced a crowd filled with cowboy hats, American flags, and secessionist T-shirts (I WOULD RATHER CUT OFF MY OWN ARM THAN LIVE IN TYRANNY). "This is not about parties," he told the masses who had been silent under eight years of the previous administration. "It's about moms, dads, people going out and working jobs every day." Without offering any numbers, he warned that Barack Obama was preparing to double the deficit—"again." Beck offered no charts or chalkboard lessons to back up the claim. And for good reason. Any official numbers would have demonstrated that just 3 percent of the coming year's federal deficit was caused by Obama's domestic policies.[8] Most of the rest could be traced to the Bush tax cuts, two Bush wars, and the fiery crash of the Bush economy that drastically reduced state revenues—a direct result of the same deregulatory philosophy championed by Beck. But this afternoon at the Alamo was not a day for boring facts. It was about emotional release, threatened secession, and Beck pretending to be David Letterman. "Ted Nugent is my Paul Shaffer!" exclaimed the emcee. Appearing via satellite from another Tea Party rally, Fox's Neil Cavuto upped the ante and called it Beck's "Evita moment."

Flattering, but a moment named after Argentina's Evita Peron is not what Beck craved. He wanted his moment on the National Mall. His "Martin Luther King moment" was now five months away.

Alas, it was not to be. On August 13, Beck announced that he would not attend the march in Washington scheduled for September 12. He would instead anchor coverage from the Fox News studios in New York. Despite his frequent and loud claims of independence, Beck is a creature of the corporation, and the corporation did not want him to attend. Fox had taken heavy criticism for its blatant promotion of the April protests, including several on-air plugs for "FNC Tax Day Tea Parties." Having Beck headline the September protest was one step too far. Visibly dejected, he described the decision in a way that suggested it had been his own:

> I have been asked to speak. And I prayed about it. Then I went to Fox and asked them if they'd help me do my role. Here's what I feel. Now I could go and speak, and then hope that someone in the media would cover it. Or, I could stay here in New York, and not only cover Washington, but some of the other big rallies that people want to go, and be a part of taking their country back. So, on nine-twelve, I will be anchoring live coverage here, of the biggest nine-twelve Tea Party yet, on Capitol Hill, on September twelfth. No matter where you are, there or here, we will see each other then.

Passions ran high in the month between Beck's announcement and the march. The Van Jones affair was approaching full boil. Health-care town halls were erupting in YouTube-ready shout-downs across the country. Then, in the week before the march, President Obama announced his plan to address the nation's schoolchildren with a motivational message of hard work. Beck and the rest of Real America were not happy.

Discussing a bas-relief that supposedly represented an Italian fascist tableaux on Fox News (see chapter 12), Beck said, "Gee, who's having indoctrination next week? Oh, yeah, that's right, the president—completely unrelated. This represents, at the time this was made, Mussolini. This was Mussolini. By the way, the artist that made this—his son—ironically and tragically died fighting the army of Mussolini years after this was made."

Indoctrination of the young. Gathering fascist clouds. Around the country, the nine-twelvers fed on Beck's paranoia like sharks on blood. A member of the Tampa 9.12 Project, who posts under the name

"Patriot Sherry," posted this call to action online the day after Beck's comments:

> Urgent! He is coming after our kids now!!!!! Does anyone read history anymore? Does anyone care? Who in the past has "reached out" to students like this? Indoctrination??? Who has tried to build a "youth movement" in the past??? Mark the date down, Sept. 8, 2009, Barack Obama will address to all students Pre-K to 6th grade! This is unprecedented, never before has this taken place in America anyway! On September 8, 2009, I will be keeping my children home and reading them excerpts of the "5000 year leap", "The American Patriot's Almanac: Daily Readings on America", and The Constitution. I declare September 8, 2009, Freedom from Oppression Day! NO OBAMA, YOU WILL NOT INDOCTRINATE MY CHILDREN!

Similar sentiments were found on signs carried to Washington on the overcast afternoon of September 12. It was the first big Tea Party event since the tax day protests. It seemed that the protesters' main enemies were Russian history and apostrophes: 32 CZAR'S, WASHINGTON IS THE NEW KREMLIN.

The placards of September 12 told the story. There were hammers and sickles and swastikas. There were crosses and coiled snakes. There were machine guns paired with taunts like COME AND TAKE IT, and WE CAME UNARMED—THIS TIME. Messages on T-shirts read, THE CURE FOR OBAMA COMMUNISM IS A NEW ERA OF MCCARTHYISM and MCCARTHY WAS RIGHT THEN AND HE'S RIGHT NOW. Some called for waterboarding the president. There were the requisite references to Satan and the New World Order. Dozens of signs called for the nine-twelver dream ticket: BECK/PALIN 2012.

It was a prospect that Palin herself would publicly entertain during her book tour later that fall. In the meantime, the nine-twelvers had work to do. Before 2012, there was 2010. Nowhere was this date being watched more closely than in Florida, birthplace of *The Glenn Beck Program* and home to the busiest Tea Party hives in the land.

On the morning of December 16, 2009, Charlie Crist, the Republican governor of Florida and a newly announced candidate for the Senate, stood behind a podium in a vacant grass lot on the edge of downtown Tampa. He was there to praise and sign a controversial transit bill that had been the subject of vigorous local debate for more than a decade. Along with boosting budgets for the state's existing commuter rail infrastructure, HB-1B would fund the first leg of a modern high-speed rail system linking Tampa, Orlando, and Miami.

By committing to building the base of this triad, Florida would qualify for a thick slice of $8 billion in federal stimulus funds the White House had set aside for high-speed rail earlier that year. More than 150 local politicians and businesspeople had come to witness the signing, held on the craggy field that was destined to host the Tampa hub of the proposed system.

"Jobs, jobs, jobs," Crist told the assembled to polite applause. "Jobs—that's what this is really all about." No one doubted that Florida's economy could use all the help it could get. The state's unemployment rate was rapidly approaching 12 percent; only Michigan was shedding jobs faster. Although Crist's speech was held blocks from Tampa's downtown business district, the only signs of commercial activity were a roadside snack shack and a Jamaican restaurant, long since closed. "Especially in these difficult times," said Crist, Florida needed "the fifteen thousand construction jobs and millions in revenue" that the transit stimulus would provide.

More polite applause accompanied Crist's signing of the bill. But the acclaim was not unanimous. At the back of the scene, behind the seated local notables and the camera crews, a knot of dissenters had been making its displeasure known. As soon as Crist assumed the podium and began talking up the rail bill, the hecklers' gallery responded by yelling slogans ("Less government! Less taxes! More freedom!"), and rejoinders ("You lie!").

The dissent was bold and loud and familiar. It drew cold stares from the seated and prompted several police officers present to raise their chins, whisper into walkie-talkies, and take a few steps toward the source of the noise. The dissenters stood out as visibly as they did audibly. Surrounded by suits, they wore jeans, shorts, and T-shirts that read AMERICAN PATRIOT and 1776. At the center of the group, which included two men and a woman in matching Harley-Davidson jean jackets, a man was waving a giant white flag. DON'T TREAD ON ME, it read, LIBERTY OR DEATH.

As Charlie Crist knew it would, the Tampa chapter of the 9.12 Project had come to shame him.

More than any other group in Florida, the nine-twelvers hated the passenger rail bill. They hated everything about it. But what they despised above all was the man who signed it. Crist could have visited Tampa to cut the ribbon at a new animal shelter run by nuns, and the nine-twelvers still would have appeared waving the DON'T TREAD ON ME flag. For the nine-twelvers, Crist was the prize beast in the great "RINO hunt" of 2010. In the terminology of Tea Party conservatism, Crist was a "Republican in Name Only." The sins that led to this designation were legion. To close budget shortfalls, he had raised the cigarette tax, increased fees on a number of city services like license registration, and, worst of all in the 9.12 view, supported the Obama stimulus package. And now here he was pushing a big-government rail bill.

The nine-twelvers' hatred of Crist was matched only by their affection for his upstart Republican challenger in the looming Senate primary: a thirty-seven-year-old state representative from Miami named Marco Rubio. More than just the darling of the Florida Tea Party scene, Rubio had emerged as the Cuban American icon of non-RINO Republicanism nationwide.

On the morning Crist signed the rail bill, a number of indicators suggested that the nine-twelvers were not alone in hoping that Rubio could unseat Crist. A new Rasmussen poll released that week showed Rubio for the first time running even with Crist among Republicans statewide. There were also signs of rising Tea Party power within the establishment it claimed to oppose. Hours after Crist's podium was dismantled in Tampa, in Washington Republican Party chairman Michael Steele held an "RNC Tea Party" in praise of the new grassroots movement.

And so it was with confidence that a Tampa nine-twelver named Kevin Wright, wearing Terminator sunglasses and an END THE FED T-shirt, issued the Florida governor a grim promise as he signed the bill: "Say goodbye to your political career, Charlie. It's *gone*. Rubio 2010!"

Not twenty feet away, a smiling Crist began shaking hands and pretended not to hear the taunt. If his deaf act looked convincing, it should have. Throughout the previous months he'd had plenty of practice ignoring the nine-twelvers. He wasn't alone. Groups affiliated with the Tea Party movement, of which the 9.12 Project is but the largest in Florida, had begun the previous summer to routinely shadow the movements of local Democrats and accused RINOs throughout the state.

If Democratic senator Ben Nelson was scheduled to appear at a breakfast fundraiser, a knot of self-styled patriots waited for him across the street with signs urging the senator to go to Cuba. When Tampa's Democratic representative Kathy Castor held a health-care town hall, the local nine-twelvers came out in force and shouted her down. And if the governor ventured in public to sign a passenger rail bill in downtown Tampa, the nine-twelvers would be there, screaming about socialism and waving a DON'T TREAD ON ME flag, bullhorns in hand.

After Crist disappeared inside his chauffeured SUV, the assembled local media flocked to the nine-twelvers. The previous summer, members of Beck's organization had become a story unto themselves. And they were always good for spicing up an otherwise dry story about a transit bill. In this case, one of them came off very well informed about the issue at hand.

When asked about the passenger rail bill, nine-twelver Kevin Wright, still in his Terminator glasses, articulated a strong and coherent case for the opposition. There was, he noted, a suspicious contracting scandal about the rail line that smelled of corruption. Some parts of the city and surrounding areas don't yet have adequate buses. And because of Florida's balanced budget requirement, the bill would cause cuts in other vital services. What's more, Wright said in closing, the bill was rejected by 60 percent of voters in a 2004 referendum. "These fat cats getting back into their limos will never take the train," said Wright, sounding perfectly sane.

But then the man standing next to Wright said, "Just like they're never going to have to face the death panels."

The voice belonged to Fred Brownbill, a hulking white-haired fifty-four-year-old "private law enforcement" professional. Alone among his peers that day, Brownbill's shouts at Crist carried the distinct accent of his native Zimbabwe, which he left after the civil war ended white rule in the late 1970s. According to Brownbill, he is now hearing the same rhetoric and seeing the same government actions that turned his native land into a bloody tyranny. "I'm running out of countries to escape," he said. "There's not a shadow of doubt, that's where we're headed—twenty thousand dead. I've seen this before."

With half a dozen of his fellow nine-twelvers nodding in agreement, Brownbill continued. "Obama's a puppet of the Marxist regime behind the scenes," he said. "He's also a usurper who doesn't meet the qualifications of president. If he does, then why not just produce the birth certificate?"

To understand the shadowy forces running the country, Brownbill suggests, "start by looking into the Vanderbilt Group" (he meant Bilderberg). He also warned of a planned "National Water Act." He wasn't sure exactly how it would work, but he suspected that it would be unleashed on the American people sometime in the coming year. "If Obama gets his way," he explained, "the federal government will control every drop of water in the country. The nationalizations are coming."

Like Glenn Beck, Brownbill and his fellow nine-twelvers worry that time is running out. It is partly because of what they see as Beck's brave patriotism that they remain hopeful. Several of those listening to Brownbill chimed in when he mentioned Beck. "I love him to death!" said Joan Hall, a fifty-three-year-old St. Petersburg homemaker. "He's kinda crazy, but he's *so entertaining.* He's stirring us up, and they don't like it."

When asked to define "us," Hall paused. "The taxpayers," she said. As Hall had learned from listening to Beck, the country is divided into two groups: taxpayers and "social justice street organizers" like Van Jones.

"Glenn is a real conservative," added nine-twelver Toni Armstrong, a forty-six-year-old homemaker from nearby Apollo Beach. "The two-party system would work fine in Washington if you had real conservatives like Glenn, and real liberals. The problem is you have all these gray areas in between."

As proof that Beck is waking people up, Brownbill pointed to the previous September's 9.12 march on Washington. "There were 2.62 million protesting in Washington that day," he said. "Think about that."

When presented with the official D.C. Fire Department estimate of between sixty thousand and seventy thousand, Brownbill huffed. "A lot of people couldn't find the Mall because the roads around the city were so clogged," he said. "But they were there."

It was then time for Brownbill and his fellow nine-twelvers to hit the road themselves. There was a big Tea Party gathering in nearby Plant City. It was being held in celebration of the 236-year anniversary of the original Boston Tea Party. Hundreds of local patriots would be there. Marco Rubio was headlining.

The suburbs and exurbs of Tampa and Orlando are among the nation's busiest hubs of Tea Party–related activity. As of December 2009, the Tampa chapter of the 9.12 Project was the nation's largest, with nearly two thousand active members and enough rolling donations to run recruitment ads on the station that launched Beck's talk-radio career, WFLA-970. The surrounding area is also home to growing chapters of the Tea Party Patriots, FreedomWorks, "Freepers" (activists aligned with the hard-right Web site FreeRepublic.com), and the Save America Foundation. It is not for nothing that when it came time for Beck to unveil "the plan," he chose the Disney Belt retirement community known as the Villages, roughly equidistant between Tampa and Orlando. Tampa Bay's Pinellas and Hillsborough counties are to the Tea Party movement of today what Orange County was to the Far Right of fifty years ago.

Among the groups rallying around the Tea Party flag, The 9.12 Project is arguably the most antiestablishment and least compromised by ties to groups funded and led by GOP operatives and lobbyists. But this relative independence has not stopped it from collaborating with groups of suspect grassroots pedigrees. The November 2009 Tea Party Express Bus Tour—funded and organized by Sal Russo, a veteran California GOP consultant—chose Orlando's Lake Eola Amphitheater for its massive final rally, which was supported and attended by local nine-twelvers. That same month, when Fred O'Neal, an Orlando-area lawyer with no ties to the Tea Party movement aside from backing from local GOP consultant Doug Guetzloe, officially registered the "Tea Party" Party with Florida's secretary of state, the nine-twelvers celebrated the event.

The nine-twelvers and their compatriots share a demographic with earlier bursts of antiestablishment conservatism. Like the fervent anti-communists who once gathered in the John Birch Society, the typical nine-twelver is white, suburban, and belongs to the less educated sectors of the broad middle class. Most were proud Republicans prior the rise of the Tea Party right; very few were politically active; almost none had ever hoisted signs and chanted. They are against government spending in most cases (other than the military) and favor tax schemes that would most benefit income brackets far above their own. Lurking beneath the movement—and to some extent driving it—is what conservative *New York Times* columnist Ross Douthat charitably calls "all kinds of inchoate cultural resentments."[9]

Along with protests and outings, the nine-twelvers like their lectures. The rise of the 9.12 Project has been a boon for conservative speakers like Rebecca O'Dell, a Tampa Bay appellate attorney who has become a regular on Florida's 9.12 scene. Using Cleon Skousen's *The 5,000 Year Leap* as the basis of her talks, O'Dell travels the state speaking on the Constitution, the "rise of judicial tyranny," and the American Civil Liberties Union, whose sole purpose, she believes, "is to champion the transformation of the United States from a Judeo-Christian nation into a secular humanist 'anti-religion' state patterned after the Soviet Union."

Often 9.12 Project events feel as social as they do political. This was always Beck's intention. On Independence Day weekend in 2009, the Tampa and the Pinellas County chapters cosponsored a series of barbecues and a Fourth of July "patriotic boat parade." The two boats that best represented an article or an amendment of the Constitution won a $500 prize. The nine-twelvers gather weekly in mall food courts for Saturday morning coffee klatches. And on the semiannual evenings when local theaters feature a simulcast of a Glenn Beck stage performance, the nine-twelvers meet at casual dining chains, where they discuss the news of the day before heading for the cinema. After the show, they haunt the exits with flyers that explain their nine principles and twelve values.

Then they get into their cars, turn on WFLA-970, and drive away.

Epilogue

The Bullet Train and the Rocking Chair

The morning of January 28, 2010, started out bright and warm in central Florida. The weather marked the end of an historic cold snap, and the mood was festive on the manicured campus of the University of Tampa. Thousands of students in T-shirts and flip-flops were lined up with tickets in hand for entry into the Bob Martinez Sports Center. Among the university buildings they shuffled past was the opulent old Tampa Bay Hotel, now a museum and administration building. At the turn of the last century, Teddy Roosevelt and his fellow Rough Riders drank and whored in the hotel before sailing off to wrest San Juan Hill from Spain.

On this morning, another American president was in town to begin a rough ride of his own, his goal to retake a different kind of high ground. At noon, an embattled and newly combative Barack Obama, fresh off his first State of the Union address, was scheduled to announce a development fiercely opposed by the local nine-twelvers: Florida would receive $2.5 billion in federal stimulus funds to build the region's first high-speed rail track. The result, claimed boosters, would be thousands of badly needed jobs and bullet trains flying between Tampa Bay, Orlando, Disney World, and regional airports.

In the week since the presidential visit was announced, the nine-twelvers lay in wait, sharpening their organizational knives. "Lets [*sic*]

252

greet Obama and Biden with a hardy Tampa 912 spirit," read a typical e-mail blast. "We need to show them that We The People will be heard. Bring your signs and flags!"

Bring them they did. Hours before the presidential motorcade's expected arrival, knots of angry nine-twelvers began gathering on nearby street corners. They asked passing cars to "honk for freedom" and hoisted the familiar signage. WHERE IN THE CONSTITUTION DOES IT MENTION CZARS? asked one placard in red, white, and blue. WE ARE TAK-ING BACK OUR COUNTRY declared another. There was also the usual collection of spitefully rendered caricatures on display. One hand-painted sign illustrated Nancy Pelosi in a Soviet-themed bikini, her cartoon breasts sagging under the exaggerated effects of age and gravity. NOT EVEN OBAMACARE CAN FIX THIS! read the accompanying message. Who said conservatives lacked a sense of humor?*

The nine-twelvers weren't alone in the streets. Freepers, Tea Party Patriots, and staff from the GOP-connected FreedomWorks also prowled the scene. Especially busy was FreedomWorks' Florida field coordinator, Thomas Gaitens, who milled about the crowd in search of interviews in progress. Part of his job, it seemed, was to keep the nine-twelvers on message. This was no easy task. Robert Cygan, a nine-twelver whose business card lists his occupation as "senior patriot," told me that the Securities and Exchange Commission had orchestrated the 2007 financial crisis in order to install a communist (Obama) in power, in accordance with the New World Order designs of the Bilderberg Group. "They don't even allow cameras into the annual meeting, you know," Cygan said. Though Beck himself has dismissed grand theories of Bilderberg power, Cygan still thinks Beck is the best commentator on TV and credits him with his recent political awakening.

Standing near but apart from the nine-twelvers was Bobby McCoy, the business manager of Local 140, Tampa's carpenters union. The union supports the president's stimulus plan in general and the high-speed rail project in particular. McCoy did not have a ticket to attend Obama's speech but came out to see the protests. "These people don't have a clue," said McCoy, gesturing at the protestors. "It was their hero, Ronald Reagan, who started gutting and bankrupting this country."

---

*Actually, Glenn Beck said this in a July 2009 interview with *GQ*.

When a nine-twelver placed an antistimulus leaflet in McCoy's hand, he examined its argument (and illiterate grammar) with dismay. "Have they seen the unemployment rate?" he asked. "My men need jobs to support their families. How do they think the railroads and freeways were built? By antigovernment small business owners?"

Though few of the participants on either side of this political set piece knew it, there was symbolism in the location of the president's announcement. The White House had originally attempted to reserve the University of South Florida's ten thousand–seat Sun Dome. But the president's advance team was told the venue was not available. It was already being prepped for another event scheduled for the following day: the Bold and Fresh stage tour starring Glenn Beck and Bill O'Reilly.

Obama and Beck. One year after ascending the biggest stages in their respective professions—the White House and the Fox News madhouse—the scheduling collision in Tampa, and its outcome, seemed all too appropriate.

By most metrics, the year had been kinder to Beck. The host began 2010 with his base energized and united; the president, not so much. If the polls were to be believed, Beck was also picking off independents, coming up fast in the president's rear view in approval ratings. Beck ended 2009 by displacing Jay Leno as the nation's second-most popular TV personality and was said to rank high among the men Americans respected most—higher than the pope. Beck's celebrity surge mirrored that of the movement he had done so much to nurture and shape. Generic Tea Party candidates were beginning to outpoll generic GOP and Democratic candidates in hypothetical 2010 and 2012 match-ups. But perhaps nothing captured Beck's new stature better than his upcoming keynote address at the 2010 Conservative Political Action Conference—the ultimate symbol of arrival and juice on the Right.

Meanwhile, Obama had stumbled. Throughout 2009, anger and frustration mounted amid a stalled recovery and Democratic feckless-ness. Playing no small part in his woes was the rise of a conservative protest movement that threatened to tag as a RINO any Republican who attempted to work with him. As Obama struggled to make the case for a future symbolized by bullet trains, Beck was focused on restoring the past. As he prepared for the speech of his life at the granite feet of Abraham Lincoln, he pined for nothing so much as his grandfather's rocking chair.

Hours after Obama departed Tampa following his high-speed rail announcement, Beck's private Gulfstream touched down. The following afternoon, he would perform two sold-out stage shows with Bill O'Reilly. But first he had a radio show to do. On the morning of the twenty-ninth, he was driven to his former Clear Channel studio complex on Gandy Boulevard, home of "the station that started it all," WFLA-970. From there he broadcast *The Glenn Beck Program*, just like the old days. "Tampa is my home away from home," Beck told his oldest fan base at the start of the show. "It's always great to come back here."

During the program's second hour, Beck monologued about his next big event scheduled for 2010: his August 28 rally at the National Mall—Restoring Honor.

A few days earlier, Beck had discussed the rally at length for the first time since the unveiling in November. In the intervening months, Beck changed the hook. No longer, he explained, was the rally pegged to *The Plan*, his forthcoming book based on his two-city American Revival education convention tour, a megachurch approach to the conservative training seminar. Nor was the date any longer tied to the anniversary of Martin Luther King's "I Have a Dream" speech. Someone at Americans for Prosperity must have sent Beck a memo on King's progressive politics, because now Beck claimed he chose the date to align not with the calendar of Martin Luther King Jr., but with that of Clark Griswold.

"I picked August twenty-eighth," said Beck, "because this is the last week before the August holiday is over, and I wanted you to be able to bring your kids. And I want you to bring your friends. And I want you to help me get the word out. Restoring honor. August twenty-eighth. Please mark it down on your calendar. Make plans to join me now." No longer tied to a detailed policy agenda, the march was now designed around a campaign of oratorical oatmeal, Beck's specialty. "Restoring honor," said Beck, was about "remembering":

> If we remember, then we have to choose. Are we going to be part
> of the solution or part of the problem? The solution is to just always

tell the truth. The way to fix Washington is not through politics but through each of us as individuals. That's why I ask you to join me at the steps of the Lincoln Memorial in a program called Restoring Honor.

Beck talked about the funding of this restoration of national honor on *The Glenn Beck Program* on January 25.

When I had this idea about restoring honor, and you can read all about it at GlennBeck.com, we started running some numbers and it looks like it could cost like two million to produce this thing. I hope to God not, but that's what they said. And I was faced with a choice: Not do it, go to sponsors—you know, go to say, hey, Goldline, you want to cough up a couple of million dollars, and it would be the Goldline "Restoring Honor" thing—or come to you. We want to put on an amazing historic event. And believe me, we will. But I want to do it for the cheapest amount we can. . . . I brainstormed with Bill O'Reilly a little bit on Saturday and we have "Restoring Honor Starts Here" merchandise—doormats and T-shirts.

Any money raised in excess of the amount needed for this self-promotional motherlode, Beck explained, would go toward a charity benefiting the children of U.S. Special Forces soldiers killed in action.

A few days later, sitting in his old Tampa studio, Beck returned to the subject of the march and elaborated on the concept of "restoration." The inspiration for the march and its operative metaphor, he revealed, was his grandfather's favorite rocking chair.

The ghost of Beck's grandfather is a regular character on his shows. Beck's fans know that the old man was a gritty Iowa farmer, "a Depression person, not a rich guy," with calloused hands that never once took a handout. Grandfather Beck had simple tastes, a profound sense of honor, and didn't take any lip. Beck claims that he inherited the old rocking chair in which granddad spent his adulthood watching *The Lawrence Welk Show*. For years, Beck told his audience, he was afraid to touch the chair. But recently he decided to call an expert and have it restored. Beck discussed watching in awe as the wood was sanded and refinished, its parts reinforced and made structurally sound once again—like a nation born anew.

Staring at the refurbished piece of furniture, Beck experienced an epiphany. As he described it that morning in Tampa, "We need to restore the Constitution, the way I restored that rocking chair." Thus was born the vision behind Beck's march on Washington: The Republic as a divinely inspired episode of *This Old House*.

Taken literally, Beck's "originalist"-inspired metaphor would take us back to a time when the country had a rural population of less than four million people. If our understanding of the Constitution and the power of the federal government were restored like his grandfather's rocking chair, and the analogous state shrunk to the size and activity of Beck's Iowa yeoman grandfather, the United States of 2010 would not fit. Indeed, the chair would crumble on impact, sending splinters into the collective ass of three hundred million Americans. This is the plain reality that has driven reform figures and movements throughout American history, particularly those whom Beck hates the most, those grouped under the term "progressive." Conversely, it is the refusal to admit this reality—not to mention the consequences of self-delusion— that makes Beck's politics so fundamentally unserious.

Beck is the latest in a long tradition to prove that a vision needn't be serious to package and sell. It need only be compelling on its own deformed terms. His brand of righteous antistate conservatism tantalizes so many precisely because of its operatic nostalgia, opiatic history, and tin-can Orwellian imagination. It is a vision of America as a rugged farmer with no need or care for subsidies, who watches *The Lawrence Welk Show* from a rocking chair in the heartland of a country whose birth God Himself performed. In this America, patriots choose Chevy trucks over bullet trains, an immutable Constitution over case law, and extremist, conversation-stopping rhetoric over informed, reasoned debate.

This America keeps a geriatric tempo with grandfather's rocking chair and stays warm with grandmother's blanket. Given the Janus-nature of Beck's media business, it is no doubt only a matter of time before he turns this rocking chair and blanket into a novel of patriotism, loss, and redemption. For everyone who loved *The Christmas Sweater*, Radio Mercury Arts presents *The Constitution Quilt*.

Rack it up as a future Glenn Beck best seller. It's all over but for the printing.

ACKNOWLEDGMENTS

The first order of thanks goes to Eric Nelson, my editor at John Wiley & Sons. Along with rescuing me from the bottom floor of broke, Eric helped me keep perspective on the subject and offered sharp editing suggestions at every turn. This book does not exist without him. Also at Wiley, Kimberly Monroe-Hill oversaw the editing and production process with much-appreciated skill and care. Judith Antonelli copy-edited the book with owl eyes.

Many friends old and new provided moral, intellectual, and psychopharmacological assistance. My original partners in 1990s zinedom, Adam Bulger and Cedric Howe, blood both, were my earliest sounding boards. Jan Frel, my longtime editor at AlterNet.org, published the essay that led to the book. My old *Prague Pill* and *New York Press* colleagues Joshua Cohen and Jeff Koyen helped me tighten some flabby writing. Former *eXile* comrades Mark Ames and Yasha Levine steered me away from at least two clichés. Michael Pool of WMFU, aka the Professor, provided a handle for the Tampa talk radio scene of yore. Mark Schone helped craft the biography chapters for *Salon*, where they first appeared. David Harding and Ernie Lazar provided generous research assistance on the life and work of Cleon Skousen.

Thanks also to Adrienne Ammerman, Josh Bernstein, Jonas Brier, John Caulkins, Kate Crane, Eric Follen, Ross Ford, Joe Gamble, Josh Goldman, Mark Grueter, Mattie Harper, Don Hazen, Nanci Heim, David Holthouse, Barbora Horackova, Jeremy Hurewitz, Micah Jayne,

Chris Ketcham, Jim Knipfel, Josh Kucera, Alex Lawson, Chris Lord, Michael Manville, Dan McCarthy, Rob Morrison, Jason Nesvet, Tim Parsa, James Pitkin, Milla Riggio, Matt Zoller Seitz, Bonnie Sultan, Matt Taibbi, Tedd Webb, Russ Wellen, Christopher Winner, my sister Allison, and the rest of the Zaitchik clan. The memory of Alex Barber is strong.

I researched and wrote this book during eight months holed up in Tampa's old cigar district, Ybor City. During most of that time, I could be found at King Corona on Seventh Avenue, sipping *cubanos* and puffing Padrons. King Corona is every writer's working-café dream come true. Thanks to Angela, Theresa, Sarah, Joe, Don, Nick, and Christina for letting me occupy the middle table by the window for the better part of 2009, rent-free. Thanks also to 88.5-WMNF, Tampa's listener-supported independent station, which helped me stay sane while listening to at least three hours of 970-WFLA every day.

Thanks to two true masters of the radio monologue, Bob Lassiter and Joe Frank. Thanks to Junior Wells, Atari Teenage Riot, and Erik Satie.

I never understood the publishing convention of leaving the girl for last. Now I understand it even less. It was the girl, Brenda Kathleen Terry, who turned a potentially hellish project into something approaching pure joy. Thanks for everything, baby. I promise to never mention Glenn Beck again.

NOTES

Introduction: The Man with the Plan

1. *The Glenn Beck Program*, June 10, 2009.
2. Ibid., January 21, 2010.
3. *Glenn Beck*, April 16, 2009.
4. Neil Harris, *Humbug: The Art of P. T. Barnum* (Chicago: University of Chicago Press, 1973), 26–27.
5. Richard Hofstadter, *The Paranoid Style in American Politics* (New York: Vintage, 2008), 44–45.
6. Brian Stelter and Bill Carter, "Fox News's Mad, Apocalyptic, Fearful Rising Star," *New York Times*, March 29, 2009.
7. David Brooks, "The Wizard of Beck," *New York Times*, October 2, 2009.
8. A rare and unexpected confrontation with reality occurred when Rubio appeared on *The Glenn Beck Program* on January 14, 2010. When Beck asked the Cuban American candidate if the United States was turning into communist Cuba, Rubio demurred rather than serve up the red meat Beck was hunting for. Rubio, who grew up and lives among Cuban émigrés in Miami, understands the difference between a Democrat and a dictator. "I'm always careful about those comparisons," said Rubio. "Fidel Castro imprisoned people. He executed people. He divided families. He created a Diaspora and exile community, and so, I mean, he's a straight-out criminal and a thug and he was before he even took over the country. So I'm always careful about those comparisons."

1. Portrait of a Young Deejay

1. Glenn Beck, *The Real America: Messages from the Heart and Heartland* (New York: Pocket Books, 2003), 194.
2. Looking back from the vantage point of Glenn Beck's crusade against activist government, one can see an irony in the young Beck launching his radio romance with inspiration from Orson Welles and other golden age radio legends. The literary productions that so enthralled Beck did not fall from a free-market tree. The 1930s and

261

1940s may have been the golden age of the sponsor, but they were also the golden age of a liberal and activist Federal Communications Commission (FCC). Beginning in the early New Deal, an alliance of academics, nonprofit cultural foundations, and labor groups crusaded against the unregulated commercial radio culture of the 1920s, which they rightly considered a cultural cesspool teeming with low humor and crawling with huckstering pitchmen. Sympathetic to this crusade, President Franklin D. Roosevelt and Congress worked to fulfill radio's loftier democratic promise. (They also wanted to put unemployed stage actors and writers to work.) In 1934, the FCC was created to promote better programming and to regulate the airwaves, and it was backed by the real threat of nationalization. This pressure, together with funding from federal cultural programs, resulted in what radio historian Simon Callow calls "the transformation of the networks into Gonzagas and Medicis of the air." See Simon Callow, *Orson Welles: The Road to Xanadu* (New York: Penguin, 1995), 370–371.

3. Pamela Davis, "Working Nerves in the Afternoon," *St. Petersburg Times*, March 17, 2000.

4. Liz Curtis, meanwhile, underwent her own metamorphosis. Beck's former Louisville piñata eventually became an internationally known motivational speaker and best-selling writer of fiction about biblical women, including such titles as *Really Bad Girls of the Bible* and *Slightly Bad Girls of the Bible*. How ironic that once there was actually something funny about Liz Curtis, Glenn Beck had probably become her biggest fan. Thus did the paths of Louisville radio's two most successful alums intersect.

5. That music director, Kevin Weatherly, is now a senior executive at CBS radio.

6. Weddings seemed to inspire Beck and Hattrick. When their general manager, Mike Horne, announced his engagement in June 1988, the duo handcuffed him to an olive tree outside his office and offered cash to female listeners to come to the station parking lot, strip, and kiss the shackled Horne. "Our offices were just a stone's throw from Van Buren, home to the majority of the city's prostitute population, so what ensued was pretty disgusting," remembers Horne.

2. Last Stop on the Top 40 Train

1. Stacy Wong, "Station Apologizes for Mocking Asians," *Hartford Courant*, October 20, 1995.

2. "Is Rush Limbaugh Good for America?" *Time* cover, January 23, 1995. Richard Corliss, "Look Who's Talking." Nearly fifteen years after the Limbaugh story, *Time* ran a cover story about Glenn Beck with the opposite title: "Is Glenn Beck Bad for America?" David von Drehle, *Time*, September 19, 2009.

3. The Luckiest Loudmouth in Tampa

1. Davis, "Working Nerves in the Afternoon."

2. Ibid.

3. Some famous exchanges are available on numerous online shrines to the Cult of Lassiter. Perhaps the most remembered of these is known as "Mr. Airstream," archived at YouTube, which has entered the annals of talk radio as one of the greatest calls of all time. For twelve minutes an unhinged elderly man living in an Airstream trailer rips into Lassiter for criticizing Jim and Tammy Faye Bakker.

4. *The Glenn Beck Program*, February 4, 2005.

5. Ibid., March 9, 2001.

6. It's possible that Beck harbored an especially deep hatred for Jackson as well as Al Sharpton for the duo's leading role in organizing a boycott of one of his talk-radio heroes, Bob Grant.

7. Beck would return to the theme of responding to terrorist attacks with nukes later in the show when an Indian American caller explained that Osama bin Laden has been funding jihadi groups in Kashmir. "Why isn't India, a country with nukes, responding?" Beck asked the caller.

8. A critics' poll by *Rolling Stone* magazine ranked the song the third most annoying song of all time.

9. It was thus a poetic touch that Beck crossed the threshold into megastardom the best way he knew how: under a red, white, and blue waterworks display. When he cried during the introduction of his initiative known as the 9.12 Project in March 2009—"I'm just a guy who loves my country"—he came full circle from the original 9/12.

4. It's Always about Glenn

1. Beck would not get three hours of airtime in New York City until June 2009, when WOR began running Beck's entire show.

2. Where Welles was stingy about sharing writing credit, Beck acknowledges coauthorship and even no authorship. Beck has admitted that he no longer writes any of his show's comedy sketches, and he has listed up to ten coauthors on his best-selling books.

3. The featured guest that night was Al Jolson, whom Hope knew from his own early career in vaudeville performing in blackface.

4. The concert cited by Beck would grow into an annual Freedom Concert series hosted by Hannity. Featuring Oliver North and country music stars, the concerts raise money for a scholarship fund to help the children of soldiers who have been wounded or killed in Iraq and Afghanistan.

5. Beck's "Follow us" line later reemerged as "Follow me," the welcome line on his Fox News show. I learned the term's origins the first time I wrote about Beck. Among the letters I received was a note from an army veteran named Larry Shields, who wrote: "I don't watch this guy but I have seen his opening monologue and how he ends it with 'Follow Me.' I find it pretty damn offensive as a former U.S. Army Infantryman that this sniveling little idiot uses it. In army training, one of the cadence songs (when I was in) was 'Follow Me, Patch on My Shoulder!' It's a reference to the old Infantry saw 'Queen of Battle' that concludes with 'Follow Me!' The Rangers use it today. I wouldn't follow that jerk-off across an empty street. I'm sure I'm not the only vet who has picked up on this."

6. As the people recited the Pledge of Allegiance, they placed their hands over their hearts, a modern tweak to the pledge ritual made by FDR. The original hand gesture, known as the Bellamy Salute, involved an outstretched arm and an open hand.

7. Beck would later falsely claim that no reporter ever called him to comment on the allegations. "They got so much wrong, and that was my first taste of how irresponsible the 'responsible journalists' are. No one ever made a phone call to me, and they never asked for the facts," Beck told Reed Bunzel, author of *Clear Vision*, an official corporate history of Clear Channel.

8. Although Ivers was the author of *The Random House Guide to Good Writing*, which includes an entire chapter dedicated to diction, he could not prevent Beck from confusing *dichotomy* with *dilemma*.

9. Victoria E. Johnson, *Heartland TV: Primetime Television and the Struggle for U.S. Identity* (New York: New York University Press, 2008).
10. Ibid., 1–25.
11. Beck, *The Real America*, 231.
12. Ibid., 10.
13. Ibid., 154–161.
14. Ibid., 147.
15. Ibid., 100.
16. Ibid., 145.
17. Ibid., 188.
18. Ibid., 191.
19. Glenn Beck, *The Real America*, paperback ed. (New York: Pocket Books, 2005), 260–261.
20. Frank Rich, *The Greatest Story Ever Sold* (New York: Penguin, 2006), 121.
21. "One Thousand Clear Channel Radio Stations Respond to Katrina," Clear Channel Communications press release, September 1, 2005.

5. This Is CNN?

1. The campaign also gave birth to Beck's deep personal hatred for Olbermann, which continues to express itself in vindictive personal attacks that go beyond even the loose standards of cable news spats.
2. The MSNBC press release that announced Savage's hiring would later be echoed in CNN's announcement of Beck's hiring. MSNBC president Erik Sorenson described Savage as a "brash, passionate, and smart [commentator who offers] compelling opinion and analysis with an edge."
3. Beck, *The Real America* (2003 edition), 85.
4. A year into the show, Beck would create one of his earliest YouTube classics when in the middle of a discussion about nude celebrity photos, he asked a female guest, "Dina, I've got some time and a camera. Why don't you stop by?"
5. The next night, Beck followed the Ellison comment by expressing his surprise that a letter written by an American criticizing Al Qaeda was written by a Muslim.
6. The January 16 letter further began: "We are gravely concerned that ABC News has hired Glenn Beck as a regular commentator on *Good Morning America*. As a talk-radio host and during his tenure with CNN, Beck has consistently fueled his commentary with vitriol and falsehoods aimed at stirring resentment toward Arabs and Muslims. His addition to *Good Morning America* would disseminate his prejudiced, openly hostile, and ignorant commentary to an even broader national audience, and diminish the credibility of your reputable and highly rated news show. To provide a platform for his hateful speech is dangerous and irresponsible, and we strongly and urgently implore you to reconsider this move."
7. Jim Tharpe, "70 Years of Ted Turner," *Atlanta Journal-Constitution*, July 18, 2009.
8. Jautz was the second person to attempt an overhaul of the network. In 2001, general manager Teya Ryan spruced up the sets and hired *Falcon Crest* and *NYPD Blue* actress Andrea Thompson to read news for a 6 p.m. soft news magazine program featuring live in-studio musical acts. Shortly afterward, 9/11 put a spike through the overhaul.
9. Quoted in Scott Collins, *Crazy Like a Fox: The Inside Story of How Fox News Beat CNN* (New York: Penguin Group, 2004), 169.

10. Jessica Pressler, "The Dr. Maddow Show," *New York*, November 2, 2008.
11. Scott Leith, "CNN Headline News Bets on Chat Show with Up-and-Coming Conservative Radio Host," *Atlanta Journal-Constitution*, January 18, 2006.
12. Joel Topcik, "Glenn Beck Recalls Radio Days," *Broadcasting & Cable*, December 4, 2006.

6. A Rodeo Clown Goes Large

1. John Zogby, Huffington Post, February 2, 2007.
2. Noam Cohen, "With Brash Hosts, Headline News Finds More Viewers in Prime Time," *New York Times*, December 4, 2006.
3. David Segal, "The Right and the Wrong," *Washington Post*, January 26, 2007.
4. Beck quickly seized on the notice by the famous author and put his words on a T-shirt, which he continues to sell at Glennbeck.com.
5. "50 Most Loathsome Americans," *The Beast*, no. 113, January 2007.
6. Brian Stelter, "A Folksy Guy, in Recovery, Is about to Land Millions," *New York Times*, November 5, 2007.
7. Davis, "Working Nerves in the Afternoon."
8. On radio and television, Beck's shows have always been friendly havens for experts funded by the energy industry as well as the politicians who love them. His favorite analysts have included Chris Horner of the Competitive Enterprise Institute, conservative TV meteorologist James Spann, and Oklahoma senator James Inhofe, who once described global warming as "the second-largest hoax ever played on the American people, after the separation of church and state."
9. Spencer Wynn, "Who's Still Cool on Global Warming?" *Toronto Star*, January 28, 2007.
10. www.realclimate.org/index.php/archives/2007/04/the-lag-between-temp-and-co2/.
11. Beck does not deny that the climate is changing. He just doesn't think it's man-made; and even if it is, it still doesn't justify raising taxes. Listeners to Beck's radio program know that Beck's lack of anxiety might have something to do with his belief that the Real American heartland will escape the worst. As he joked on the radio a month after hosting the special, "Does anybody really care? I mean, come on. Shanghai is under water. Oh, no! Who's gonna make those little umbrellas for those tropical drinks?"
12. http://blogs.discovermagazine.com/badastronomy/2007/10/26/glenn-beck-idiot/.
13. "Glenn Beck's Weak on CNN," Newscorpse.com, July 10, 2007.
14. Special report, "Glenn Beck Wants You," *Newsmax*, October 2009.
15. Gregory A. Prince, "The Red Peril, the Candy Maker, and the Apostle: David O. McKay's Confrontation with Communism," *Dialogue: A Journal of Mormon Thought* 37, no. 2 (Summer 2004): 37–94.
16. Michael D. Quinn, "Ezra Taft Benson and Mormon Political Conflicts," *Dialogue: A Journal of Mormon Thought* 26, no. 2 (Summer 1993): 1–87. When the third-party effort stalled, Benson sought the number two slot on George Wallace's 1968 presidential ticket. Retired Air Force general Curtis LeMay ultimately got the nod.
17. Michael D. Quinn, *The Mormon Hierarchy: Extensions of Power* (Salt Lake City: Signature, 1997), 98.
18. Robert Gottlieb and Peter Wiley, *America's Saints: The Rise of Mormon Power* (New York: Harcourt, 1986), 75–76.

7. Beck Unbound

1. http://panerairelicawatches.blogspot.com/2009/06/great-right-hope.html.

2. Dahlia Lithwick, "The Fiction behind Torture Policy," *Newsweek*, August 4, 2008.

3. *The Steve Malzberg Show*, August 27, 2009.

4. For example, *The Glenn Beck Program*, January 14, 2009.

5. www.youtube.com/watch?v=jw3o3y77MaA.

6. Editorial, "Politics of Attack," *New York Times*, October 8, 2009.

7. Patrick Allit, *The Conservatives: Ideas and Personalities throughout American History* (New Haven, CT: Yale University Press, 2009), 18–19.

8. Sam Tanenhaus, *The Death of Conservatism* (New York: Random House, 2009), 37.

9. Editorial, "Defining Problems with Socialism for the Post–Cold War Generation," *Investor's Business Daily*, October 27, 2008.

10. Matea Gold, "Fox News' Glenn Beck Strikes Ratings Gold by Challenging Barack Obama," *Los Angeles Times*, March 6, 2009.

11. David Horowitz, "Obama Derangement Syndrome," *National Review Online*, December 8, 2009.

12. Chris Steller, "Bachmann Fears Re-education Camps," *Minnesota Independent*, April 6, 2009.

13. *Glenn Beck*, March 30, 2009. Beck must have realized that thanks to fellow Mormon superstar Stephenie Meyers, the author of a vampire romance series, there's nothing Americans love more than overprotective, hunky vampires.

14. Glenn Beck (with Joseph Kerry), *Common Sense* (New York: Mercury/Threshold, 2009), 9.

15. Craig Nelson, *Thomas Paine: Enlightenment, Revolution, and the Birth of Modern Nations* (New York: Penguin, 2006), 262.

16. Christopher Hitchens, *Thomas Paine's Rights of Man* (New York: Atlantic Monthly Press, 2006), 110–122.

17. *Common Sense*, 58.

18. Ibid., 106.

19. Ibid., viii.

20. Ibid., 102.

21. Steve Krakauer, "Tipping Point? Glenn Beck Fan Arrested with Guns and Ammo," *Mediate*, August 7, 2009. According to the measure suggested in *Common Sense*, Genovese was a useful barometer of trust in government. On page 87, he proposes the following "trust indicator": "When the sales of guns and bullets go down, it means the American people have more trust in their government. It's just common sense, right?"

22. Beck, *Common Sense*, 21.

23. Ibid., 34.

24. Ibid., 50.

25. Ibid., 84.

26. Ibid., 58–59.

27. Ibid., 87–88.

28. Ibid., 7.

29. Ibid., 79. Leaving aside the fact that most Americans support what's known as "commonsense" gun legislation, this is odd coming from a man who has spent the last ten years of his life inside gated compounds. In Tampa, then in Connecticut, he took on local ordinances to build taller walls than those allowed. See John Cook, "Paranoid Faux Populist Glenn Beck Walls Himself Off from Humanity," gawker.com, May 27, 2009.

30. Beck, *Common Sense*, 39.

31. Ibid., 42–43.
32. Ibid., 45.

8. False Victory

1. https://members.premiereinteractive.com/ows-img/glennbeck/pages/28585/41410.htm.
2. *The Glenn Beck Program*, July 23, 2009.
3. Phil Kerpen, "How Van Jones Happened and What We Need to Do Next," *Fox Forum*, Foxnews.com, September 6, 2009.
4. Ben Smith, "The War on Beck," Politico.com, October 14, 2009.
5. *The Glenn Beck Program*, August 11 and 14, and September 1, 2009.
6. See Harriet A. Washington's *Medical Apartheid: The Dark History of Medical Experimentation on Black Americans from Colonial Times to the Present* (New York: Doubleday, 2006).
7. Van Jones, *The Green Collar Economy: How One Solution Can Fix Our Two Biggest Problems* (New York: HarperCollins, 2008), 23.
8. Ibid., xiii.
9. Ibid., 3–4.
10. Beck, *Common Sense*, 13.
11. Eric Lantz and Suzanne Tegen, "NREL Response to the Report *Study of the Effects on Employment of Public Aid to Renewable Energy Sources* from King Juan Carlos University," U.S. Department of Energy, August 2009, 5.
12. Running more or less parallel to Beck's campaign against Jones was Color of Change's campaign against Beck's Fox advertisers. Since Van Jones was a cofounder of Color of Change, many assumed that Beck and Jones were waging proxy wars of revenge. But the timelines don't quite match. Color of Change had already started a campaign around Fox News' race-baiting when Beck first mentioned Van Jones. Beck, meanwhile, began attacking Jones just days before the Color of Change campaign was launched.

9. "A Deep-Seated Hatred for . . . the White Culture"

1. The look on Doocy's face was reminiscent of actor Mike Myers's expression during a 2005 public service appearance on NBC, when his on-air partner Kanye West declared, "George Bush doesn't care about black people." West's outburst, delivered in the wake of Hurricane Katrina, was the last time a public figure had appeared on national television and accused the president of the United States, point-blank, of racism.
2. Katie Couric, CBS News online interview, September 21, 2009.
3. *The Glenn Beck Program*, June 17 and June 30, 2009.
4. Ibid., May 29, 2003.
5. Quoted in Johnson, *Heartland TV*, 86.
6. James Shortridge, *The Middle West: Its Meaning in American Culture* (Lawrence: University Press of Kansas, 1989), 5–20.
7. Rick Pearlstein, *Nixonland: The Rise of a President and the Fracturing of America* (New York: Scribner, 2009), 331.
8. Max Blumenthal, "Hannity's Soul-Mate of Hate," *The Nation*, June 3, 2005.
9. www.youtube.com/watch?v=G_vmQrTi3aM.
10. Joe Garofoli, "Louisiana's Jena Six Beating Case Galvanizes S.F.'s 'Black Moveon,'" *San Francisco Chronicle*, September 22, 2007.

11. Brian Stelter, "Host Loses Some Sponsors after an Obama Remark," *New York Times*, August 14, 2009.
12. Robert Seidman, "Big Beck," TVbytheNumbers.com, August 27, 2009.
13. David Duke, "Whites Are People, Too," DavidDuke.com, September 8, 2009.
14. www.stormfront.org/forum/showpost.php?p=7213067&postcount=100.
15. www.stormfront.org/forum/showpost.php?p=7213821&postcount=104.
16. www.stormfront.org/forum/showpost.php?p=7214447&postcount=113.
17. www.stormfront.org/forum/showpost.php?p=7214770&postcount=122.
18. www.stormfront.org/forum/showpost.php?p=7211864&postcount=69.
19. www.stormfront.org/forum/showthread.php?p=7258048.
20. Ibid.
21. www.stormfront.org/forum/showpost.php?p=7214009&postcount=111.
22. "DefendGlenn.com Launches," WorldNetDaily.com, August 16, 2009.

10. ACORN

1. *Sean Hannity,* Fox News, September 14, 2009.
2. Lachlan Cartwright and Jeremy Olshan, "Duo Who Turned This Trick," *New York Post*, September 16, 2009.
3. Scott Harshbarger and Amy Crafts, "An Independent Governance Assessment of ACORN: The Path to Meaningful Reform," Proskauer Report, December 7, 2009. The report can be downloaded at www.proskauer.com/news/press_release/report/.
4. In some offices, ACORN staff members called the police. In others, they didn't provide advice; they just listened patiently and, perhaps, too sympathetically. The videos do not show at what point the pair mentioned its prostitution scheme. In some offices, it would make sense for ACORN staffers to listen and offer advice if they hadn't yet heard about the prostitution angle. In San Diego, it appears that the ACORN staffer was confused about what the two were proposing, since he mentions that he has friends in the district attorney's office and knows some local police. In San Bernardino, the ACORN staff was clearly aware of some sort of scam and tried to scam the two back. In no ACORN office did any staff even begin to fill out any forms or applications for the pair. Some ACORN staffers acted stupidly, but it isn't clear that they provided useful advice to the pair in more than two offices. It is possible that O'Keefe and Giles doctored the film in ways that distort what actually happened. Since they won't release the unedited videos, it is impossible to know. As the *Los Angeles Times'* media critic asked in one of the few pieces to put the videos in context, "Who knows what we might find—either damaging or benefiting ACORN's image—if we could see the unedited video of these encounters? The raw material could be posted on YouTube for all to see."
5. Along with posting the videos, Breitbart has posted memos recovered from ACORN's garbage. One memo, posted in November 2009, discussed how to get local municipal governments to install speed bumps on busy streets where pedestrians had been injured or killed.
6. Public Policy Polling, "Acorn," publicpolicypolling.blogspot.com/2009/11/acorn.html, November 19, 2009.
7. The attacks continued after the convention. On the Sunday after Palin's speech, Giuliani appeared on *Meet the Press* and linked Obama to the father of modern community organizing, Saul Alinsky, and Alinsky to "share the wealth" socialism.

8. Peter Dreier and Christopher R. Martin, "Manipulating the Public Agenda: Why ACORN Was in the News, and What the News Got Wrong," http://departments .oxy.edu/uepi/acornstudy, September 2009.

9. Teresa James, "Caging Democracy: A 50-Year History of Partisan Challenge to Minority Voters," ProjectVote.org, September 2007.

10. Chandler Davidson, Tanya Dunlap, Gale Kenny, and Benjamin Wise, "Protection or Minority Vote Suppression—or Both?", Center for Voting Rights & Protection, September 2004.

11. Dreier and Martin, "Manipulating the Public Agenda."

12. Greg Gordon, "Death Threat, Vandalism Hit ACORN After McCain Comments," McClatchy Newspapers, October 17, 2008.

13. Robert Fisher, ed., *The People Shall Rule: ACORN, Community Organizing, and the Struggle for Economic Justice* (Nashville: Vanderbilt University Press, 2009), 3–61.

14. The Home Mortgage Disclosure Act was passed in 1975, and the Community Reinvestment Act in 1977.

15. www.businessweek.com/investing/insights/blog/archives/2008/09/community_reinv.html.

16. Barry L. Ritholtz, "A Memo Found in the Street," *Barron's*, September 29, 2008.

17. Jeremy Scahill, "The ACORN Standard," *The Nation*, October 14, 2009.

18. Ben Smith, "The War on Beck," Politico.com, October 14, 2009.

19. David Sears, Colette van Laar, Mary Carrillo, and Rick Kosterman, "Is It Really Racism? The Origins of White Americans' Opposition to Race-Targeted Policies," *Public Opinion Quarterly* 61 (1997): 16–53. See also Martin Gilens, *Why Americans Hate Welfare: Race, Media, and the Politics of Antipoverty Policy* (Chicago: University of Chicago Press, 2001).

20. Senate Judiciary Committee report, "The Militia Movement in the United States," http://books.google.com/books?id=CZ0ObAxvzrcC&source=gbs_navlinks_s, June 15, 1995.

21. Doug Ross, "Red Alert: ACORN and the Obama Youth Corps," Directorblue.blogspot. com, March 28, 2009.

22. *Glenn Beck*, March 18, 2009.

23. Ibid., February 18, 2009.

24. Ibid., March 25, 2009.

25. Ibid., September 21, 2009.

11. Brother Beck Presents: Mormon Masterpiece Theater

1. Sarah Lenz, "Stadium of Fire Flag Burning Was Fake," *Deseret News*, July 9, 2009.

2. *Glenn Beck*, February 5, 2009.

3. Michael Idov, "81 Minutes with Glenn Beck," *New York*, April 13, 2009.

4. Ibid.

5. *Glenn Beck*, January 8, 2008. What Beck asks his audience to grant him, he denies to women. After Hillary Clinton's voice cracked while she was speaking with voters at a diner in Portsmouth, New Hampshire, Beck guffawed like a master counterfeiter presented with a sloppy batch of phony fifties. "Hillary Clinton isn't just running for president, she's also making a run for the best actress nomination," he said. "I don't buy the hype of the tears. I don't think you should, either. Believe me, I know what it's like to get caught off guard and break down occasionally. I mean, I cry on this freaking show like every ten minutes, so I get it. . . . You're losing, and this is some sort of bizarre,

last-ditch strategy to ingratiate you with women, maybe? Or make you seem less like the Terminator?"

6. Susan J. Douglas, "Letting the Boys Be Boys: Talk Radio, Male Hysteria, and Political Discourse in the 1980s," *Radio Reader: Essays in the Cultural History of Radio* (New York: Routledge, 2002), 485–503.

7. Daniel H. Ludlow, ed., *The Encyclopedia of Mormonism* (New York: Macmillan, 1992), 1470–1472.

8. Whether one is listening to the church hierarchy address the flock or is reviewing the works of orthodox Mormon culture, it is hard to avoid the sense that to be Mormon is to live in a never-ending LDS Church–produced after-school program. The results are predictable. In 2008, Mental Health America ranked overwhelmingly Mormon Utah the most depressed state in the country, with more residents on antidepressant drugs than in any other state by twice the national average. After two studies on this were released, a former president of the Utah Psychiatric Association told *ABC News* that there was "a cultural factor" behind the numbers. See Russell Goldman, "Two Studies Find Depression Widespread in Utah," ABC News, March 7, 2008.

9. Beck, *The Real America*, 221–222.

10. Joanna Brooks, "Mormon Sentimentalism: A History," www.askmormongirl.com/sentimentalism.

12. The Ghost of Cleon Skousen

1. As usual, Beck's history was bunk. Nelson Rockefeller, who hired Rivera only after Henri Matisse declined the commission, had explicitly asked the muralist not to include Bolshevik iconography in *Man at the Crossroads*. When Rivera disobeyed his employer's wishes, the mural was draped and soon thereafter destroyed.

2. Richard Lacayo, "Glenn Beck: Crack(ed) Symbolist," Time.com, September 4, 2009.

3. Steven Heller, *The Daily Heller*, www.printmag.com/Article/Glenn-Beck-Art-Hysterian, September 4, 2009.

4. Beck, *The Real America*, 117–122.

5. Beck, *An Inconvenient Book*, 282.

6. Beck, *Common Sense*, 110.

7. J. Bracken Lee, letter to Mrs. Elizabeth Laine, August 1960, http://ernie1241.googlepages.com/skousen.

8. Special report, "The Ultras," *Time*, December 8, 1961.

9. Quoted in W. C. Sullivan, memo to A. H. Belmont, January 1963, http://ernie1241.googlepages.com/skousen.

10. Robert Welch, *The Politician*, 1958, unpublished, 267.

11. The parallel between Skousen's defense of Welch's Eisenhower accusation and Glenn Beck's charge of racism against Barack Obama is striking. Both resulted in an exodus of corporate support, even though Beck's desertion by advertisers was instigated by a public campaign.

12. Quinn, *The Mormon Hierarchy*, 82–85.

13. Rudy Maxa, "The Professor Who Knew Too Much," *Washington Post Sunday Magazine*, March 23, 1975.

14. Though no conspiracist, Quigley was known as something of an eccentric. He was famed at Georgetown for the following three-hour final exam question: "Please

describe the development of civilization since the retreat of the Wurm glacier." Among his Georgetown students to later sing his praises was Bill Clinton.

15. Cleon Skousen, *The Naked Capitalist*, 5th ed., self-published, 1971, 65–66.

16. "Roundtable Review: The Naked Capitalist," *Dialogue: The Journal of Mormon Thought* 6, no. 3 (Autumn/Winter 1971): 99–116.

17. "Mormon Media Image," *Sunstone*, July/August, 1981, 58–59.

18. Ibid.

19. Anson Shupe and John Heinerman, "Mormonism and the New Christian Right: An Emerging Coalition?" *Review of Religious Research* 27, no. 2 (December 1985): 146–149.

20. "Mormon Media Image," 58–59.

21. Neil J. Young, "The ERA Is a Moral Issue: The Mormon Church, LDS Women, and the Defeat of the Equal Rights Amendment," *American Quarterly* 59, no. 3 (September 2007): 623–644. This same Mormon activist playbook would be used to even greater effect during the 2008 campaign against California's gay marriage ballot initiative, Proposition 8. Although Mormons make up fewer than 3 percent of California's population, they contributed more than half of the funds and volunteers for the successful effort to defeat Proposition 8.

22. Crucial to the growth of his institute was Skousen's unlikely friendship with the Korean mogul and self-declared prophet Sun Myung Moon. When Skousen arrived in D.C. at the dawn of the Reagan era, Moon was energetically showering the nascent Christian Right with cash. Skousen made sure that the Freemen Institute benefited from Moon's largesse, and before long the humble Mormon had established a close working friendship with the billionaire cult leader and tax felon, whose claims of a direct line to God mirrored those of Mormon founding prophet Joseph Smith. This odd couple became an even more bizarre trio with the addition of former Black Panther Eldridge Cleaver, who was baptized a Mormon in 1983 and soon became friendly with both Skousen and Moon. Cleaver, one of Mormonism's most famous midlife converts prior to Glenn Beck, gave lectures under the Freemen Institute banner until 1986.

23. O. Kendall White Jr., "A Review and Commentary on the Prospects of a Mormon New Christian Right Coalition," *Review of Religious Research* 28, no. 2 (December 1986): 182–185.

24. Two of Cleon Skousen's sons, Harold and Paul, currently sit on Wythe's board.

25. W. Cleon Skousen, *The 5,000 Year Leap: A Miracle That Changed the World* (Malta, ID: National Center for Constitutional Studies, 1981), 88–92.

26. Ibid., 14–18.

27. Ibid., xix.

28. Ibid., Ronald Reagan, back cover.

29. "In God We Trust," *Time*, February 9, 1987.

30. W. Cleon Skousen, *The Making of America* (Washington, DC: National Center for Constitutional Studies, 1985), 728–740.

31. *Glenn Beck*, July 25, 2007.

32. *The Glenn Beck Program*, September 24, 2007.

33. Ibid., November 21, 2007.

34. According to Paul Skousen, Cleon Skousen's son, Beck first came into contact with the book in Skousenite fashion: as an anonymous gift. "As I understand it," the younger Skousen says, "Glenn Beck was given a copy of *Leap* by a friend in Canada. When Beck read it, suddenly the effusive and disembodied principles of freedom that he had

been trying to dig up and put together all came together and he could make sense of them. He was so excited about the clarity it brought that he began mentioning it on his show." Around the same time, the Skousen family was ready to respond to the Beck-inspired demand. "We as a family," says Paul Skousen, "were preparing to publish another edition, so I contacted his office with the request that Glenn write a foreword. He was gracious and kind and did just that. That is the version we're now publishing."

According to James Pratt of PowerThink Publishing, publishers of the thirtieth-anniversary edition of *Leap* with the Beck foreword, the new edition was intended to replace the version that the Beck show was already touting through links on its Web site. Pratt says that the previous version was not authorized by the family. "It was presumed by Mr. Beck and staff that copyright authority was in effect with that edition," he says, "and as an author I must say I had also assumed the same thing. . . . I was more than a little surprised this was going on, to the tune of hundreds of thousands of copies." PowerThink secured the agreement of the Skousen family to create the current edition of *The 5,000 Year Leap*, which was published on March 1, 2009. Pratt says that a federal lawsuit "is in process to secure the copyright authority in an 'authoritative' way" to stop anyone but PowerThink from publishing the book. In March, with the new edition available, Beck invited Skousen's nephew, Mark, onto his Fox show. Mark would later say that between commercials, Beck told him that a friend had sent him *Leap* and that the book "changed his life."

35. *The Naked Capitalist*, 67.
36. *Common Sense*, 11.
37. Ibid., 104.

13. The 9.12 Project

1. Michael Tomasky, "Something New on the Mall," *New York Review of Books*, October 22, 2009.
2. Ibid.
3. Rick Moran, "The Santelli Rant: A Red Bull Rush," February 22, 2009.
4. Chris Matthews, *Hardball*, MSNBC, February 20, 2009.
5. Mark Ames and Yasha Levine, "Is Santelli Sucking Koch?" ExiledOnline.com, February 27, 2009.
6. *The Glenn Beck Program*, November 12, 2009.
7. The nine principles and twelve values are taken from www.the912Project.com.

> **The 9 Principles**: America Is Good
>
> I believe in God and He is the Center of my Life
>
> I must always try to be a more honest person than I was yesterday
>
> The family is sacred. My spouse and I are the ultimate authority, not the government
>
> If you break the law you pay the penalty. Justice is blind and no one is above it
>
> I have a right to life, liberty and pursuit of happiness, but there is no guarantee of equal results
>
> I work hard for what I have and I will share it with who I want to. Government cannot force me to be charitable

It is not un-American for me to disagree with authority or to share my personal opinion

The government works for me. I do not answer to them, they answer to me.

The 12 Values: Honesty, Reverence, Hope, Thrift, Humility, Charity, Sincerity, Moderation, Hard Work, Courage, Personal Responsibility, Gratitude.

8. David Leonhardt, "America's Sea of Red Ink Was Years in the Making," *New York Times*, June 10, 2009.

9. Ross Douthat, "The Tea Parties," *Atlantic,* http://rossdouthat.theatlantic.com/archives/2009/04/the_tea_parties.php, April 16, 2009.

INDEX